# CHOSEN

A Memoir of Stolen Boyhood

## STEPHEN MILLS

Metropolitan Books
Henry Holt and Company
New York

Metropolitan Books
Henry Holt and Company
*Publishers since 1866*
120 Broadway
New York, New York 10271
www.henryholt.com

Metropolitan Books® and ⬛® are registered trademarks of
Macmillan Publishing Group, LLC.

Library of Congress Cataloging-in-Publication Data

Names: Mills, Stephen Tukel, author.
Title: Chosen : a memoir of stolen boyhood / Stephen Mills.
Description: First edition. | New York : Metropolitan Books, Henry Holt and
    Company, 2021.
Identifiers: LCCN 2021060762 (print) | LCCN 2021060763 (ebook) |
    ISBN 9781250823212 (hardcover) | ISBN 9781250823205 (ebook)
Subjects: LCSH: Mills, Stephen Tukel. | Adult child sexual abuse victims—
    United States—Biography. | Sexually abused boys—United States. |
    Child grooming (Child sexual abuse)—United States.
Classification: LCC HV6570.2 .M55 2021 (print) | LCC HV6570.2 (ebook) |
    DDC 362.760973 [B]—dc23/eng/20220127
LC record available at https://lccn.loc.gov/2021060762
LC ebook record available at https://lccn.loc.gov/2021060763

Our books may be purchased in bulk for promotional, educational, or business use. Please
contact your local bookseller or the Macmillan Corporate and Premium Sales Department at
(800) 221-7945, extension 5442, or by e-mail at MacmillanSpecialMarkets@macmillan.com.

First Edition 2022

Designed by Kelly S. Too

Printed in the United States of America

1   3   5   7   9   10   8   6   4   2

To Susan
Truly, madly, deeply

In memory of my father, with love for my son

I'm always afraid of being hurt: and to me, while I live, the force of that night will lie in the agony which broke me, and made me surrender. . . . I wanted to put it plain in the book, and wrestled for days with my self-respect . . . which wouldn't, hasn't, let me.

—T. E. Lawrence, letter to Charlotte Shaw, March 26, 1924

# CONTENTS

The names and identifying details of some victims and witnesses in this book have been changed.

# CHOSEN

Part One

---

# PREDATION

# Prologue

## 1959

I WAS AN ONLY CHILD until the weekend came. Then our small house filled with aunts and uncles, great-aunts and great-uncles, cousins of all degrees, and my father's Army Air Corps friends—a tribe so large and so loud I never felt alone in their presence. They came to talk at my father and help my mother. *Hey, boychick, how's the old man? Steve-a-rino, siddown and tell me what's cookn. Hello, doll, give your aunt a big wet kiss.*

In the summer, they gathered in the backyard beneath towering oak and maple trees, surrounding my father like a Jewish hydra with twenty heads, yakking about Jack Benny, Israel, and astronauts. They stopped gabbing and gesticulating only to consume bagels and Chock full o'Nuts.

My father sat at the center of their coiled embrace in a sturdy metal wheelchair, elbows resting on padded blue armrests, hands folded stiffly across his stomach. His two legs listed to the left, as if stuck to the frame. The white short-sleeve shirt he wore was newly ironed, his thinning brown hair carefully trimmed by the Italian barber who came to our house every month to take care of him and me. My father's face was smooth on the weekend. My mother shaved him on Friday mornings. She pretended to shave my face, too.

I could always find my father—he never moved. My uncles played ball with me and carried me on their shoulders, but my father was for hugging. On summer days, I liked to climb up on his lap and sit at the center of the family circle. I slumped against his chest, his arms around me.

Every few minutes he'd let loose a kind of strangled cackle, his distinctive laugh, because the men in this circle were all kibitzers. They lived to tell jokes, to surprise with the punch line. Uncle Harold, who taught me to sing Broadway show tunes and dance around the Maypole. Uncle Milt, who sold girdles and made me memorize the names of philosophers to study when I grew up: Ponty, Husserl, and Arendt. Great-uncle Jorge, who smoked a big smelly cigar, composed music, and built pianos.

I didn't understand their jokes, but my father loved them. His bony legs quaked beneath my thighs. His right hand twitched against my ribs. When he laughed, his large nose, crooked grin, and tortoise-shell sunglasses all scrunched up together.

The women of the tribe were arrayed opposite the men. Aunt Delle with jet-black hair, smoking a Parliament that she'd set aside in the ashtray, kissed with red lipstick. Aunt Fran, her eyebrows heavily penciled, clutching a shiny gold cigarette case and pitching her hundred-decibel voice. Great-aunt Jean, whose impossibly large lips were painted like apples or oranges.

They flanked my mother, who relaxed in an aluminum-frame lawn chair. She wore navy blue slacks and a plaid shirt. Enormous round sunglasses shaded her eyes from the high noon sun. Her slight build and girlish bangs made her seem younger than her thirty-four years. The daughter of a learned Orthodox Jew, she was often mistaken for Irish, with her fair complexion, sandy hair, and hazel eyes.

But here, among friends and sisters-in-law, there could be no doubt of her origins. She had been an only child. Her parents,

immigrants from Eastern Europe, had long since died. When she
married Seymour Mills—known by all as Si—she was adopted by
his tight-knit clan.

On Saturday nights, they set up camp in our house. Sleeping
quarters materialized out of thin air. Fold-up cots unfolded. A sofa
and its cushions blossomed into a bed for two or three. Army sleeping bags proliferated. I had too much fun to sleep.

I KNEW MY father was different from other fathers. They didn't need
a wheelchair or visits from nurses. They didn't need to be fed by their
wives from a spoon on a yellow tray. It's how he came back from the
war, my mother said. That part confused me. I knew he had something called MS. Those two letters always hung in the air, like the
cigarette smoke that arrived with my aunts and uncles. World War II
and MS were connected but I didn't know how.

I thought my father was still in the army, because the army took
care of us. In the early 1950s, they had built my parents a custom
ranch house in Wantagh on Long Island. It had ramps in front and
back and extra-wide doorways, so my father could roll, or be rolled,
anywhere in the house. All the kids on my street wanted to run up
and down our ramps. I was almost as popular as Tommy, whose
father was a Mister Softee man and parked his ice-cream truck in
their driveway.

Our car was different, too. The army had outfitted a big blue
Plymouth sedan with hand levers so my father could operate the gas
and brake pedals without using his feet. That was before I was born.
I never saw him drive. When my mother took over the driving, they
removed the back seat so my father could fit there in his wheelchair
when we went to visit our relatives.

On shopping trips, I sat in the front with my mother, pretending
to be older, straining to see over the dashboard. Every Friday we
drove almost an hour to Fort Totten, an army PX in Queens near
the Whitestone Bridge. She loved the low prices for army families

like ours. I was more interested in the soldiers with holstered guns who guarded the entrance. When we stopped at the gate, they would look in the car and ask my mother about the hand levers. She explained how they worked. The soldiers pointed and nodded, impressed.

On the nights when my father had to go to the hospital, my mother would wake me, kneel by my bed, and tell me which aunt or friend would be staying over till morning. Sometimes they stayed for days. I had nightmares about sirens. I'd wake up panicked, sure that the siren I'd heard was real. Sometimes it was but usually it wasn't. I'd clutch a small stuffed leopard to my chest and listen hard.

One night, there were strange sounds coming from my parents' bedroom. I grabbed my leopard and padded across the hallway to their closed door. When I opened it, I was hit with a blast of warm, menthol vapor that poured out of a round, green glass contraption sitting on the dresser. The machine was always running, magically producing steam like the morning fog that hung above the pond at Forest Lake Elementary School.

I stood in the doorway for a moment, searching for my parents through the mist before moving closer. My father was sitting up in bed, his skinny body wrapped inside a white harness. My mother stood next to him, pushing up and down on a long metal lever that operated a big hoist.

Each time she pushed down, my father rose a few more inches above the bed. She was strong. When he was clear of the bed, she grabbed the harness with both hands and swung him over to the wheelchair. Then she worked the lever again, lowering him into it. His legs fell to one side as they always did, and his head hung down.

"Why are you up, sweetheart?" my mother asked when she saw me. "Did you have a bad dream?"

"I heard a siren, Mommy."

"There was no siren, just a dream. Go back to bed. I'll tuck you in after I take Daddy to the bathroom."

"I want to stay in here," I said, hugging my leopard.

She rolled my father past me and through the wide bathroom door. I stood by the green machine and closed my eyes, letting the steam fill my lungs. After a minute, I turned to my father's typewriter, a blue-green IBM electric.

I pressed the gray ON button, and the machine came to life with a reassuring hum. I loved to press the square white keys, which responded with an electric click when you barely touched them, as if they knew what you wanted. I wasn't allowed to type if there was no paper in the roller, so I ran my fingers back and forth over the bumpy keys, then pressed the OFF button.

An army shortwave radio sat at the end of the dresser. I turned the fat black dials back and forth on the gray metal box, moving a vertical red tuning stick across the names of faraway places. Uncle Harold, my father's younger brother, had read the names to me: Tunis, Naples, Calcutta, Peking. He said my father had gone to these places during the war.

The bathroom door opened and my father rolled out, my mother behind him. When they reached the bed, she repeated the hoisting operation in reverse. Then she waved me over.

I climbed on the bed and gave my father a hug. He was wearing soft blue pajamas and smelled like menthol. He put his hands on my cheeks and kissed my head.


MY FATHER WAS in the hospital again. It was winter, just before my fifth birthday, and I was staying with Aunt Delle and Uncle Harold. Theirs was my home away from home. It was a big old house where I learned that hot stoves shouldn't be touched, that basement coal bins made great playpens, that fireflies could be caught in jars, and that I could get away with a lot more bad behavior than my cousin David. He was eight months older than me. We spent so much time together he was more brother than cousin.

A blizzard was moving in and there was no school. My uncle made waffles, and, after breakfast, I went upstairs to use the closet-sized bathroom on the second-floor landing. I could see through the small window that snow was starting to fall. I pulled down my red flannel pajamas and sat on the toilet.

I was imagining what Dave and I would do that day. We'd have a snowball fight with the other kids up on the big mountain of dirt where someone was building a new house. We had dirtball fights there—ten kids slinging dirt grenades until someone got hit in the head, started crying, and the game would end.

I was deep in the snowball reverie when I heard the front door slam and snow boots clomping up the stairs. It had to be my mother. Who else could it be? But she was coming straight up without stopping to speak with my aunt and uncle. Then she screamed my name so loudly I startled.

"I'm in the bathroom, Mommy," I yelled. She burst through the door in her long winter coat and fell to her knees. There was snow in her hair and tears streaming down her face. I'd never seen my mother cry. She grabbed my hands and squeezed them.

"Daddy died, sweetheart. Daddy died."

I didn't know what the words meant but they jolted me. I tried to steady myself, holding on tight to the toilet seat.

She saw my confusion.

"Daddy's not coming back."

I could tell she didn't mean that night.

"You mean, ever?"

"He's never coming back." She was shaking her head from side to side. "He's never coming back."

Then she was sobbing and hugging me. After a minute, she released me and trudged down the stairs. I cracked the door open and heard her talking to my aunt and uncle. I couldn't make out the words, but my uncle was crying.

I washed my hands, then went to the room where I'd slept. The snow was falling hard, harder than I'd ever seen it snow. The trees were barely visible. I felt sad, and the snow was making me sadder because it wouldn't stop. It might never stop.

Dave came in the room, put his arm around my shoulder, and we watched the snow come down without saying a word.

I knew animals died. I'd seen it in cartoons like *Bambi*. I saw people die in TV shows like *The Lone Ranger*. Half the mothers in fairy tales were dead before the story started. But these animals and people were on television or in books. My father wasn't in a cartoon or a book. He was real, so he had to be out there somewhere. He would come back.

That night I developed a high fever. I was sick for days and missed the funeral. My father was buried on my mother's thirty-fifth birthday. An aunt took care of me at home, but I don't remember any of that.

# 1

THE FIRST TIME MY MOTHER brought up my father's death was eight years later—the night of my bar mitzvah.

The day had gone just the way she and Ken, my stepfather, had planned. If it had been up to me, a few things would have been different. I would have gotten the shiny green suit that cost only ten bucks. I would have had the reception at the synagogue, like most of my friends did, instead of at home. That way there would have been room for fifty or sixty people and I could have invited some of the girls in my class. Then they would have noticed me, maybe even liked me. They didn't *not* like me. It was more like I didn't exist.

In fifth grade, I'd gone steady with a skinny girl with long dirty-blond hair. I never asked her to go steady, but her best friend and my best friend said we were, so I figured it was true. I broke up with her—my friend told her friend—when she cut her hair to look like Twiggy and I thought she looked like a boy. By then I was stuck on a raven-haired Italian girl who had thirteen brothers and sisters. I felt sorry for her because she wore the same yellow sweater with holes in it every day, but I loved her sad brown eyes.

Based on some test, I was placed in the honors track in junior high, and the girls here were different. In biology and geometry, the two toughest classes, their hands shot up and they always had the right answers. They wore miniskirts that showed off their tanned legs, and sometimes their white underwear, too, when they were sitting down. They traveled between classes in packs of four or five.

I watched them from across the room at a few bar mitzvahs that fall. They were usually lined up on the dais, flanking the boy of the moment. My own bar mitzvah was coming up in March. I pictured the girls there, arrayed on either side of me.

The shiny green suit would help. It was a pale green, nothing too crazy. But I loved the way it shimmered—*like shark skin*, the salesman said. When I put it on and stood before the enormous, three-paneled dressing room mirror, I saw three shiny green Stephens at once. I was dazzled.

The suit brought out my green eyes. I had my mother's fair complexion and freckles. People saw me and guessed Irish, like they did with her. I'd grown my hair a half inch longer than my usual crew cut so it was just touching my ears, and my bangs swooped down the right side of my forehead.

Standing before the mirror, I puffed out my chest, held my breath, and turned to check the back of the suit. I was relieved to see the jacket covered my ass nicely. Some boy had made a joke about my butt being too big for a skinny kid. I was always trying to suck it in.

"Oy vey," my mother groaned as I admired myself.

"What?"

"I mean, if that's what you really want." That was her way of saying, there's absolutely no way you're getting that suit. Ken didn't say a word. He didn't have to because he always agreed with my mother.

I'd been sure the low price would do the trick. She liked to remind me that she had grown up so poor and hungry she was still surprised to wake up in a nice home with food to eat. Her father, a Talmudic scholar, had invested in Brooklyn real estate and owned many homes. But he lost them all in the Depression, then suffered a series of strokes. Her mother was already ailing from the tuberculosis she'd contracted as a teenager.

By the time my mother was nine, she was taking care of two disabled parents. When her father died three years later, she and her mother moved to a cramped, cold-water tenement. *The rathole*, she called it. They shared a bed and scrimped to survive on eight dollars a week from Home Relief. Bookish and whip-smart, my mother graduated high school at sixteen. She dreamed of going to college but she went out to work instead.

I knew she must have hated the shiny green suit if she was willing to shell out for a pricier one. She showed me a dark blue suit for thirty-seven dollars. The salesman preferred it, too. *It's very sharp*, he said. It would have to be tailored, but Ken said we'd get that done for free at his dry cleaning store, where I worked every Saturday, manning the cash register.

The suit didn't matter. There were no girls at my bar mitzvah anyway. There were ten boys, sitting around a fold-up aluminum table in our wood-paneled basement, drinking Best Yet Cola from the discount liquor store and eating my mother's roast chicken. Eight of them were cousins or family friends. The whole thing felt like every other birthday party I'd had in the basement, which seemed right somehow since I was still only twelve. The synagogue was scheduling bar mitzvahs early that year.

After everyone left, my mother said they wanted to talk to me. She and Ken led me into the den. It was clogged with rented tables covered with gold tablecloths, white floral centerpieces, and empty wineglasses. I sat down with a thwack on the maroon Naugahyde sofa and felt the cushion flatten under me. I knew this talk would be serious, because serious conversations happened on this sofa, not the one in the living room.

"Now that you're a man," my mother began, sitting opposite me in a metal folding chair, "we thought this is the right time to tell you about something." *Oh, shit*, I thought. *Please not a sex talk.* My friend and I had found a copy of *Playboy* lying on the ground in Salisbury Park a few months earlier. We'd been trading it back and forth every weekend. This was the wrong week for my mother to discover Miss June under my mattress.

"There's money set aside for you in a savings account," she said. *Thank God, it's not Miss June.* "I set it up a long time ago. When Si died, the Veterans Administration began sending me money each month to help support you. I spent some of it, but over the last few years I've been depositing it in the bank. When you turn twenty-one, the savings account will become yours."

MY MOTHER HADN'T said a word about my father's death since she'd remarried when I was six. Sure, she'd mentioned him plenty of times. How could she not? When the conversation veered into some bit of family history, she'd say his name. *Yes, Si and I lived in Tucson in the early fifties. We went there for his health.* She started calling him that—Si—after her marriage to Ken. Before that she'd always said "Daddy" or "your father."

In my new family, I was told to call Ken "Dad." *He's your father now*, my mother said. I also had a new brother and sister: Alan and Donna. Alan was twelve, six years older than me. Donna was ten. Their mother had died of leukemia. They were told to call my mother "Mom." The three of us kids knew never to use the words stepfather, stepbrother, or step anything. We were going to be a real family, just like any other.

At first, this felt to me like acting, pretending these strangers were family. But I liked them, and I wanted them to like me, especially since my mother and I had moved into their house in East Meadow, nearby on Long Island. Where would I go if they *didn't* like me? I'd said goodbye to my friends and classmates. I knew I'd never see them again.

Secretly, though, I wanted things to go back to how they'd been before. In my new first-grade class, I daydreamed about rescuing my mother on horseback. I took my story lines from *Ivanhoe*, the television version starring Roger Moore, which I watched in reruns every day after school. I always took my mother back to the house in Wantagh. It would be just her and me, the way it had been in the year after my father died, when we went everywhere together in the big blue Plymouth. She drove me to Jones Beach, where I took swimming lessons in the saltwater pool and drank foamy root beer floats. We went food shopping every Friday and talked to the nice soldiers in the white helmets. We took the ferry to Fire Island and stayed for a week with friends who had a bungalow by the beach. I wanted life to be like that again.

Instead, I had to watch Ken kiss my mother on the living room sofa. I started calling him Dad anyway, like I was told. It was hard not to like Ken. He took me to the circus and bought me a pen-light. He played catch with me in the street and helped break in my new baseball mitt. When I had a day off from school, he took me along to his job in the garment district in New York, where he sold "notions," which were needles and buttons and things. That was before he opened the dry cleaning store.

Ken was a good guy. But I knew he wasn't my father. I didn't like it when my mother said "Si" at the dinner table. She made it sound like he was the stranger, not these people I'd just met. It was as if our life before had never happened, as if I'd never had a father and Donna and Alan had never had a mother.

Our dead parents were these two uninvited ghosts who might drop in at dinnertime then were shown the door as quickly as possible. Otherwise, they weren't discussed and there was no sign of them in the house. Donna kept a photo of her mother on top of her dresser, but Ken told her to put it away. It was time to move on, he said. It would make her new mother feel more at home.

I had no photos of my father to put away. His typewriter and shortwave radio arrived with all our other stuff in the moving van, and I watched my mother stash them in a basement closet.

I wanted to know about my father. Where did he grow up? What

was he like as a kid? Why did he join the army? I knew better than
to question my mother, but Uncle Harold would tell me stories if
I asked.

One weekend, he took Dave and me to the Polo Grounds to see
the New York Mets for the first time. To get there, we had to drive
through the Bronx, where my father and his brothers had grown up.
Uncle Harold sang in the car. He had a beautiful voice and could
whistle like a bird. In between songs he'd stop and point things out.

"See that old brick building on the corner?" my uncle said. "That
was the family grocery. We lived upstairs. Every day after school,
your dad and I crated the eggs and ladled the milk into metal con-
tainers." My uncle showed us the park where their Boy Scout troop
had met. "Steve-a-rino, your dad was the one who turned our troop
into a drum and bugle corps. He taught me to play the military
drum and the baritone bugle."

At the Polo Grounds, he pointed to where they used to sit in the
cheap seats and root for the New York Giants in the 1930s. "I was
just a little shaver when your dad took me to see Carl Hubbell pitch
for the first time. King Carl, that's what we called him." After the
game, on the ride home, I asked why my father joined the army.

"Well, kiddo, it was early 1941. The war was on but America
wasn't in yet. Your dad kept saying it was just a matter of time. He
didn't want to get drafted and be told what to do. If he was going to
be in the service, he wanted to learn a trade. He had golden hands,
your dad, could build or fix anything. He wanted to be an engineer,
so he joined the Air Corps to learn about aircraft engines. I still
remember the day he came home and told me."

My uncle got quiet. "I was only sixteen," he went on, choking
back tears. "I looked up to him. Right then, I decided I was going
to enlist in the army. But the navy got me first."

Back at his house, Uncle Harold took Dave and me down into
the basement, dug out an old photo album, and showed us pictures
of my father at an air base in North Africa. He had been a crew chief,
and his job was making sure the planes would fly.

There was a photo of him in uniform. He was standing at ease, hands on hips and smiling broadly, in front of a fighter plane that said "Miss Sea Bay" on the side. Uncle Harold said my father had done the lettering. I carried that picture around in my head for a long time.

I was sure my father would come back. He was up there listening to everything I said, watching everything I did. He wanted me to be good and help my mother. I knew all this because I saw the movie *Carousel*. The main character, Billy, watches his wife and daughter from wherever it was that dead people went, and in the end he returns to the land of the living and visits his family.

I figured my father would come back to Wantagh, not East Meadow, and I wanted to be there when he returned. In the basement of my new house, there was a small window with painted glass above Ken's workbench. The week we moved in, I dreamed that I climbed out through this window and discovered a secret tunnel leading to Wantagh. When I woke up, I ran straight downstairs, got up on the workbench, and used all my strength to pry open the window. I was sure I'd find the tunnel but all I saw was the driveway.

I didn't give up. One night, Ken heard noises downstairs, and he found me in the basement closet. I had turned on the overhead light and was standing in front of my father's shortwave radio, turning the dials back and forth, as if searching for a signal or sending an SOS. Ken tried talking to me but I didn't respond. I was sleep-walking.

Then I did it again, and again. Finally, Ken moved the radio higher in the closet, where I couldn't reach it. The next time he found me, I had brought my own radio down to the basement and was talking into it.

When I entered second grade my mother told me the five of us would be going to court to make ourselves into one family.

"Dad is going to adopt you," she said. "You'll have his last name and become Stephen Tukel."

"Isn't calling him Dad enough?" I asked. I didn't want a new last name. My father was watching all this from his invisible realm, and he'd be upset.

"I know you like your name," she said. "But it will be better if we all have the same one. Then everyone will know you belong to this family."

"But I do belong to this family."

"If you have a different name you may feel left out."

"I don't feel left out." This was true and also a lie. I felt included, but I had to be ready to leave the minute my father returned.

"Well, you may not understand now," she said, "but one day you will."

The night after we went to family court, I crawled under my desk and shined my circus penlight on the floor-to-ceiling white peg-board. Using a pencil, I wrote my old name—Stephen Mills—over and over on the white board. No one would ever see it, but I knew it was there. One day it would be my name again.

I'm not sure when I stopped waiting for my father. About a year before the bar mitzvah, my bedroom got painted. When the paint-ers moved my desk, I saw my name all over the pegboard. It was like a message from the old me. I asked them to leave it.

I had stopped dreaming about rescuing my mother. At some point I no longer even liked her. She had begun fighting with Alan soon after we moved in, always trying to get him to do something he didn't want to do or stop him from doing something he wasn't supposed to do. One day they had a huge blowup and she smacked him across the face. When it was over, she came looking for me—I was hiding under the bed.

For a while, I was caught in the middle of their war, trying to make peace. Eventually, I took my brother's side. I admired his rebellion, the way he stood up for himself. I didn't have it in me to defy my mother. I was scared of her anger, not to mention her open hand, which sometimes hit my left cheek with a crack. Her out-bursts were unpredictable. I could tell they had more to do with her mood than with anything I had done. After getting hit a few times, though, I was always on guard.

Around the time my room was painted, Alan and I formed a secret society called the Mommy Revenge Squad—M.R.S. That's how we signed postcards and letters when one of us was away from home. This two-person club had no mission apart from commiseration.

The year he left for college, I started junior high. To my new friends I was Stephen Tukel. They didn't know I had moved to East Meadow from Wantagh. They knew nothing about my father. My mother's prediction about changing my name had come true: *Everyone will know you belong to this family.*

"When Si died," my mother said after the bar mitzvah party, holding out a savings bank passbook. On the den sofa, I fidgeted with my cuff links, feeling confused. Ken, who was tall and lanky, usually leaned back in a chair with his legs crossed. Now he was sitting straight up, looking as serious as my mother. They were waiting for me to speak, but I didn't know what I was allowed to say.

I focused on the money, which seemed like a big deal. I was a man now, sharing responsibility for my financial future. My father and the US Army were counting on me.

"How much is it?" I asked.

My mother handed me the passbook and I flipped through the pages. There was a little more than four thousand dollars in there.

"Whoa, that's a lot of money," I exclaimed.

"Yes, but it's not everything," my mother said. "The VA will help pay for your college when the time comes. If you want to go to a private college, you can do that."

"That's really cool," I said. Private schools were expensive. I'd assumed I'd go to a state school, like my brother and his friends.

"Well, we know you'll make the most of it, Stephen," she went on. "You're such a great student. We're very proud of you."

"Yes, we are," Ken chimed in, nodding.

When I went to bed that night I realized that no one had mentioned my father the whole day, not even Uncle Harold, until that talk in the den. It was as if he were there but everyone pretended he wasn't. During the bar mitzvah service, though, Rabbi Satlow had called me to the Torah by my Hebrew name: Shlomo ben Shimon. Shlomo, the son of Shimon. According to Rabbi Satlow and Jewish law, Shimon—Si—was still my father and always would be.

# 2

My cousin Dave and I had gone to Camp Ella Fohs twice before, and we returned that summer. It was a coed, sleepaway camp in northwestern Connecticut, outside the town of New Milford, set amid rolling, wooded hills that encircled a small, man-made lake. We always stayed for one of the three-week sessions.

There was nothing fancy about Ella Fohs, but we loved it. UJA-Federation, a Jewish philanthropy, had founded the camp to give the children of immigrants a chance to get outdoors. Most of the campers were Jewish, but there was a smattering of Blacks and Puerto Ricans. A few of us were from Long Island and Brooklyn, while the majority were from the Bronx. They lived in apartment buildings on Jerome Avenue or the Grand Concourse or in Co-op City, where their parents were teachers, civil servants, and shopkeepers. Every July, a hundred of us would gather outside the East Tremont YMHA in the Bronx, lugging canvas duffel bags, and pile onto school buses that drove us two hours to Ella Fohs.

In the summer of 1968, my cousin and I were bunking with two other boys in the camp's "tent city," where twelve-to-fourteen-year-olds lived in four-man tents that sat atop sturdy wooden platforms. Our counselor, a college student named Roy, had long hair and a wispy goatee, and spent most of his time playing the sitar, which the Beatles had just made popular. He didn't take off his sunglasses all summer, even indoors.

Dave and I played a lot of softball. We had a good five-man team that was undefeated against teams of nine. Then one day it rained hard and we stayed in our tents, reading comics and practicing card tricks. Before lunch, Roy told all the boys in tent city to report to the rec hall for a sex education movie. I joined the stampede to claim spots on the wooden benches as close to the front as possible. The screen was the portable, pull-down kind. There was a din of talking and laughing.

The camp director, Dan Farinella, stood in front of the screen, hands on hips, waiting for us to simmer down. He was forty-ish, of medium height and large build. His big shoulders, powerful arms, and broad chest, all atop short legs, gave the impression he was just a torso. His dark T-shirt hugged an impressive gut. He had a pack of cigarettes rolled up in his left shirtsleeve and wore khaki shorts to the knees along with white Keds sneakers.

Farinella had become the camp's director the summer before. The first time I saw him I thought he might be Rodney Dangerfield's Italian twin brother. His dark basset-hound eyes and big lips gave him a perpetual hangdog look.

He was growing impatient. When he motioned for the room of rowdy boys to quiet down, it got noisier.

"Okay, shut up ya faces!" Farinella boomed, putting on his Bronx tough-guy voice. The rec hall fell silent. A couple of kids in front began heckling him about his haircut, which looked like someone had placed a bowl over his head and shaved around it.

"Hey, don't make fun of ugly people!" he deadpanned to loud laughter, feigning a hurt look. "It's nice to be nice. Don't forget that." It was one of his stock lines, used while breaking up fights or intervening before they started. With the room settled, Farinella introduced the film.

"As long as you're all sitting around moping, you may as well learn something for a change. I know you think you know it all, but based on the wacko stuff I've been hearing, I think some sex education would be a good idea. That's how you become mature, responsible adults. You all want to become mature and responsible, right?"

There was a murmur of agreement. Farinella looked disgusted.

"What are you, in a coma? I said you all want to become mature and responsible, *right*?"

"RIGHT!" we screamed.

"That's what I thought. You guys in the front row, don't get too excited, there's no nudity in this film. Like they say on *Dragnet*, it's just the facts. Try to contain yourselves and save the questions for your counselors."

The film opened with two men, dressed in suits and ties, sitting in big chairs. They looked like newsmen on TV. They answered "normal questions" about masturbation and menstruation. There was a diagram showing the female reproductive system. For something so simple on the outside, it sure seemed complicated on the inside.

When the film was over, we ran through the pouring rain to the mess hall. Lunch was macaroni and cheese, my favorite, washed down with purple bug juice. I had just finished eating and was about to leave when someone tapped my shoulder. I figured it was my cousin, but when I turned my head, Farinella was looming over me.

"C'mon, I want to talk to you," he said, nodding toward the front door. He didn't look happy.

My stomach lurched. *What the hell did I do wrong?*

I followed him down the center aisle, between the long rows of tables. My mind was replaying the morning's events, searching for what I'd done that might have gotten the director's attention. I'd

never said a word to him before. That would have been like speaking
to the school principal, something you only did if he summoned
you to his office, which had never happened to me in my life.

Farinella was nothing like Mr. Golden, who had run the camp
during my first summer. Golden stuck to his cabin and his office.
Not Farinella. He prowled the grounds day and night, appearing
without warning at the waterfront, in the dining hall, and during
bunk activities. He addressed all one hundred campers at flagpole
each morning, stood over the cooks in the kitchen, barked orders at
the lifeguards, and scanned the woods after dark with his high-beam
flashlight, hunting for night raiders from the boys' bunks. Farinella
was everywhere. He knew everything.

I stared straight ahead as we walked toward the big screen doors,
avoiding eye contact with the other kids. They knew I was in trouble. Once outside, I trailed behind him down the soggy path. It had
stopped raining. Farinella said nothing, but when we got to the dirt
road, he turned to be sure I was keeping up. Finally, he spoke.

"Don't worry, you didn't do anything," he said. "I just like to get
to know our campers."

I exhaled loudly, as if I'd been holding my breath the whole time.

"Oh, good, I was a little worried," I confessed.

"How's camp going for you?" he asked. "You having a good
time?"

"Yeah, I like my tent. It's my cousin and two other guys."

When I told him the names, he said he knew their families in the
Bronx. We had reached the junction in the dirt road and could keep
going straight toward the infirmary or turn right to the other side of
the lake, where there was a camp for low-income, Jewish senior citizens. Farinella was the director of that camp, too. He turned right.

The senior side was off-limits to junior campers, but we could see
the old folks across the lake every day: bubbes and zaydes in rickety
beach chairs talking and waving their arms. In the afternoons, pairs
of them circled the lake in rowboats, their teenage waiters pulling
the oars.

The grounds on the senior side were mysterious. There was an enormous redbrick mansion at the top of a grassy hill that rose gently from the lake's shoreline. We all knew the Fohs family had once lived in that house. Every summer I heard campfire stories about the mansion: that it was haunted, that there were sex parties in the attic, that people still lived in the basement. I didn't believe these tales any more than I believed the one about a child-eating monster named Cropsy that roamed the surrounding woods.

But there was one story I'd heard so many times from so many counselors that I thought it might be true. They said that Ella, the family's teenage daughter, had drowned in the lake, which is why the lake and the camp were named for her. One counselor told me that a spooky portrait of the dead girl still hung in the mansion. I could have asked Farinella, but I didn't want to sound ridiculous.

Once we crossed to the senior side he turned onto a footpath that ran down to the lake. Now I could see the junior waterfront across the water—its canoes, boathouse, and flagpole. It was strange to see them from this side, like a postcard of my camp.

"Tell me about your family," Farinella said.

"I don't know. Like what?"

"Brothers and sisters?"

"Yeah. I have one brother and one sister. They're older."

"How much older?"

"He's nineteen. She's seventeen." Then I said, "They're my stepbrother and stepsister." I wasn't sure why I added that part.

"You lose a parent?"

"Yeah. My father died just before I turned five. My mother remarried."

"You get along with your stepdad?"

"Yeah, sure."

"How about your brother and sister?"

"I like them. I'm close with my brother . . ."

"But?"

"He and my mother fight a lot. That's hard."

Farinella nodded, like this was a problem he was familiar with. We all knew he was a social worker.

We were down at the shoreline now, walking side by side through the tall marsh grass.

"What'd you think about the film this morning?" he asked.

"I thought it was good. Better than the one we saw in school this year." Actually, I thought the film was lame, but all those films were lame.

"So you already knew all that stuff?"

"Not really," I said. "I'm sure there's a lot I don't know."

"What do you think about masturbation?" he asked.

I kept walking and didn't answer. Was this a test? The film had said masturbation was normal, but there was no way I was going to admit jerking off to a grown-up, much less the head of the camp. What if he thought masturbation was depraved?

"Well, I wouldn't condemn anyone who did it," I finally said. "Condemn" was one of those words I'd picked up reading the *New York Times* every day. I worried whether I'd used it properly. I sounded like a goddamn lawyer.

"You know it's totally normal, right?" he asked.

"Yeah, sure."

I thought I should explain my hesitation. So I told him what had happened the previous fall—a story I'd never shared with anyone. Three days before Dave's bar mitzvah, he called saying he had started pissing blood. He and I were sure the problem was too much jerking off, and I'd probably start bleeding next. Dave told his father, who took him to a specialist, who said it might be a tumor. He recommended an exploratory procedure right away, but my aunt refused to postpone the bar mitzvah. There were a hundred people coming, she said.

Dave went through his bar mitzvah weekend thinking he was going to die. I was terrified. The following week, he went to the hospital and had a cystoscopy. It turned out there was nothing wrong with him. The bleeding had probably come from a bad hit he'd taken during football practice. Jerking off had nothing to do with it, the doctor told him. That was our all-clear signal, but I still wondered.

By the time I finished talking, Farinella and I had done a loop on the path and were back at the dirt road. He shot me a funny look, like maybe he thought I was nuts.

"Masturbation is a natural and healthy thing," he said. "It's nothing to worry about or feel guilty about, okay?"

I nodded, glad to hear that from another adult besides Dave's doctor. I was even gladder to move on to another topic. Then I realized our walk was over.

"You better get back to your bunk," he said. "If you ever need anything, you let me know."

I wanted to thank him, but I wasn't sure what to call him. I knew him only as Farinella. The counselors called him Dan. The kids from the Bronx called him Danny. I thought Dan was safer since I wasn't from the Bronx.

"Okay, thanks, Dan," I said.

"All right," he answered. Then he headed up toward the mansion, and I returned to the junior side by myself.

WE RETURNED FROM swim period one day to find that a bed in our tent had been smeared from top to bottom with peanut butter. The boy who slept in it wasn't too popular. Every night he snacked on peanut butter after lights-out. He kept a supply of the stuff in a duffel bag under his bed. We weren't supposed to have food in the tents—there were raccoons and skunks around. Plus, it was annoying as hell to hear and smell him eating his Skippy.

Still, I was sure that my cousin and our other tent mate weren't behind the peanut butter attack. That would have been too obvious. Besides, neither of them had said anything to me. It had to be a kid from another tent.

Solving the crime was too much for Roy, our counselor, so Farinella was called in. I thought he'd line everybody up, the way they did in school, and make us stand there or threaten some collective punishment until the guilty one confessed. But Farinella didn't do that. Instead, he sat in our tent and summoned each boy in our bunk, one by one, to talk with him. When it was my turn, I went in and sat on the bed opposite him.

"Well, at least I know it wasn't you," he said.

"How do you know?" I asked. I was sure I'd be a suspect.

"You don't have it in you," he replied.

"How will you figure out who did it?" I asked.

"Easy. Someone's story won't line up with everyone else's. There'll be holes. I'll know in thirty minutes."

I was impressed. He was like a detective who'd taken me into his confidence. I was on the inside, part of his team. He told me to get in touch if I saw or heard anything, but I never had the chance. It only took twenty minutes for him to finger the culprit. It was my cousin.

I WAS LYING on my bed during free period reading a *Batman* comic when Farinella stuck his head in the tent.

"Okay if I come in?" he asked.

I was confused to see him there.

"Sure," I said.

I put down the comic and sat up. He lowered himself onto the bed facing me, then leaned forward, planting his large hands on the mattress. He was too big for the tent.

"Your cousin needs to respect people's property," he said.

"Yeah, he told me you're docking him from canteen."

"It's okay not to like somebody, but you got to find other ways to settle your differences."

"I know," I said.

"Have you two always been pals?"

"Yeah, since we were little kids."

"That's good. It's good to have family. Lets you appreciate the differences in people."

"What do you mean?" I asked.

"Every person's different. That's what makes the world go round. You and your cousin are opposite personality types, so it's good you can get along."

"What's his personality?" I asked.

"The kind that would play the trombone. You know, big and brassy."

"How do you know he plays the trombone?" I asked, amazed.

"He told me," Dan replied. "He's a very confident guy. Maybe a little too confident."

"I guess," I said. "I never noticed till this year, when he started playing quarterback and bragging."

"He's just compensating for some deep insecurity. Boasting helps him feel okay about himself." I'd never thought of Dave as insecure but what did I know? Dan was a social worker.

"So what kind of personality am I?" I asked.

"You really want to know?"

"Yeah."

"You got a piece of paper and a pencil?" he asked.

"Sure, why?"

"Just get 'em and let's go for a walk."

I grabbed them out of my cubby and followed him outside. He headed toward the rec hall and I trotted to catch up before he turned onto the softball field. I had no idea where we could be going—this was a dead end. But he crossed the field and led us into the woods on a well-hidden trail that went steeply uphill. After a few minutes, he stopped and pointed to a fallen log.

"Let's sit here," he said.

The log had a good view of the lake. I could see kids in their canoes and old people in their rowboats. I felt special to be up here with Farinella, like we were on some secret mission.

"All right," he said, pointing at the paper, "I want you to draw me a picture of a family."

"A family or *my* family?" I liked to be clear when I was taking tests.

"Whatever you think about when I say family," he replied.

"I'm bad at drawing."

"It could be the worst drawing in history," he said. "Doesn't matter."

While he watched the lake, I drew five figures: a mother, father, and three kids—a boy, a girl, and a baby. When I finished, I studied it for a minute, trying to guess what it might mean. I handed the drawing to Dan and he glanced at it for two seconds.

"You're a scared rabbit," he said.

That sounded bad.

"How can you tell?"

"You drew yourself as helpless, a baby. And you see how you're off to the side? It's almost like you're not in the family at all, like you're trying to disappear."

I was amazed he'd figured that out from a drawing, but I didn't like being called a scared rabbit.


AFTER THAT WALK in the woods, I felt like Dan was my friend. He knew stuff about me that no one else knew. Only a week before, he'd been Farinella, the ruler of camp. Now we were buddies.

One afternoon during swim period I saw him on the waterfront horsing around with two older boys in their bathing suits. I went over to them, something I wouldn't have done a week earlier.

"Hey, Steve," Dan said, "you're just in time. Give me a hand with these two tough guys." He pretended to cower as the two fourteen-year-olds flailed away with their fists at his shirtless upper body, laughing at his weak attempts to cover up.

"Let me show you how to take care of bullies like this," Dan said to me. "First you use the shark bite. You know what that is?"

"No," I said.

His right hand shot out and grabbed the fleshy part of one kid's stomach. "Shark bite!" he yelled. Then he twisted the handful of flesh and the boy hollered in pain until Dan let go.

"If that doesn't work, you blivitz 'em."

He turned toward the second kid and delivered a quick knee to the outside of his thigh. "Blivitz!" The boy hobbled away, dragging his leg in circles, desperate to make the spasm stop.

"The worm has turned!" Dan exclaimed, with obvious satisfaction. "You two give up yet? I'm rough and tough!" He flexed his biceps like he was Mr. Universe.

"No!" they screamed, then began attacking him all over again. It was like watching two puppies try to take down a buffalo.

"Hey, Steve," Dan said, peeking through his arms. "You got to help me here."

There was no way I was going to side with him. I'd seen enough of these fights to know the rules. It was everyone against Dan. The bigger the gang, the more he loved it. I stepped in and delivered a blivitz to his right thigh. He howled.

"You traitor! I thought you were my friend," Dan cried.

The bell rang, signaling the end of swim period.

"All right, enough!" he yelled, throwing us off him one at a time. "Get ready for dinner. I'm not going to hold it against you, Steve. You turned on me, but we're still friends, right?"

He put out his hand to shake mine. I wasn't going to fall for it. I'd seen him squeeze a kid's hand till he screamed in pain.

"No way," I said, shaking my head.

"What do you think, I'm going to hurt you? I'm trying to make peace here. You can't refuse a handshake when someone's making peace. Come on now."

I extended my hand and he shook it, then slowly tightened his grip until it hurt. Then he tightened some more. The pain was excruciating, like my bones were breaking.

"Stop!" I screamed.

He didn't stop. I started crying.

When he saw my tears, he let go. Then I turned and ran as fast as my legs would fly. My hand was throbbing, my face flushed with shame. I was a weakling, a scared rabbit. I flew into the first open door: Dan's cabin.

I dashed into the bathroom, slammed the door shut and locked it. I stood hunched over, hands on my knees, trying to catch my breath and stop crying. I hated Dan Farinella. I'd been such an idiot to trust him. The betrayal hurt worse than my aching hand.

A minute later, he was talking to me through the door.

"Hey, I'm sorry. I didn't mean to hurt you. Come on out now."

He sounded sorry but I didn't care. I wasn't coming out.

"I promise, I'll never do that again. I made a mistake. I'm sorry."

He kept talking and apologizing, but I didn't say a word. His tone grew more and more pleading. After twenty minutes or so, my resolve weakened. I couldn't stay in his bathroom all night. I opened the door.

"You all right?" he asked.

"Yeah, I'm fine." I didn't want him to think I was a baby. "But don't do that to me again."

"I won't," he said. "I promise."

My friends and I were passing the director's cabin when I heard Dan call my name. He was outside on his deck, smoking a cigarette.

"Hey, Steve," he yelled. I liked when he singled me out. I walked over to him.

"Come on inside," he said. "Have some milk and cookies. It'll make you feel better."

"I feel okay."

"Well, it'll make me feel better. I feel bad about the other day."

He put out his cigarette, and I followed him into the cabin's small kitchen. There was a boy from a younger bunk sitting there and a plate of chocolate chip cookies in the middle of the table.

"Steve, this is Howie. We just solved all his problems. Right, Howie?" The boy nodded. "Okay, you better get back to your bunk," Dan said to him. "They're probably wondering where you are." Howie took another cookie, then got up and left.

Dan poured me a glass of milk and I picked out a cookie with a lot of chocolate chips.

"So?" he asked, standing over me.

"So what?" I replied.

"Sew buttons on overcoats."

"Very funny," I said, sarcastically, in between bites.

"Hey, that's one of my best jokes."

"Then you need some new material."

"Jeez, you're tough on a guy," he said. "How's the cookie?"

"It's good. Better than the ones in the mess hall."

"So are we friends again?" he asked.

"Yeah, I guess."

"Good, then I'm happy. You want to know a secret?"

"What?"

"You can get most kids talking with milk and cookies. They don't teach you that in social work school, but it works like magic."

# 3

THE FIRST TIME DAN CALLED my house I was sitting at the kitchen table after school, eating pecan sandies and drinking a glass of milk. When the phone rang, my mother left off unpacking the groceries from Waldbaum's and grabbed the yellow, corded receiver off the wall. I could tell it wasn't a friend or a relative because she didn't say anything for a few seconds.

"Oh, hello, Dan," she finally said, sounding flustered. "Of course I know who you are."

It was a girlish tone, the one she used when speaking to someone important. In my mother's world, no one was more important than social workers. They ranked just below Freedom Riders, Bobby Kennedy, and Martin Luther King, those who had been martyred in the cause of a more just society. Social workers were in the trenches every day, advocating for low-income housing, teen pregnancy programs, and drug rehab. She worked as a secretary and office manager for the Family Service Association. Her branch was located in the basement of an all-Black, public housing project in Freeport.

My mother's boss at county headquarters was Sal Ambrosino,

the dean of progressive social work on Long Island. She idolized Sal. He was the son of Italian immigrants, a man of the people who had devoted his life to the downtrodden. Sal had no patience for bureaucrats or agencies that patronized the populations they served. He was all about changing things from the bottom up. "Empowering the poor," he called it. His name was spoken with reverence at our dinner table.

To my mother, Dan Farinella was the second coming of Sal Ambrosino—another scrappy Italian kid off New York's mean streets who was serving the less fortunate. She had never been to camp or met Dan. Each summer she drove me to the Bronx and put me on the bus. But Dan's reputation extended beyond camp. He was a counselor at Oyster Bay High School on Long Island, where he was known for reaching the hardest-to-reach kids, no matter their race, class, or drug of choice. He was partial to tough love, cutting through bullshit and talking straight.

Speaking to Dan on the phone, my mother was rapt, chiming in with the occasional "uh-huh" and "I see."

"That's very nice of you, Dan," she finally said. "Let me discuss it with Stephen and his father and we'll get back to you."

I couldn't imagine what we needed to discuss. It was November. I wasn't going to camp for another eight months. And why would Dan be calling about camp anyway? He was the director. I was just a camper.

She hung up the phone, looking pleasantly surprised.

"Dan Farinella is inviting you up to Ella Fohs with him next weekend. It'll just be you and him. He wants you to help out with some projects there."

"Really?" I said, amazed.

Sure, I'd gotten to know Dan a little bit over the summer, but so had plenty of other kids. I was just one more camper who called him Dan or Danny. But getting chosen to visit camp with him in the off-season was a whole different thing. It was like winning a prize I didn't know existed.

"Yes, imagine that," my mother said. "I guess you're not that bad after all. You're going to go, right?"

"Yeah, of course."

My mind was flooded with questions. What would we do there? What was it like at camp when no one was around? Where would we sleep? What would we eat? What would Dan and I talk about for two days? For the next week and a half, the trip to camp was the last thing I thought about at night and the first thing in my head when I woke up.

That Friday, I told my friends I wouldn't be around on the weekend to play touch football or our usual marathon game of Risk.

"The director of my summer camp needs my help up in Connecticut," I said, trying to sound casual, like it was a big deal but also no big deal.

After school, I packed a gym bag and sat on the living room sofa, tapping my foot. When the doorbell finally rang, I vaulted off the sofa and opened the front door. Dan was standing there in chinos, a button-down shirt, and his usual white Keds. I'd never seen him out of shorts and a T-shirt before. He was holding a large white bakery box, like he had brought dessert for the holidays.

"So, you going to let me in or what?" he asked through the screen door.

"Yeah, sorry." He came in and shook my hand. Then my mother appeared.

"Hi, Sydell. I'm Dan," he said. "Very nice to meet you."

"It's an honor to meet you, Dan," she said. "We've heard such great things about you and Camp Ella Fohs."

He was very courteous with my mother, not like the tough guy at camp who took charge and issued orders. He sheepishly offered up the large white box with both hands.

"I brought you some cannoli," he said.

"Wow!" my mother exclaimed, her arms sagging under the weight of the box. "That's a lot of cannoli."

"There's a few other pastries, too. It's from a place in Yonkers. I know my cannoli, and I won't get them anywhere else."

"Would you like one before you go?" she asked. "I could make some coffee."

"I'd love some black coffee. Thank you, Sydell." Everyone called my mother Syd. Sydell sounded strangely formal to me.

My mother showed Dan to the living room, where he sank into the sofa. Then I followed her into the kitchen to get a look inside the box. She cut the delicate red and white string and opened the lid. I was looking at more Italian pastry than I'd ever seen in one place outside Borrelli's restaurant. My mother piled an assortment on a plate.

In the living room I offered it to Dan but he waved me off, patting his gut. I put the cannoli on the coffee table, sat down opposite him, and waited for my mother to appear.

"You gonna eat one or what?" Dan asked. "Go ahead, *mangia*!"

I lifted a cannoli off the pile and took a bite. It was so good—crunchy on the outside, sweet and creamy inside. My mother came in with two cups of coffee and handed one to Dan.

"Okay if I smoke, Sydell?"

"Of course." She passed him a shiny blue ashtray I'd made at camp. Then she sat down near me on her favorite upholstered chair.

Dan lit a cigarette, took one puff, and laid it down in the ashtray.

"I hope you're going to help us eat these, Dan," my mother pleaded, pointing at the plate.

"No, thank you, Sydell. You enjoy."

My mother chose a biscotto and dunked it in her coffee.

"So where are you from originally, Dan?" she asked.

"The Bronx. Near Arthur Avenue. You know it?"

"Of course. That's the real Little Italy."

"That's right. But I'm not a real Italian—just half. My mother was Jewish. So I'm a mutt. I know how to get along with everybody. That's probably why I became a social worker."

My mother turned serious. "We need more of that. I don't understand what's happening to our country." She meant the killing of Bobby Kennedy and Martin Luther King. They fell silent, and I stopped eating my cannoli.

"It's all about respect, you know what I mean?" Dan said. "You got to respect yourself before you can respect others. That's what we teach at camp. A lot of these kids, they don't know their own heritage. Blacks, Puerto Ricans, Irish. They don't have a clue. We try to make them feel good about where they come from, so they can appreciate where others come from."

"I liked Soul Food Day last summer," I said. "The barbecue was good." I took a second cannoli.

"Everybody's got to eat," Dan said. "The best way to another culture is through the stomach."

"That's so true," my mother agreed. "My culture was matzoh balls, chicken livers, and schmaltz. All the foods that give me heart-burn now."

"Where did you grow up, Sydell?" Dan asked.

I'd heard this conversation between native New Yorkers a million times. I knew my mother's answer before she said it.

"Brownsville in Brooklyn. It was the dregs of the dregs. Terrible poverty. I once took Stephen there to see it. He was shocked."

"Yeah, no Jews there anymore," Dan said.

"The Jews fled when the public housing got built in the fifties," my mother explained. "I can't blame anyone for running from pov-erty. I married young partly to get out of there."

That was news to me. I wondered how old she and my father were when they got married. I imagined they had met after the war but I wasn't sure.

"How about you, Dan?" my mother asked. "Are you married?"

"Yep. One son. He's ten."

"Oh, that's wonderful."

"This is great coffee, Sydell," Dan said. "Just what I needed to get me going. Speaking of which"—he turned to me and put his cup down—"we should get a move on. There's always traffic on the Taconic."

"Okay, you two go," my mother said. "I'll start inviting people over to eat all these cannoli. It was so nice to meet you, Dan. Thanks for giving Stephen the chance to help out."

"I should be thanking you. I'm going to put him to work."

I pictured myself repairing tent platforms and clearing trails. I was going to prove myself. I wanted Dan to know he'd made the right choice by inviting me.

IN THE CAR, Dan asked me how eighth grade was going and quizzed me about things at home. Then he told me about what he had to do in the off-season at camp: order supplies and fix up cabins and hire counselors.

Whenever we stopped at a toll, he asked the tollbooth collector for a receipt. He had to keep track of his expenses, so the camp could pay him back. They paid for everything on these trips. I thought that was pretty cool, getting paid for staying at camp.

By the time we pulled into New Milford two hours later, the sun had set and I was starving. Dan said we'd eat at the Italian restaurant. It was a small place with wooden booths and red-and-white-checked tablecloths. The owner greeted Dan by name and seated us. I ordered lasagna. Dan got the spaghetti and meatballs.

"This place makes good meatballs, decent sauce," he said. "Not as good as my father's but not too bad."

"Your father cooked?" I asked.

"He had no choice. He hated my mother's cooking. Most Italian men can't boil water. They'd starve to death without their mamas. My father married a Jew, and she didn't know how to cook his food. So he learned how to make spaghetti and meatballs. It's probably the only thing I picked up from him."

"What kind of work did he do?"

"He was in the mob. A small-time hood—real son of a bitch."

"Huh." I wasn't sure what else to say.

AT THE ENTRANCE to Ella Fohs we pulled off Little Bear Hill Road and followed the shoreline of the lake. A minute later, as we neared the center of camp, our headlights picked up two figures sitting by a small fire at the waterfront.

"Now what?" Dan said.

He pulled up to the office, just above the lake, and cut the engine. I could make out a man and woman by the fire. As we walked down the slope, I recognized the woman: she was the nurse in the camp infirmary.

"Isn't that Carol?" I asked.

"Yep," Dan said. "And Jim, my new maintenance man. Looks like he's *shtupping* my nurse." I was surprised to hear him use the Yiddish.

Jim jumped up to greet us. "Well, howdy, Dan!"

He was a muscular guy in his late twenties, with a crew cut, US Army T-shirt, and tattoos on both arms. He looked kind of scary. He hoisted a bottle in our direction. Carol got up more slowly.

"Howdy?" Dan mimicked. "I'll tell you what's howdy. Howd'ya explain what you mental midgets are doing out here drinking?"

Jim grinned, like a kid caught by his parents, and he suddenly seemed less scary.

"Hello, Dan," Carol chimed in. She was wearing jeans and a sweater. I hadn't noticed during the summer how voluptuous she was.

"I don't give a damn what you two do at home," Dan said, "but there's no drinking or drugs in my camp, even in the winter."

"Yes, boss," Jim said.

Dan turned to Carol.

"I didn't expect to see you. You're not in the infirmary, are you?"

"No." She paused. "I'm in Jim's cabin."

"That'll work," Dan said. "We'll be in the infirmary tonight." He motioned to me. "This is Steve. He's helping me out."

I could tell Carol didn't recognize me. I was glad—she seemed embarrassed.

"What the hell is that gun for, Jim?" Dan suddenly asked.

I scanned the ground and saw a rifle lying by the fire.

"Heck, I was just hoping to get us some dinner, Dan."

"What kind of dinner? It's not deer season."

"I thought I might bag a turtle and then Carol here could make us some soup. I love turtle soup, but no sign of one yet."

"That's 'cause those turtles are a lot smarter than you," Dan said.

"Sure looks that way. I've been stalking them for days."

In my three summers at camp I'd yet to see a turtle on top of the pile of mud and sticks known as Turtle Island that sat thirty yards offshore.

"I'm going to make apple pie tomorrow," Carol said, changing the subject. "I picked the apples myself on the way up. Would you two like some?" She was smiling at me with piercing blue eyes and a kind face.

"I love apple pie," I said.

"Make sure that fire's out when you're done," Dan said, gruffly.

"You got it, boss," Jim replied.

Dan turned and walked toward the car. I followed behind.

"I'm running a goddamn resort for rednecks," he said, just loud enough for me to hear.

We were halfway up the hill when it hit me I was at camp. I stopped to gaze up at the sky. It was blanketed by a million stars.

WE DROVE PAST the Main House, the director's cabin, and the dining hall. They were empty and dark. The whole place was like one of those ghost towns I'd visited out West with my aunt and uncle. Our headlights sliced through a stand of trees that had lost most of their leaves. It was creepy. I started thinking about the ghost stories I'd heard at camp.

"That was kind of weird," I said. "I mean, Jim having a gun."

"Jim's okay," Dan said. "He's a local kid, just got back from Vietnam. I'm trying to help him adjust." Then, he added: "Looks like he's adjusting a little too well."

"Yeah, it looks that way," I said. I didn't really know what we were talking about, but I liked that Dan didn't hide adult things from me, like guns and sex and booze.

"I'm not worried about the rifle," he went on. "The nurse is what worries me. She could get knocked up before camp starts. Or those two lovebirds could run off. I don't like it, but she's a smart cookie, that one. She'll come to her senses when she realizes her stud has nothing between the ears."

"Huh," I said, at a loss for the second time that night.

Dan eased the car into the driveway and pulled up to the front steps of the infirmary, which was set back in the woods. When he turned off the engine, it got dark, almost pitch-black.

We grabbed our bags, then he turned on a flashlight and aimed it at the steps. The front door made a loud creaking noise when I opened it. I stopped for a second, inhaling the disinfectant smell. Dan followed me in and turned on the lights. There were exposed wooden beams overhead, lots of shuttered windows, and walls lined with supply cupboards. It was so cold I could see my breath.

"We'll stay in back," Dan said.

I followed him to a small room. He pulled the chain on a hanging bare bulb, revealing two metal beds about three feet apart. There were big partitioned windows on one wall. I could see our reflection in the glass. Dan seemed to take up most of the room.

"Pick a bed," he said. Each bed had a thin mattress made up with sheets but no blankets.

I threw my bag on the farthest one from the window and collapsed on it, exhausted. "Brrrrrr," I said, wrapping my arms around myself and shivering.

"Yeah, it's colder than a witch's tit in here," Dan said. "I'll get us a heater and some blankets."

He disappeared for a few minutes, then came back with an electric heater and plugged it in. When he returned the next time, he had an armful of gray woolen blankets, which he dumped on his bed. There were two magazines on top of the pile. He picked them up and tossed them in my direction.

"There you go," he said.

I propped myself up on one elbow and eyed the magazines next to my leg. The one on top was called *Mirage*. There was a naked woman on the cover, lying on her back, her knees drawn up and falling to either side. Her bush was exposed and it looked bigger than her head. The photo was gritty, like it was taken in someone's basement.

I pushed the magazine aside and looked at the one underneath. It showed a naked girl lying on her stomach, doing the splits, shot from behind. There was a yellow disk hiding her vagina.

Dan was standing over me. What did he want? Was I supposed to like these magazines or not like them? It seemed like a test, like when he'd asked me what I thought about masturbation.

"Well?" he asked.

I sat up and reached for *Mirage*, then leafed through it, slowly. There were lots of naked women with their legs spread. It was gross—nothing like *Playboy*. I had never seen a vagina before. The barrage of them was unrelenting.

I turned the pages faster. *I'm not supposed to be seeing this*, I thought. *I wish I wasn't here.* By the time I got to the last page, I was nauseous. I didn't want to do the wrong thing, and throwing up was definitely the wrong thing. I closed the magazine and set it down.

"What do you think of that?" he asked.

"I don't know," I said. "They're okay."

I made myself look up at him, but I didn't see any clue in his face at all. Blank. That scared me. He always had something to say. Maybe he was just showing me what adults did, like the way he told me about Jim and Carol screwing. If that's what this was, I didn't want any part of it.

"I'm so tired," I said, stifling a fake yawn.

"All right," he said. He took the magazines and left. I grabbed a blanket off his bed and dove under the covers wearing all my clothes. By the time he came back, I was curled up in a ball, facing the wall.

"Don't want to brush your teeth?" he asked. "It's good to brush your teeth."

"Too tired. I'll do it in the morning."

"All right," he said. "Good night."

Once he got in his bed, I lay awake for a long time, listening in case he moved. When I did fall asleep, I was plunged into a hallucination of rampaging ghosts and armed men bent on destroying me. But I kept waking up. Each time I opened my eyes, I was still in the small room with the large man in the metal bed next to me. Then I'd fall back into the same berserk nightmare of ghosts and armed men.

In the middle of this endless night, I opened my eyes and moonlight was pouring in through the window. Dan had kicked off the blankets and was lying on his back, wearing only his white briefs. He was snoring, and his enormous belly, lit by the moon, was rising and falling with each loud rattle.

Could this be the same person who had brought my mother cannoli that afternoon? He was a stranger, and I was alone with him in the woods, far from home. What did he want with me?

The full moon cast a cold, white light through the naked trees. Their bony, outsized shadows danced across the walls. This place was haunted.

I pulled the blanket over my head and began whispering: *Just make it to the morning. Just make it to the morning.*

# 4

THE NEXT TIME I woke up, it was light outside and Dan was gone. Then I remembered the magazines. Had any of that really happened?

I put on my shoes, grabbed a sweatshirt, and walked into the main room. Dan was on the front steps, smoking a cigarette. He came in, carrying a coffee cup.

"Sleeping beauty's up!" he said in a cheery tone.

"Morning."

"I brought you some hot chocolate," he said, handing me the cup. "It'll get you warmed up."

"Thanks." It tasted good, the same kind we had at camp in the summer.

"Sleep okay?" he asked.

"All right. Except you were snoring."

"Sorry. Just sock me if I do that. That's what my wife does. I'll roll over and stop." I knew I'd never do that.

He didn't say a word about the magazines. After I drank my hot chocolate, we went to the dining hall. The kitchen storeroom was stacked high with single-sized servings of Frosted Flakes, Cocoa Puffs, and Fruit Loops—all the sugar cereals I wasn't allowed to eat at home. I sliced open a box of Frosted Flakes, poured in some milk, and devoured it. I followed that with a box of Cocoa Puffs and then some Fruit Loops. Dan didn't care, but he said that I still hadn't brushed my teeth.

For the next hour, we took inventory of the storeroom. I stood on a ladder and counted off the giant, gallon-sized cans of peaches, pears, and tomato sauce. Down below, he wrote everything on a clipboard.

From there, we went to the senior side of the lake. I'd only been there that one time, after the sex education movie. The senior dining hall was like the cafeteria at school, with fluorescent lights and linoleum tile. We all wanted to be waiters or kitchen boys here when we turned fifteen. I heard you could make two hundred fifty bucks in a summer.

Dan and I repeated the inventory procedure. It went faster because there weren't as many cans to count.

"You're okay, Steve," Dan said, as we stood at the counter, eating tuna sandwiches he'd made. "You want to work here next summer?"

"I don't think I'm old enough. I'm only thirteen."

"When's your birthday?"

"May."

"So you'll be fourteen. You've got more on the ball at thirteen than most of the head cases I had here this year. We'll talk about it next spring, okay?"

"All right," I said. I loved the idea of saving money.

Back at the infirmary, Dan sat in the main room, working on his inventory sheets. I lay on my bed and read *Call of the Wild* for a book report due in English class. After a while, Dan came into the bedroom. He grabbed a pillow from his bed and threw it at me. I caught it and hurled it back at his head.

"Oh, you're a tough guy, huh?" he said. "Come on, take me down. Do your best."

I'd never had a fight with Dan by myself. I had zero chance against him but I knew he'd play the punching bag.

"C'mon, I'm rough and tough," he said, flexing his biceps.

I stood up, cocked my right fist, then came in low with a blivitz, burying my right knee in his left thigh. He howled for a couple of seconds, most of it an acting job.

"I'm built like a brick shithouse," he said, "You gotta do better than that."

"That's all I got," I said, shrugging.

"Did I ever show you where a horse bit me?" he asked.

"No." I pictured the huge teeth on a horse. That had to hurt.

He pulled down the collar of his T-shirt, revealing his left shoulder. Then he crouched down, told me to have a look, and I leaned in close. Suddenly, I felt his hand on my crotch and his body push into mine, dropping me to the bed.

*What about the horse bite?* I thought. I was pinned, on the wrong end of a wrestling move I'd learned in seventh-grade gym. His hand was rubbing my dick through my jeans. This wasn't wrestling. I couldn't see—his body was too big. The side of his head was in my face and I could smell the Brylcreem on his slicked-back hair.

"You give up yet?" he asked, still rubbing. "You give up?"

His voice sounded faint, as if it were coming from far away. I was frozen, unable to move, unable to speak. But my dick was getting hard.

"What's that in your pants?" he asked. He unsnapped my jeans, pulled them down, and continued pawing me through my underwear.

"Whoa, that's big. But I'm tough, I can take care of it."

*No, no, no,* I thought.

He released the hard-on from my briefs. Then it was in his mouth. He was sucking and slobbering. I closed my eyes and prayed. *I'm not here. I'm not here.*

When I opened my eyes, I was floating, looking down at my body, as if it belonged to someone else. There was pleasure coursing

through that body. I was going to come soon and somehow Dan
knew it.

"Hand or the mouth?" he asked. "You want the hand or the
mouth?"

*No hand. No mouth.* But the lifeless boy on the bed couldn't
speak. I climaxed, a powerful wave of pleasure followed by an even
longer wave of revulsion and shame.

When it was over, Dan sat up, holding my limp cock like a con-
quering hero.

"Pacified!" he exclaimed.

I clenched my eyes tight, unable to look at him. When he moved
off me, I opened my eyes and found myself in the bed again, gazing
up at the ceiling. A moment later, he reappeared, holding a white
washcloth.

"Clean yourself up," he said, tossing it to me.

I wiped around my stomach and pulled up my jeans. Rolling
onto my side, I saw *Call of the Wild* on the floor. I stared at the cover
for a long time. It seemed strange, like it belonged to some other
life—a life I wasn't in anymore.

Dan went back to his paperwork, and I heard him light a cigarette. I found the place in the book where I'd left off and read the
page over and over. No matter how many times I read it, I couldn't
follow anything.

Then I heard Carol's voice at the front door.

"You guys here?"

"Hey, Steve!" Dan called out. "Carol brought us some pie."

I didn't want any pie, but my body carried me into the other
room.

"Sorry, there's no ice cream," Carol said, gesturing to two slices
of pie on paper plates. I tried to smile.

"Are you feeling okay?" she asked. "You look pale."

"He's fine," Dan assured her. "He's just whipped. He's not used
to working so hard."

"Well, nothing that some pie can't fix," Carol said. "And if that doesn't do it, we're in the infirmary. I'll take care of you."

I sat at the table next to Dan, who was eating and making happy grunting noises.

"That Jim is one lucky guy," he said.

I lifted a small forkful to my mouth. Carol stood behind me, squeezing my shoulder. I wanted her to take care of me, to cover me with her kindness. But I didn't move a muscle.

WE ATE DINNER that night in the same booth of the same Italian restaurant as the night before. It seemed impossible that only twenty-four hours had passed. Everything had changed. Or rather, everything seemed the same on the surface: the red-and-white table-cloth, the Italian menu, Dan sitting across from me. But behind all that was some hidden realm, ghoulish and terrifying. I had no idea how I'd gotten here. I had no idea how to get out.

"Cat got your tongue?" Dan asked.

"I'm thinking about what to eat."

I didn't want lasagna, ever again. I decided on manicotti because my mother made it sometimes. The food came and we ate in silence. Then Dan smoked a cigarette, paid the bill, and got his expense receipt.

We had just arrived back at the infirmary when we heard the rifle report—a single shot that echoed off the hills surrounding the lake.

"Fuckin' Jim," Dan said. "C'mon."

We jumped in the car and drove to the waterfront. Dan trained his headlights on the lake and left the engine running. Jim was standing by the shoreline, holding a large turtle upside down by a tail nearly as long as the dark green shell.

"It's a snapper," Jim said when we reached him. The turtle's mouth was frozen open, the hooked beak protruding downward, as if poised to defend itself. "These guys almost never come out of the water this time of year. They just hang out on the bottom."

"You want to hold him?" Jim asked me.

I'd never seen a snapper this close. I took the turtle with both hands.

"Whoa, it's heavy," I said.

"Yeah, twenty, twenty-five pounds. I bet he's forty years old, maybe more."

I brought the turtle to my body and cradled it. The shell was covered with a blanket of slimy lake moss. That's why the turtle looked dark green, almost black. The odor of lake muck was strong. I stroked the soft, squishy coat. If this turtle was forty years old, he had been living in the lake before there was a camp. Maybe he was sitting there on Turtle Island, watching, when little Ella Fohs dove in and never resurfaced.

Why did Jim have to go and kill it? I thrust the turtle back at him, and he pointed at my sweatshirt, his eyes wide. I looked down and saw a jagged streak of dark red blood that ran from my chest to my belt.

"Looks like you got shot," Dan said. "That'll come out if you wash it at home tomorrow." He turned to Jim, who was admiring his prey.

"Hunting season's over, Jim. You got to stop with the guns. This isn't goddamn Vietnam."

"Whatever you say, boss. No more guns."

THERE WAS NO way I was going to change into my pajamas in front of Dan. When we got back to the infirmary, I grabbed them from my bag and went right to the bathroom. I studied my bloodstained sweatshirt in the mirror. It was freaky-looking. I peeled it off slowly, trying not to touch the blood.

After I put on my pajamas and brushed my teeth, I walked quickly to our room. Dan was lying on his bed, and I stopped in the doorway.

"Need anything?" he asked.

"No. Just some sleep."

"Did you brush your teeth?"

"Yeah."

"All right. Sweet dreams," he said. That sounded weird. It was something my mother said.

"Okay. Night."

I got under the covers, faced the wall, and hugged my knees to my chest.

"Is the light going to bother you?" he asked. "I may read for a bit."

"No, that's okay." I knew I wouldn't sleep, light or no light.

I lay awake, thinking about wrestling and the dead turtle. I worried about the book report I had to write. The next thing I knew, the sun was up.

Dan was still sleeping, the covers pulled up to his neck. I was glad—I didn't want to see his underwear again. I changed into my clothes and went outside. It was freezing. Then I walked back and forth, watching my breath till Dan got up.

After breakfast, he said he had to meet with Jim, so I wandered around camp. I climbed Junior Hill and found my first bunk. The maroon-colored wooden barrack was set into a steep slope, held up in front by four tall columns of cinder blocks.

Inside, the windows were shuttered and the light was dim. I went over to my old metal bed and sat on the lower bunk. The coils creaked under the thin, worn mattress. I'd been so nervous that first night away from home when I was ten. On the second day of camp, I met the director, Mr. Golden. He was a nice guy, like my schoolteachers.

Dan had seemed nice, too. Then he showed me those gross magazines and grabbed my dick. Then he was nice again. What did he want from me? I planted my elbows on my knees and held my head between my hands.

He had trapped me. I'd done something so awful I could never tell anyone. If I hadn't gotten a hard-on, this wouldn't have happened.

It was my fault. He could hold it over me. He could even tell my parents.

But why was he doing it? I remembered about his father being in the mob. Maybe Dan was in the mob, too. It seemed crazy, but why not? A well-known Mafia family lived a few blocks away from us in East Meadow. They seemed normal. I knew their kids. But I heard they were dumping bodies all over the place. For all I knew, Dan had kidnapped me. I might never be going home. Or if he did take me home, and I told anyone, he might kill my whole family.

I was rocking back and forth on the bunk bed, wishing things could be the way they were before.

WHEN I RAN into Dan at the waterfront, he had my gym bag. He said we had to get going because after he dropped me on Long Island, he'd have to double back and drive another hour to his house in Yonkers.

We didn't say a word in the car. In New Milford, he pulled into a diner and said we were getting lunch. I was relieved. If he was going to kill me, he probably wouldn't buy me lunch first.

We ate our sandwiches at the counter and watched a football game on the black-and-white TV.

"I never understood this game," he said. "Bunch of goons beating the crap out of each other. Reminds me of where I grew up."

"Did you get beat up when you were a kid?"

"Sure. Who didn't? Most of the time I did the beating. I hated bullies, always picking on weak kids. I was the guy who got your lunch money back, you know what I mean?" I pictured Dan, with his powerful arms, pulverizing the older toughs who tormented me in grade school.

When he paid for our check, Dan asked if I wanted candy, and I picked out some Juicy Fruit gum. As soon as we got in the car, I opened my book and pretended to read. But after a while, I gazed out the window, trying to smother my fear. What was his plan?

When I finally saw the sign for the Long Island Expressway, I relaxed a little, knowing I'd be home soon. I hoped Dan wouldn't come in the house. But when we pulled into the driveway, he cut the engine and said, "I should say hi to your folks."

I jumped out, grabbed my bag, and headed to the front door, wanting everything to seem normal. My parents were in their chairs, reading the Sunday *Times*. After my mother kissed me, she introduced Dan to Ken and they shook hands.

"How'd it go up there?" my mother asked me.

"Good."

"We got a lot done," Dan said. "Steve was a big help. We took inventory in both kitchens."

"Nice work," Ken said, smiling proudly.

The three of them went on for a while about the Bronx and Brooklyn. I gripped my gym bag with the bloody sweatshirt inside. I'd wash it while my mother was at work the next day. I could tell she didn't suspect a thing.

"Steve, let me know when you've got another weekend free," Dan was saying. "I get a lot more done when you're up there."

My parents smiled, waiting for me to respond.

"Okay," I said.

He reached out his hand and I shook it. After he left, my parents went on about what a great guy he was.

# 5

I WOKE UP AT SEVEN, downed some Wheaties with milk, and avoided my mother. At a quarter to eight, I yelled goodbye and trudged to school, lugging several fat textbooks under my right arm.

At the bus gate, I said hey to some kids who sat on the same square of sidewalk every morning, smoking. Once inside, I flung open my hallway locker with a clang and stared at the books, Twinkie wrappers, loose change, and crumpled-up paper. It all looked familiar but different somehow, as if I were seeing my life through glass, like one of those dioramas of ancient man at the Museum of Natural History.

I grabbed what I needed and headed to homeroom, dodging anyone I knew along the way. I didn't want to get asked about the weekend. In class, someone was impersonating Tiny Tim, singing "Tiptoe Through the Tulips" and pretending to play the ukulele. I made myself laugh along with everyone else.

At lunch, I sat with my friends and ate a sloppy joe before we cleared our trays and played penny hockey on the long, smooth tabletop. I scored a couple of goals and threw my hands in the air but felt nothing.

As soon as I got home I threw the bloody sweatshirt in the washer with a full cup of detergent and set it on hot. An hour later there was only a faint stain. I put it in the dryer and left for my clarinet lesson.

My teacher, Abe, lived four blocks away. He was a professional clarinetist and conductor. I'd been taking lessons in his basement for years. Abe was strict, but patient and funny, and looked like a big, bearded teddy bear.

When I sat down next to him that day, though, he seemed different, more sinister. I kept my eye on him as I put my clarinet together. Did he always sit this close? My hands felt clammy as I gripped the instrument. I'd been practicing Bach's Chaconne for months but the sheet music in front of me, a hodgepodge of black marks, looked unplayable. I began and my fingers somehow found the notes.

When I was done, Abe cringed and said, "Uh, where'd Stephen go?"

Walking home, I was alarmed to realize that Abe looked like Dan: big guy, black hair, swarthy complexion. How come I hadn't noticed it before? I pushed the thought away. Abe was a great guy. But that's what I had thought about Dan. What if Abe's friendliness was an act? I was alone with him in his damned basement. I mapped out the windowless room in my mind. There were two staircases I could use to escape if he ever tried something.

That night I was lying in bed when Miss June called to me from her hiding spot under my mattress. I closed my eyes, picturing her and stroking myself. Five seconds later, her image vanished, replaced by the back of Dan's greasy head and the loud drooling noises he made.

I stopped. How did he even know how to make me come? How did he know my body like that? This had been so easy before. I never had to think about it. I was going to come now if it was the last thing I ever did. I shut my eyes tight and focused on Miss June. She wanted to make me happy.

It was over in less than a minute. But I knew: this would never be the same.

Dan called a month later. My mother yelled to me that he was on the phone.

"Hurry up," she said.

The second I heard his voice—*Hey*—I was trapped, helpless. He wanted me at camp that weekend.

"Yeah, okay," I mumbled. When I hung up, I felt a burning sensation in my stomach, like I'd swallowed a hot coal.

Dan showed up Friday afternoon after he got off work at Oyster Bay High. He said we'd stop at his house in Yonkers on our way to camp. An hour later he parked in front of a small, two-story home and I followed him up the front steps.

"Betty!" he bellowed.

"I'm in the kitchen," his wife yelled back.

I stopped in the living room, brought up short by the sofa and easy chairs. They were covered in thick, see-through plastic, like they were on display in a furniture showroom. Dan saw my confusion.

"That's to protect them and make sure no one sits on them," he said, frowning.

"Aw, what do you know?" Betty said sharply. She was standing between the living and dining rooms, holding a kitchen knife at her side.

"I know plenty," Dan said. "I know you were barefoot when I found you in the gutter in the Bronx. Now look at you! You think you're the Queen of Sheba with your plastic sofa."

"I'm as close to the queen as you're ever going to get," she shot back.

Betty was younger than Dan, maybe thirty or so. Her minidress hugged a stout, curvy body. She wore her reddish hair in a bobbed cut and had on eye makeup and a gold necklace, like she'd just gotten home from work. She didn't seem like someone who would be spending much time at camp.

The way they talked to each other reminded me of the "rank-out" contests we had at Ella Fohs. You'd insult someone's mother— *Your mother wears army boots*—and the other kid would have to top it—*Yeah, your mother's so fat, when she goes camping the bears hide their food*. I'd never heard a married couple rank each other out.

"And who might you be?" Betty asked, as if she'd just noticed me.

"This is Steve," Dan said. "Remember? I told you he's going to help me at camp this weekend."

"Right. Camp always comes first," she said, rolling her eyes.

"Hey, girlie, mind your own business!" Dan yelled. He sounded dead serious but also the opposite, like when he told campers not to make fun of his haircut. Then he asked, "How about feeding us before we go?"

I thought Betty might throw the knife at him. Instead, she turned toward me, a maternal look on her face.

"Are you hungry, Steve?"

"Actually, I am."

"Okay, you two get lost and I'll put something up."

"Let's go downstairs and I'll get the stuff I need," Dan said to me.

The basement was finished with wood paneling. There was a workbench covered with tools in one corner and a desk against the far wall. Dan grabbed some papers off the desk.

Then he went to the middle of the room, glanced up at the low ceiling, and punched out one of the white perforated tiles. He reached into the empty space, and his hand came back down with two super-8 movies.

"This is where I keep my special ones," he said, showing them to me. The first had "Danish" in the title—there was a naked woman on the front. The second one showed a naked man and woman. She had her arm around a German shepherd.

"That's so gross," I said, covering the picture with my hand.

Dan laughed. "We love this one with the dog. We watched it with the neighbors."

I didn't want to know what the German shepherd did in that movie. I couldn't believe the woman cooking our dinner upstairs would watch this. Their neighbors had to be from a different planet than ours. I prayed Dan wouldn't bring the movies with us, so I was relieved when he put them back in their hiding spot.

On our way up the stairs it occurred to me that the world might be much weirder than I thought. Maybe our neighbors were just like Dan and Betty's neighbors. I mean, if Betty Farinella watched dirty movies, then who wouldn't? She was like someone in a commercial. She covered her sofa in plastic, for Christ's sake.

DAN PULLED OFF Route 202 at a liquor store in Brookfield, the town before New Milford. He cut the engine and told me to wait in the car. When he returned, he pulled a pack of cigarettes out of a brown paper bag, then tossed the bag on my lap.

"That's for you," he said. He lit a cigarette, while I reached in the bag and pulled out a *Playboy* magazine. I was confused. Did he know I had a copy of *Playboy* at home? Did he know everything? This was only the third issue I'd ever seen. I had goose bumps just holding it, but I was too embarrassed to open it. I put the magazine back in the bag, and Dan drove off without saying a word.

When we got to camp, it was getting dark. Dan passed the waterfront and turned right to the senior side. I was glad we wouldn't be in the infirmary. He went straight up the hill and followed the dirt road all the way to the end: a gravel parking area in front of the Fohs mansion.

I'd never seen anything like the massive, two-story brick house, except when my family had visited Monticello in Virginia. This place didn't have white columns or a dome on top, but the brick façade and partition glass windows reminded me of Jefferson's house. The home had three or four wings, all with different roof levels. There was a brick chimney on either side of the dark, ornately carved wood door.

Dan let us in with a key and turned on the lights. We were in a circular hall beneath a grand curving staircase. It was like something out of *Gone with the Wind.*

"Go look around," Dan said. "I'll put on the heat." It was freezing cold.

I wandered deeper into the house and found myself in a vast living room with floor-to-ceiling windows that framed the lake below. There were a few pieces of old furniture but it seemed as if no one had lived here for a long time.

From there I entered a parlor, pressed the switch on the wall, and an overhead light came on. A worn orange sofa with an ottoman faced a stone fireplace. High above the mantel hung a large, formal portrait of a girl and her mother in a gilt frame. This was the painting I'd heard about for years—the portrait of Ella Fohs.

Ella looked like she was twelve or thirteen, my age. She and her mother were in a forest clearing, with a blue lake and steep hills and dramatic clouds in the background. The girl was wearing a gauzy pink jumper that stopped a few inches above the knee. She was flat-chested, like a boy, with her hair cut in the sort of short bob I'd seen in pictures from the 1920s. She stood behind her mother, who was seated, wearing a severe black dress with a cape, as if she were in mourning.

Ella's mother was glaring at me, as if to ask: *What the hell are you doing here?*

Dan walked in, stopped in front of the portrait, and twisted his face in mock horror. Then he sat down on the sofa and lit a cigarette.

"Creepy, huh?" he asked.

"Very. How long has that been up there?"

"A long time. Ella died in the 1920s."

"When did they move out?"

"A few years ago. They donated the land for the camp."

Dan finished his cigarette, threw the butt in the fireplace, and left. I stayed put with Ella and her mother. I figured out that if the girl had lived she'd be about sixty and sitting on this sofa, and I wouldn't be here. Instead, she had a camp named after her and she'd be up there on the wall forever.

"Hey, get up here!" Dan yelled.

I turned off the light and found my way back to the big winding staircase, which brought me to the second floor. I followed the long hallway until I got to the only room with a light on.

"You can sleep there," Dan said, pointing to a bed, already made, with an arched wooden headboard. It looked a hundred years old and big enough for three people. I dropped my bag and sat on the foot of the bed.

Dan tossed me a pack of playing cards and told me to look inside. It was a regular deck—Jack, Queen, King, Ace—but when I turned the cards over there was a picture of a different naked woman on each one. They were more like the women in *Playboy* than the scary ones in *Mirage*. I lingered for two seconds over a beautiful ass, shot from behind. And just like that, I had a hard-on.

"That was fast," Dan said, grabbing at me with his right hand. "I guess you like those cards."

Without letting go, his left hand pushed me down until I was flat on my back, with my feet still on the floor. His body loomed over me and he tugged at my zipper. I clutched the playing card, holding up the naked woman to block out the man pulling down my jeans. Then he had me in his mouth.

I closed my eyes, wishing I were out of my body like last time. But it was too late. I reached into my gym bag and grabbed the *Playboy*, which was a lot bigger than the playing card. I held it above my chest and focused on Miss January. I could fit my entire body into the soft crevice between her breasts.

A minute later, Dan was saying, *Hand or the mouth?* I blotted him out, fixing my entire attention on Miss January until I came.

Dan got up, but a few seconds later, his hands were on me again, cleaning me with a washcloth. His belly was bursting out of his white T-shirt.

"Damn, that was a big load," he said. "Don't you ever jerk off?"

I didn't answer. I was thinking about Ella and her mother hanging on the wall beneath us. What if the two of them had seen what just happened? I covered my face with my hands. Ella's mother knew everything. I'd done something awful in her bed. It was unforgivable.

I felt the burning in my stomach again. This time it was intense, urgent. I pulled up my jeans and rushed to the bathroom. I had diarrhea. I sat on the toilet, studying the floor: black-and-white tile with lots of pieces missing. There were rust stains in the ancient bathtub and peeling paint on the walls. The place creeped me out.

I went to the bathroom twice more until there was nothing left in my gut.

"I'll make you some white rice," Dan said. "It's binding. That's what you need."

In the senior kitchen he got an enormous bag of rice out of the supply room. After cooking some on the stovetop, he served it to me in a small bowl. I ate in the dining room by myself while Dan made himself dinner.

Then I went right to bed. Dan slept in some other room. The next day, all I ate was white rice.


When I woke up on Sunday, it was snowing hard. Dan turned on his transistor radio and we heard that a big storm was moving in.

"Do you think we can make it out?" I asked. I didn't want to get stuck in the mansion with Dan and the rusty bathtub and Ella's portrait.

"Yeah, if we leave right now. I've got chains for the tires if we need them."

He disappeared, then returned with his bag. He grabbed the

*Playboy* off the floor and put it in his briefcase. Halfway down the mountain we got out of the station wagon and he showed me how to put on chains.

By the time we were on Route 7, the snow was blinding. I watched it pile up along the road and kids build snowmen in their front yards. It usually took twenty-five minutes to reach Danbury, where we'd pick up Interstate 84, but after an hour we still weren't there. Finally, we got to the entrance ramp but it was closed. A police officer told us they'd shut it down.

"Looks like we'll be staying here," Dan said.

"Where?" I asked.

"Right there," he said, pointing to a Howard Johnson's on the other side of Route 7. The orange roof was blanketed in white. "They've got a restaurant, too," he added.

I liked Howard Johnson's. My family went to a HoJo's near our house every so often for fish and chips. The orange and blue colors reminded me of the New York Mets uniforms. But I didn't want to stay in a Howard Johnson's with Dan. I wanted to go home.

At the front desk, a woman handed Dan a pen and asked him to fill out a registration card. She was wearing horn-rimmed glasses with pointy corners that made her look like a cat.

"Where are you fellas heading?" she asked me.

"Long Island," I said.

"You should have no problem making it tomorrow. The snow is going to taper off tonight."

Dan pushed the card toward her, and she studied it.

"I see you have different last names. Are you two family?"

"No," Dan said. "He's the son of a friend."

"Your room is just up the stairs," she said, handing him the key. "The restaurant is open if you're hungry."

The motel seemed new and the room was clean. There were two beds and no rust in the bathtub. Dan reached for the phone on the nightstand and called my mother to tell her about the roads being closed.

"It's snowing there, too," he said after he'd hung up.

"I hope there's no school tomorrow," I said. If there was school and I missed it, I'd have to explain my absence. What would I say? That I was stuck in a HoJo's with the director of my camp? That would sound strange even in the summer. In the winter it didn't make any sense at all.

I'd only eaten rice for a day and was starving. Downstairs in the restaurant I ordered the fish and chips.

"You looking forward to getting home?" Dan asked.

"Yeah. I don't want to miss school."

"How are things at home?"

"I don't know."

"You sure you don't know or you're just saying that?"

"Not great."

"Why not great?"

"I want to visit my brother at college and they won't let me. Well, my mother won't let me. My father doesn't say anything."

"Sounds like your average Jewish family," he said. "Do any of your uncles call the shots at home?"

I thought about this. My aunts were definitely in charge.

"No, I guess not. It's just, she makes me do this stuff I don't want to do, like getting confirmed. And she won't let me do the stuff I *do* want to do, like visiting my brother."

"What's 'getting confirmed'?"

"It's some made-up Reform Jewish thing that keeps you going to synagogue after your bar mitzvah. I hate it."

"Well, they gotta fill the seats," he said. "Personally, I think religion is the greatest cause of hatred in human history. The world would be a better place if everyone was an atheist."

I agreed, but I'd never heard an adult say that.

"Anyway, I don't think it's fair to stop me from seeing my brother. He's *my* brother, I have the right to see him."

"Yeah, you should have that right, but your mother's a ballbuster."

"What do you mean?" I asked.

"She needs to control the men in her life. It's a psychological thing. She dominates your stepfather and she tried to break your brother. She's not going to let you do what you want."

The waitress set down the fish and chips in front of me, but I didn't feel hungry anymore. I resented Dan calling my mother a ball-buster. It sounded horrible. Still, there was something to what he was saying, like he'd pulled a blindfold off my face. I'd been pissed at my mother for years, and he'd diagnosed the problem in ten seconds.

"Did I kill your appetite?" he asked, digging into his food.

"Kinda."

"You're in a tough spot, kid. Your brother escaped, so you're going to bear the brunt for a while."

"Yeah. Five more years. It's like a prison sentence."

"You'll survive. My old man used to beat the shit out of me on a daily basis. Look how good I turned out."

"That's not helping," I said.

"Hey, you got a right to feel bad. But don't starve yourself to death. I have to bring you home alive and you've only eaten rice. So shut uppa ya face and eat your fish."

I picked at the plate. By the time Dan smoked his cigarette and drank a cup of coffee, I'd eaten most of it. When we got back to our room, he opened his briefcase and did camp paperwork. I sat on my bed, propped against the headboard, and started reading *To Kill a Mockingbird*. I had two weeks to write a book report.

I liked the small-town story. I related to Jem because he missed his mother, who had died when he was six. But the part about Boo Radley scared me, especially when Jem said Boo dined on raw squirrels, had bloodstained hands, and shuffled through the neighborhood in the dead of night. Boo sounded a lot like Cropsy, the half-dead creature who supposedly roamed Camp Ella Fohs, feasting on children.

When I finished the first chapter, I closed the book and sighed.

"You okay over there?" Dan asked.

"Yeah. Just reading a scary book for English class."

"A book? What the hell is that?" He made one of his crazy, bug-eyed faces. "When I was your age we couldn't afford books."

"Well, you must have learned something," I said. "You went to college, right?"

"Yeah, I fooled 'em long enough to get a degree. Actually, two. I've got a bachelor's and a social work degree. But I was never much for books. I got my education on the street. Stay in school, kid. You don't want grow up to be like me."

"What's wrong with you?"

"I can't write or talk too good. I got lots of ideas but I'm not exactly polished."

"I don't know. Polished people probably can't do what you do. They've got too much book learning, not enough experience."

He looked at me funny.

"You're a pretty sharp kid, you know that?"

He got up and approached, shadowboxing. Then he grabbed my feet and pulled me down toward the end of the bed. My body went numb and *To Kill a Mockingbird* fell on the floor. He got the copy of *Playboy* from his briefcase and Frisbee'd it over to me. I opened the magazine, positioning it so I couldn't see him.

When it was over, I waited for him to stand up before I put down the *Playboy*. I knew that whatever just happened would happen again. But why was he doing it?

"Jeez, it's almost eight o'clock," Dan said. "You want to watch *Ed Sullivan*?"

"All right," I said.

## 6

On Interstate 84, heading toward New York, Dan started talking about a family weekend he was planning.

"The Jewish group that runs Ella Fohs, they're having some kind of family powwow in the Catskills for their staff. You know, at one of those Borscht Belt places."

I wasn't sure why he was telling me this.

"Ever been to the Catskills?" he asked.

"No. My parents go there every year for a weekend with their friends. I don't know what they do there."

"They do what Jews do—eat and schmooze and listen to stand-up comics. All those summer resorts are open in the winter now. We're going to Homowack Lodge. It has ice-skating and a bowling alley."

"Sounds fun."

"You should come with us," he said, glancing at me.

I wasn't sure I'd heard him right. Was he inviting me on his family vacation? That seemed weird.

"You don't have to answer now," he said. "Think about it. I know you're looking to get out of the house. It would be good for my son to have some company. It's not easy being an only child."

"What will Betty think?" I asked. I remembered her in the living room, asking who I was.

"She likes the idea."

"You already talked to her about it? When?"

"Last night. I called her from the lobby to tell her we were stuck in Danbury. I told her I was going to invite you to the Catskills."

It seemed this had all been decided.

"Are you going to tell my mother?" I asked.

"Yep. When I drop you off today."

For the next hour I watched a blur of snow-covered fields go by.

DAN TOLD ME to bring dress clothes to Homowack Lodge. We arrived Friday night, and I was seated with Dan, Betty, and their son, Gary, at a big round table that held eight or ten people. It felt like a bar mitzvah. I had on a sports jacket and slacks. Betty was wearing a fancy dress. With his ill-fitting jacket and beige chukka boots, Dan looked like he had wandered into the wrong event.

The Sabbath was starting, so each of us took a black yarmulke from the pile on our table before they recited the Hebrew blessings.

"I've never seen you in a yarmulke," I said to Dan. "Do you think you'll fool them?"

"Not a chance. They're wondering who let the guinea in."

"Stop it, you two," Betty said, shooting us a look of disapproval since Gary was listening.

After dinner, I fell in with a group of kids my age, thirteen- and fourteen-year-olds. The girls wore minidresses and white stockings. Two other boys and I followed them around the hotel like puppy dogs.

Gary and I shared a room. On Saturday, while he went bowling with his parents, I stayed in the room and answered questions in my Constitution workbook about how a bill becomes a law.

There was a knock at the door. It was Dan.

"Hey, can I come in?" he asked.

"I thought you were bowling."

"One game was plenty," he said, heading for the bed. "I'm sorry you and I aren't getting time to talk. They're making me nutty with all these activities. How about you?"

"It's okay. The girls are cute. But I need to study. I've got two tests on Monday."

"Don't you ever stop?" he asked.

"I want to get into a good college."

"You're only in eighth grade. Have a little fun."

He reached out and gave me a weak shark bite on the stomach. When I tried to pry his hand off, he grabbed my balls with the other hand and I froze. Without letting go, he stood up and maneuvered me to the bed as if I were a mannequin. Then my pants were off. With no *Playboy* to hide him, I shut my eyes and conjured up the blonde in school orchestra who clenched a cello between her long legs. I was the cello. Three minutes later, it was over.

After Dan left, I lay on the bed, agonizing. Was I homo? Why else would I get a hard-on when he touched me? It didn't make sense. I'd never liked boys that way. I could remember every girl I'd ever been in love with: the cellist in eighth grade; the violist in seventh grade; the sad Italian girl in sixth grade; Twiggy in fifth grade. In second grade I used to kiss the girl who sat behind me, when the teacher wasn't looking.

But really, it all went back to Bonnie, our neighbor in Wantagh. I used to visit her every day when I was four, hoping to get a look at her mother's enormous pale breasts and their jutting nipples, which she pulled out of her dress one at a time and waved at her new baby. The first time I saw them I was confused. None of my aunts pulled their breasts out of their dresses, and my mother definitely didn't. It was shocking: the baby grabbing the nipple with its mouth.

Bonnie told me the baby was eating. I found this hard to believe since I knew babies drank from bottles, the kind that were always stacked up in Aunt Delle's sink. But I could never get the right view-ing angle to see if Bonnie was telling the truth.

One morning I knocked on her door and she led me by the hand to the living room. We sat on the sofa, her mother facing us in the rocking chair, cradling the baby and watching a game show on television. After a while the baby started whimpering. Without tak-ing her eyes from the TV, Bonnie's mother reached down into her blouse and released the breast from its hiding place in one dazzling movement. She shoved the red pointer between her baby's puck-ering lips. I could tell from the slurping sounds that the baby was drinking, just like Bonnie had said.

I felt a tingle in my legs and groin. I asked Bonnie if she wanted to play doctor. We went next door to my house and down to the laundry room. She stood in front of the washing machine and took her clothes off, then lay facedown on a pile of dirty laundry. She asked me to check her and I probed each of her mysterious holes with my medical instruments: dull pennies, red marbles, a plastic Civil War horse.

"Am I sick?" she asked.

"Yes, you are."

"Can you cure me?"

"Yes."

I gave her an injection with the right foreleg of the horse, and she was healed.

Nine years later, lying facedown on my bed in the Catskills, the thought of probing Bonnie's naked body still got me excited. How the hell could I be homo?

# 7

IT HAD BEEN A FEW months since I'd seen Dan when he called my mother that October, telling her that he needed my help. I hadn't gone to camp that summer. We had family friends visiting from Israel.

The mansion seemed dingier than I remembered: threadbare furniture, discolored paint, dreary curtains. Ella was still hanging in the parlor, and her mother was still glaring at me. But Dan wasn't lighting up the way he always had.

"How come you're not smoking?" I asked.

"I quit."

"Really?"

"Yup. I've been smoking since I'm thirteen. I don't want to be smoking when I'm fifty. Those things will kill you. Besides, I don't like doing it in front of the kids at school. I'm supposed to be a role model."

"How'd you quit?"

"I just stopped. It's called willpower. Same way I stopped drinking."

"You used to drink a lot?"

"I grew up in the Bronx. We drank and smoked and acted tough.

I'm done with all that crap." He glanced at his watch. "It's still early. Let's get out of here," he said, standing up suddenly.

In the car I asked where we were going.

"Torrington. They've got a big movie theater from the 1920s. It reminds me of the theaters I used to go to when I was a kid. They were like opera houses."

"What do you know about opera?" I asked.

His eyes practically popped out of his face.

"I'm Italian. That's all I need to know about opera. It's the only real music. Not like that racket you listen to."

"Yeah, well at least my racket doesn't have fat ladies and dead people in it."

"Hey, be careful, you're talking about my heritage. You might hurt my feelings."

"Yeah, right. So what's playing in Torrington?"

"*Midnight Cowboy*," he said.

"*Midnight Cowboy*? Are you serious? That has an X rating!"

"So?"

"So I can't get in. You have to be sixteen. I'm only fourteen."

"Let me handle that."

I knew he would handle it. That was the problem. I wanted to see *Midnight Cowboy* badly, but it scared me. The movie had opened that spring with one of the first X ratings under the new Hollywood system. I didn't know anyone who'd seen it, not even my parents. I could score points with my friends if I talked about it on Monday. *Yeah, I saw* Midnight Cowboy, I'd say. *It was pretty intense.*

When we got to the theater, Dan told me to wait in the car. He came back five minutes later holding two tickets. As we crossed the lobby, I walked on the balls of my feet to look taller. The old guy taking tickets didn't seem to care. Dan got us sodas and a large popcorn to share, then we went inside. The theater was cavernous, like the biggest ones on Broadway—easily a thousand seats, most of them empty. There were gold-paneled walls and a ceiling that looked like the Hayden Planetarium.

Then the movie came on. At first, I thought it was funny. The main character, Joe Buck, seemed like a joke on cowboys. The audience laughed at the sex scene between Joe and a lady with a toy poodle. I'd never heard of male prostitutes but I caught on fast. This was a comedy.

The next thing I knew, there was a creepy preacher trying to make Joe Buck get down on his knees and pray. I stopped eating my popcorn. The preacher was definitely homosexual and thought Joe was, too. He terrified me—his wild-eyed desire, his unpredictability, his menace. I held my breath, wishing the scene would be over. But as soon as it ended, Joe got a blow job from a boy in a movie theater. I squirmed in my seat. Then Joe tried to collect payment for the blow job.

I was totally lost. Why would the boy pay to give a blow job? And why would Joe get a blow job from a boy in the first place? For a movie about a guy who wanted to make easy money off rich women, there sure were a lot of homosexual scenes. I angled my body away from Dan.

Then Joe had sex with a woman he called an alley cat and I thought, *Thank God.* I'd never seen naked boobs in a movie. But they disappeared soon enough, and Joe was beating up another unhappy homosexual. I shut my eyes and opened them only to see the poor guy get his teeth knocked out. In the end, Ratso Rizzo died on a bus.

When the lights came up, Dan said, "Well, they didn't sugarcoat it." I had no idea what he was talking about. I shoved my hands in my pockets and didn't say a word. I'd thought the X rating meant we'd be seeing lots of naked women. Instead, I felt like I'd just watched Dan's dog-porn movie. The worst scenes kept replaying in my head.

When we exited the theater I had to stop and remember where I was. It was dark out and I'd never been to Torrington before.

"You hungry?" Dan asked.

"No."

"Let's clear our heads," he suggested, walking down Main Street.

After half a block, he steered us toward Woolworth's, which was still open.

"I need a couple of things for camp," he said.

Once inside, he pointed me to the record section. I grabbed *Abbey Road* off the rack of new releases, then zeroed in on *Led Zeppelin II*. I ran my hand across the plastic wrap, admiring the album art: the band in military uniforms and the familiar exploding zeppelin. I really wanted it, but I was holding six dollars' worth of albums and only had four dollars in my pocket.

Dan reappeared, carrying cleaning supplies in a bucket.

"You want those two?" he asked.

"Yeah, but I don't have enough."

"Never mind that. I'm buying," he said.

"Thanks. Do you want to see if they have any opera?" I asked, only half joking.

"Nah, they don't have my kind of records here. I love the oldies. I've got a recording of Caruso from 1902. You're not going to find that in Woolworth's."

"That's pretty cool."

"You better believe it. Sometime, you'll come over and I'll play it for you."

When we got to the checkout counter, Dan paid with cash and asked the girl for a receipt. I figured the camp was paying for my albums.

For dinner, Dan chose an Italian restaurant with white tablecloths, brick archways, and a seaside scene painted on the wall. It reminded me of those places on Long Island where families went for birthdays or graduations.

"So?" Dan asked, after we were seated and ordered our food.

"So what?"

"Sew buttons on overcoats. What'd you think of the movie?"

"It was depressing," I said.

"That's 'cause life on the street is depressing. You do what you got to do to survive."

"I guess I wouldn't survive then."

"Trust me, you would. But stay in school and you won't have to worry about it."

"I didn't get why the two characters are friends. I mean, I see why Ratso would be friends with Joe. He needs the money. But why does Joe need Ratso?"

"He's lonely. He's scared. He's not cut out for New York."

"So he moves in with a crippled con man?" I asked.

Dan laughed.

"What's so funny?"

"They're both crippled, aren't they? Joe's just crippled on the inside. He's like a lost sheep, desperate for connection."

"You mean, the way he tries to talk to everyone?"

"Right," Dan said. "I don't care who you are. We're all the same inside. We all need attention. Ratso's the first person who listens to Joe. That's a big deal."

I was starting to understand Joe Buck. I wanted to run away from home, too. Did that mean Dan was Ratso Rizzo?

"The ending was a bummer," I offered.

"Are you kidding me? Ratso gets to the promised land. Joe throws out his cowboy outfit and looks for a real job. That's two less hustlers on the street. In social work, we call that a success story."

Dan stared off into space. We were done talking about *Midnight Cowboy*, and thank God he hadn't mentioned the sex scenes.


IT WAS ALMOST midnight when we arrived back at camp. There was no sign of Jim the maintenance man or anyone else. It was spookily quiet.

Inside the mansion, I hit a switch and lit up the grand staircase. I thought about Ella and her mother and headed for the second floor, Dan right behind me. Once upstairs, I took in the long hallway with all the rooms to the left and the right.

"It's not exactly Ratso's place," I said.

"No. This is what money buys."

"It gives me the creeps."

"Why?" Dan asked.

"Because it's abandoned, like Ella's family just vanished and we're squatting here, like Joe and Ratso."

"You're a worrier," he said. "Anyone ever tell you that?"

"Yeah, my mother. She says I should have more fun."

"Good advice. You're too young to worry. Wait till you're my age. You'll have plenty to worry about."

"What do you worry about?"

"I got a list a mile long. Counselors doing drugs. My maintenance man playing with guns. Kids drowning in the lake. Seniors dropping dead during sex. The price of milk."

"The price of milk?"

"Yeah. Our milk supplier has been overcharging us and he won't even talk to me. He's got a monopoly. Do you believe that? I'm doing a slow burn over that one."

"Sounds bad."

"Hey, I'm just getting started here. There's Oyster Bay High. Pregnant girls in ninth grade, junkies in tenth grade. And the board of ed tells me I can't talk about sex or drugs. I come up here in the winter to forget all that craziness. I like the peace and quiet, the big empty house. I can hear myself think here."

"It's like your castle," I said.

"Yeah, it is my castle. No one gets in. Except you."

"It still creeps me out," I said.

"Well, go to bed and stop thinking about it."

I put on pajamas, got into the bed big enough for three people, and fell asleep instantly. I had no idea where Dan slept.

THE NEXT MORNING, there was no sign of him. I went to check on Ella and her mother, then looked to see if there was any food in the ancient kitchen. I heard the front door slam.

"Anybody home?" Dan called out.

He stood in the front foyer, holding a small square suitcase.

"I borrowed this from the office," he said. "You can play your records on it."

I'd been sure I wouldn't hear my new albums until I got home. Now I knew what I'd be doing for the rest of the morning.

Dan looked through his keys and opened a door I hadn't noticed before.

"This is my secret room," he said, stepping inside. "It's my hideout during the summer."

We were in a small bedroom with an unmade double bed. Venetian blinds were drawn over the only window and, on the opposite wall, there was a low chest of drawers beneath a mirror.

"What was this room?" I asked.

"Probably the servant's quarters. It's next to the front door and near the kitchen."

Dan put the record player on the chest and plugged it in.

"You can do the honors," he said.

I popped the latches on either side of the box and opened it, revealing a white tone arm and black rubber platter.

"We replaced the needle this summer so it should be good," Dan said.

After breakfast, he grabbed his briefcase and headed for the living room. I closeted myself in his hideout and played the music as loud as I wanted, something I couldn't do at home. I listened to *Abbey Road* all the way through, getting off the bed only to turn the record over. Then I put on *Led Zeppelin* and cranked up the volume even more.

When it was done, I played one song, "Heartbreaker," a few more times. "Some people cry and some people die / By the wicked ways of love," Robert Plant wailed. What the hell did "wicked ways" mean? The girls I knew were nothing like the girls in Led Zeppelin songs, the kind who pleaded *Daddy, I just can't wait*.

There was a knock at the door.

"Come in," I yelled.

"The racket stopped so I figured you're done listening," Dan said.

"Yeah, I'm done. I might listen again later."

He put his briefcase down next to the record player, then pulled out a magazine.

"I got you the new *Playboy*," he said. "November." He handed it to me. I glanced at the cover and he grabbed my leg.

"I'm strong like bull," he said, flexing his bicep. "Feel that."

"I don't need to, I can see it," I said.

"You know, when I was your age I was a skinny kid, skinnier than you. But I had these huge arms, as big as they are now. You know why?"

"Why?"

"I worked for a plumber. Every day after school I lugged pipe at construction sites. That's all I did, haul pipe. So my arms got real big." He struck another muscleman pose. "I looked like Popeye. It took another ten years for the rest of my body to catch up."

"Did you want to be a plumber?"

"No chance. If you know shit runs downhill you can be a plumber. I liked people. I could always read them, especially people in trouble. I liked helping them." He reached over and grabbed my thigh. "Like I'm gonna help you right now, 'cause I can tell you got girls on the brain."

"That's not fair. I always have girls on the brain."

"That's why you're easy to read," he said. I froze as he unzipped my jeans and pulled them down. "You're gonna make some girl very happy one day with that thing. But remember, kid, it's not the size of the boat that counts but the motion on the ocean."

I leafed through *Playboy* but it didn't help. It was still Dan with his hands on me. So I conjured up the woman in *Midnight Cowboy*— Joe's alley cat. I felt her lipstick mouth on my cock, working me expertly as she raked her nails down my back. God, she was wicked. I was not in the servant's room of a shabby mansion with the blinds drawn. No, no, no. I was floating, outside of space, outside of time, tangling with the alley cat. She knew exactly what she was doing, and she was going to make me come in about ten seconds.

"Pacified!" Dan exclaimed. I rolled over, my eyes shut tight.

ON SUNDAY DAN said he had to stop in the camp office to pick up some paperwork on our way home. Once inside, he opened the closet, revealing a large safe that sat on the floor. He turned the dial a few times and the heavy steel door swung toward us. Then he retrieved the *Playboy* from his briefcase and put it in the safe.

"You keep *Playboy* in there?" I asked, amazed.

"Yep. No way it's going to disappear. I'm the only one who knows the combination."

He crossed the room to the office desk, leaving the safe open, and I sauntered over to the closet for a better look. There were six or seven issues of *Playboy* in there. I took one and stashed it in my bag. I knew I was sneaking it, but wasn't I entitled? He had bought them for me.

Before we left, he put some papers in the safe and locked it.

A week later, I was doing my homework when my mother yelled that Dan was on the phone. "He's calling from camp!"

I went to the kitchen and picked up the phone.

"Hey, Dan."

"Where's my payroll?" he asked.

"What do you mean?"

"Did you take the camp payroll home?"

I thought he was putting me on, but it didn't sound like he was kidding. Was he accusing me of stealing?

"What payroll?" I asked.

"The magazine in the safe," he said. "Did you take it?"

I finally understood: payroll was code for *Playboy*.

"Yeah, I did," I said.

"Don't do that, all right? You can get me in trouble."

"Okay."

I didn't know what kind of trouble he meant. Losing a copy of *Playboy* didn't seem like a big deal, especially compared to losing the actual camp payroll. But he'd never chewed me out about anything, so I knew he was upset.

"Just get it back to me and don't take it home again, all right?"

"Sure, all right," I said.

When I hung up the phone, my mother eyed me with alarm.

"Is the payroll missing?" she asked.

"No, no. I saw it there in the office. He'll find it when he checks the safe again."

"Oh, good," she said. "I was worried."

# 8

"DAN'S COMING OVER TONIGHT," MY mother informed me one day when she got home from work.

"Why?" I asked, caught off guard.

"He wants to talk about something."

Dan appeared after dinner, carrying a large box of cannoli. While I loaded the pastries onto a plate and coffee brewed in the percolator, Dan told my parents about the lonely fights he was waging for interracial camping and against drugs in school.

"I'm taking on the bigots and the bureaucrats," he declared. My parents said they supported him one hundred percent.

When the coffee was ready, we moved into the living room. Dan sat at one end of the sofa, his legs crossed, looking a lot more relaxed than a year earlier when he'd come to our house for the first time.

I sank into the other end of the couch, my jaw tense, trying to force a smile. What the hell could this be about?

"So, what's up, Dan?" my mother asked.

"Well, Sydell, I thought I should discuss this with all of you together. Betty and Gary and I are planning a trip to the Bahamas over the Christmas holiday. We'd like Steve to come with us. It would be our treat."

I couldn't believe my ears. The last thing I wanted was to spend my vacation with Dan and his family. Why would anyone think I'd want to do that? In my head, I was screaming no. But my throat was getting tighter and tighter, like I couldn't talk at all. I began praying to my mother: *Please say no, please say no.*

"That's very generous of you and Betty," she said. "Of course, it's okay with us, if Steve wants to go."

They all turned to me. Dan was looming, three feet away. My mother was smiling, waiting for me to say yes.

"I guess so," I said quietly. My shoulders suddenly felt heavy. How come my parents didn't see this was weird?

"Great," Dan said. "Then it's all set."

Ken hadn't said a word.

"Ken, I want to make sure this is okay with you," Dan said. "I wouldn't want you to feel displaced in any way, because if you did, well, we won't do this. Family comes first, and you're Steve's father. You know what I mean."

"It's good of you to ask but there's no issue," Ken said, waving his hand as if swatting away Dan's concern. "You're just doing a nice thing for Steve. We appreciate it."

"I got to tell you," Dan said, "you two are doing something right because this guy"—he motioned to me—"is one of the finest young people I know. He's got great values, works hard, and really cares about others. That's pretty rare these days. You should be very proud."

"Well, I guess we'll keep him then," my mother said, shooting me a smile. "That's so nice to hear, Dan, especially coming from you."

WHAT SURPRISED ME most about the Bahamas wasn't the blindingly white sand or the ocean water the color of a robin's egg. It wasn't the colossal resort hotel with its fourteen stories of balconied rooms facing the beach. It wasn't the postcard palm trees or all the Black people serving tropical drinks to all the white people under thatched-roof palapas.

No, what shocked me was that my cousin Dave's French teacher, Mrs. Desjardins, was staying in our hotel. She was on our beach, with her husband, one thousand miles from East Meadow. Dan's family and I had been stretched out on towels for only twenty minutes when I spotted the couple coming toward us.

I shuddered. I'd always given Desjardins a wide berth in the school hall. She was a large, mean French woman in her forties, constantly threatening to fail Dave, who was a pathetic student of foreign language. When she was ten yards away I held my breath and she seemed to look through me. I was safe. Her husband, a stooped and balding little man in blue bathing trunks, was just as sour-looking as her.

Only then did I see their daughter, thirteen or fourteen years old, trailing a few feet behind. She was so stunningly beautiful that for a second I thought I had it wrong. There was no way that angel was the Desjardins' daughter. She was just some random girl who happened to be walking near them. But Mrs. Desjardins turned and said something, taking the girl's hand.

I couldn't believe it. How did two such unremarkable humans produce that radiant beauty? Had she been adopted? As they passed our blanket, I zeroed in on the daughter's oval face with its doe-like eyes and full lips. She had thick, dark brown hair that fell just below her shoulders, and smooth tanned skin set off by white bikini straps. She was taller than her parents, and her long legs disappeared into the skimpiest of bottoms. She walked so fluidly, so naturally, she might have been a jungle cat. And like a cheetah, she seemed unaware of how extraordinary she was. As if that weren't enough, she was French! I was in love—madly in love.

The Desjardins' daughter was lagging behind her parents again. *She doesn't want to be here, either*, I thought. Dan was lying next to me on his stomach in a plaid bathing suit. The matted hair on his shoulders made him look like some kind of beached bison. He'd been immersed in *The Godfather*, one of the fattest books I'd ever seen, since we'd gotten on the plane that morning, and he'd taken to giving us regular updates.

"They just killed Sonny," he reported. "It was Barzini, I'm telling you. I know how these goombahs think." Betty was lying on the other side of him, facedown, in a one-piece yellow bathing suit, working on her tan. Gary had gone to wade in the ocean.

If my cousin had been an A-plus French student, and if I were braver, I would have introduced myself to Mrs. Desjardins. I daydreamed what would happen next. She would ask me to join the three of them for lunch and maybe for a trip on a sailboat. I'd spend the afternoon talking with her daughter about literature and music. By nightfall I'd be making out with her under the full moon.

But there was zero chance of any of that happening. Even if I could muster the courage to talk to her, how would I explain what I was doing in the Bahamas? I had no idea what I was doing in the Bahamas.

DAN, GARY, AND I headed back to the hotel in the late afternoon to shower and change before dinner. Betty wanted more time on the beach. Gary and I were sharing a room, like we'd done in the Catskills. On the way there, he asked for the first shower. Dan said I should wait in his and Betty's room.

I followed him inside and saw two mannequin heads on the chest of drawers. One of the white foam heads was wearing a reddish wig; the other head was bare. I'd noticed that Betty changed her hairstyles and now I understood how. They looked like robot heads. While I was studying them, Dan got me in a full nelson from behind.

"C'mon, let's wrestle," he said, moving me toward the bed. I tensed, turning to dead weight.

"What's the matter?" he asked, grabbing at me through my swim trunks. *Was he out of his mind? What if Betty walked in?*

"I shouldn't be here," I said, growing panicky.

"You worry too much," Dan said. "I'm the boss." He unbuttoned my swimsuit and moved me onto the bed. I closed my eyes, playing dead. I imagined the Desjardins girl in her little white bikini. *No, no. She's too pure. Think of someone else.*

"Hand or the mouth?" Dan asked. But I'd gone mute. Just then, I heard a key in the lock, followed by the door opening. My cock fell out of Dan's mouth.

"Shit," he said, stuffing the swollen thing into my trunks. I had two seconds before Betty would pass through the foyer and into the room. I yanked up the swimsuit and rolled onto one side, propped up on a trembling elbow. My trunks were unbuttoned—too late to fix that. Dan was getting off the bed, backward, when Betty appeared, a towel around her swimsuit.

"Hey," Dan greeted her. "Steve is just here till Gary finishes in the shower." I tried to smile.

Betty stopped in her tracks, confused. After two seconds, which seemed like forever, she headed toward the bathroom.

"I'm getting ready for dinner," she said.

As soon as I heard the shower, I buttoned up and charged past Dan. A minute later, I was sitting on the edge of my bed, the heels of my palms digging into my eye sockets. I was seeing stars, the room was spinning.

When Gary came out of the bathroom, I maneuvered past him, mumbling something about a shower. I braced myself on the sink counter and stared in the mirror.

*Everything's fine*, I said to the terrified face staring back. *Everything's fine.*


AT THE BEACH the next day, Dan handed Betty his camera and asked her to snap a photo of him and me. She stood knee-deep in the ocean, the blazing sun directly above her. Dan and I took up a spot at the water's edge.

Just as he put his arm around my shoulder I saw the Desjardins girl some thirty yards off, wading into the surf. I was so ashamed I turned away, pretending to look at something in the distance, praying the girl wouldn't see me. Betty called my name and I faced the camera, wishing I were invisible. Dan's arm weighed on my back and I squinted into the sun.

Back in New York, I received an envelope from Dan in the mail with four vacation photos inside. I was expecting to see a little kid next to him on the beach, but there was a teenager as tall as him. When we'd first met, in the summer after seventh grade, Dan had towered over me. Not anymore, although I still looked about half his weight.

In the photo, Dan was relaxed, left hand on hip, his enormous right hand draped over my boyish shoulder. My arms were rigid, hands slightly cupped and frozen in place, as if rigor mortis had set in. My pale, smooth body contrasted with his hairy, olive-skinned frame. It appeared he had his arm around a statue.

The photo made me uneasy. I'd never hang it on my bulletin board. When I'd gone back to school, I'd avoided talking about winter vacation altogether.

The three other photos were all of me, standing at the water's edge, shirtless and smiling. I could recall Dan taking them, moving back and forth to get the shots he wanted. In one, Mr. Desjardins was slouching into the frame. *Just my luck*, I thought. *I get the damn father in the picture, not the daughter.*

I put all four photos in the envelope, then stuffed it in the back of my desk drawer where no one would find it.

## 9

IN THE SUMMER OF 1970, after finishing ninth grade, I packed an army surplus trunk for ten weeks at Camp Ella Fohs. My cousin Dave and I were going to work as waiters on the senior side, serving hundreds of old folks from the Bronx.

I was bringing a tenor sax, along with a pile of sheet music and a stack of albums by John Coltrane, Charlie Parker, and Sonny Rollins. Dave, who was a talented trombonist and a fixture in the high school jazz ensemble, had told me the best way to learn was to listen to those guys play a line and then repeat it over and over.

My mother hated the saxophone plan. She said I was squandering years of clarinet lessons, not to mention the money they had cost. But I knew the real reason she was opposed: she was scared I'd follow in my cousin's footsteps. Jazz was his life calling, and he was going to be a professional musician, not the lawyer his mother imagined. My mother thought nothing good could come of my spending the summer with Dave practicing jazz.

Dan had offered to drive the two of us to camp. He and his family had moved that year from Yonkers to Plainedge on Long Island, fifteen minutes from my house. When we arrived at camp and I caught sight of the woods and the lake, it all seemed so lush, almost like a jungle. I'd gotten used to being there in the fall and winter, when the trees were bare, the waterfront empty, and the mansion solitary.

Driving in, we saw rowboats and canoes stacked on the shoreline. Dozens of life preservers hung on the boathouse walls and floating lines were strung across the pool. In a few days, the place would be swarming with a hundred kids fleeing summer in the city.

We pulled up to the mansion, where Dan said we'd be bunking. Dave knew that Dan had been taking me to the mansion in the winter, and I had even told him about the portrait of Ella Fohs. I felt special, knowing all this stuff that he and most campers had never seen. But when we got out of the car, I was on edge.

"The waiters sleep in the basement," Dan said. "I bet Steve didn't know there's a basement." I was just relieved we wouldn't be upstairs where I'd stayed before.

We followed Dan down a long flight of steps. At the bottom, he pulled on a cord that lit a bare hanging bulb. We were in the middle of a windowless, concrete bunker. It was chilled and damp, and I caught a whiff of mildew. The walls had recessed areas, each one containing a bunk bed—four in all. It seemed like a dreary place to spend the summer, but I figured we'd hardly ever be down here. Dave and I chose the bed on the farthest wall, with me claiming the top bunk.

I knew a couple of the other waiters from previous years at camp. They were all from the Bronx, most of them fifteen or sixteen years old. They called our living quarters "the dungeon." The dishwashers and other kitchen boys were a little older, a mix of guys from the Bronx and Oyster Bay High School, plus a few townies from New Milford. They lived in four-man tents set up in the woods above the mansion.

The first buses arrived the next day, disgorging dozens of elderly Jews, chattering away in English and Yiddish. They hovered over a mountain of luggage rising outside the bus. Once they were assigned to a cabin, they headed off to inspect their living quarters while we schlepped their bags behind them.

Dan roamed the kitchen that night as the roast chicken was sent out. He peered over the shoulder of the cook and gave the kitchen boys grief over how they were operating the commercial mixer.

"What are you, mental midgets?" he growled, threatening them with a raised hand.

I left to serve my tables, and on my return three of the kitchen boys had Dan pinned against a steel storage shelf. He disabled each of them in turn by inflicting just enough pain to loosen their grip, while the cook watched in horror. Then he commandeered the mixer and showed them how to use it.

During the dessert course, Dan made the rounds of the tables in the dining hall, like the father of the bride at a Jewish wedding.

"*Nu*, Danny, you're looking very thin," a blue-haired grandma at one of my tables said. "Don't they feed you?"

"You need new glasses, Freyda. I'm lugging thirty pounds of pasta here," he said, clutching his belly.

"*Zie gezunt*, Danny. Sit down a little."

"No time, dear. I got two camps to run."

He moved on, working the room. After the crowd departed for their evening activity—canasta or bingo or dancing—we cleared the tables, put up the chairs, and mopped the linoleum floor. Then Dave and I grabbed our instruments and headed over to the junior side. He'd met a few counselors who'd brought some sheet music from the band Chicago's second album. We got together in their cabin and jammed on a few of the tunes. It was the last time I left the senior side for weeks.


THE MANSION WAS my world that summer. Three times a day I served meals in the dining hall and some afternoons I'd row a couple of old-timers around the lake. Other than that, I stuck to the Fohs house, moving from room to room and floor to floor.

Each morning after breakfast I'd climb two flights, pass the master bedroom where I'd slept the previous winter, and follow some narrow stairs up to the attic. That's where I played my saxophone. It was an enormous space, the length of the entire house, with open framing and plywood flooring. There were windows at either end, so it was bathed in natural light, giving it the feeling of a tree house, one with great acoustics.

Later, I'd park myself on the worn orange sofa in the parlor, beneath the portrait of Ella and her mother, and read books or write letters. Sometimes, I'd sit on the back patio, overlooking the lake. In the late afternoon or evening, I'd go to Dan's secret hideout and play my records. He only used that room when he didn't want to be found. Otherwise, he lived and slept in the director's cabin on the junior side, where Betty visited him on weekends.

I never saw anyone on the first or second floors of the mansion. The waiters came and went through a side door, and they hung out in the kitchen boys' tents. The place felt as abandoned as it had been in the winter.

DAVE HATED THE waiter job from day one and couldn't face doing it for the whole summer. Serving the seniors their early-bird breakfast meant getting up before six, and he never went to sleep earlier than one or two a.m. It didn't help that we were sleeping in a concrete crypt where you couldn't tell day from night.

When the first two-week session was over, Dan reassigned him to the kitchen on the junior side, where he'd be unloading trucks and prepping food. I helped my cousin move his trunk and trombone to tent city, where he and I had once bunked as campers.

"You got to admit, this is a hell of a lot nicer than the dungeon," Dave said as he tied up the front flaps of his tent to let in more light.

"We were turning into vampires down there. You should move over here, too, man. The kitchen crew is great. And you wouldn't have to put up with all that kvetching."

"I don't mind the seniors," I said, "and I'll make more money over there."

"Yeah, you probably will. But that doesn't mean it's worth it. Besides, all the girls are here. And some of them look pretty good, you know what I mean?"

I did know what he meant, but I didn't like that he was bailing out. We were supposed to be spending the summer together, working our first jobs. I'd made a commitment to Dan and besides, it was tough to beat my setup on the senior side, where I had the run of the mansion. Dave had made his choice to leave. I'd made mine to stay.

That night, after dinner, I was reading in the parlor when I heard the deep tones of his trombone floating across the lake. He was playing Bach, a favorite warm-up exercise. It sounded like he was standing right next to me, but I knew we were drifting apart.


DAN GAVE ME attention—a lot of attention. He took me to Conn's Dairy for ice-cream sundaes. He drove me into town to see *Woodstock*, the movie. When I wanted a new album, we'd get in his wagon and go to Woolworth's in Torrington, and he'd pay for it. One day we went to Candlewood Lake, the biggest in Connecticut, and spent the afternoon tearing across the water in a speedboat.

I spent so much time with Dan that one of the kitchen crew asked if I was his nephew. I said no, but I was glad he thought that. Everyone knew Dan had my back, so I could do pretty much whatever I wanted. Not that I slacked off. I worked hard and got along with the whole crew. But no one was going to give me grief.

Dan was running two camps at once. He oversaw dozens of staff and two hundred campers. Everyone, young and old, wanted a piece of him: some advice, a ruling, a play fight. Each day brought a series of rolling crises: an outbreak of pink eye, a missing kid, a pregnant counselor. It was like fighting multiple forest fires. No sooner did he put one out than two more sprang up. He was always on the move, never in the same spot for more than five minutes.

But if I wanted to talk about my job or my family or anything at all, he'd meet me on the back patio of the mansion or in his hideout, where he went to hear himself think. Unlike the winter, he could only get there for a half hour at a time. He'd bring his own problems, too, and he unburdened himself to me.

"Oh, we got some real winners this year," he said one afternoon as we lounged on the patio. "I hired too many ex-junkies. I can't help it. I've got a soft spot for them. They just want a chance. It'll be a miracle if we get through this summer without a disaster."

Then he ran through the list: who had drug problems, who was screwing who, who wouldn't make it to the end of the season. I had the inside story and Dan never asked me to keep it confidential. He just knew I would. His was a lonely job and he had to talk to someone, he said.

In turn, I complained about my mother.

"She wants to control everything—my hair, my music, my social life."

"Your mother's scared of men," Dan said. "She needs to have power over them. A psychoanalyst would call her the castrating type."

I felt better knowing my mother was a type, even if it was the castrating type. That meant I wasn't crazy.

"Freud said it all goes back to the first five years," he explained. "That's when our personality gets formed. Your mother is who she is. You got to take care of yourself."

"How do I do that?"

"The Greeks said, 'Know thyself.' That's a good place to start."

"That's it?" I asked, skeptically.

"What do you mean, *That's it*? I just gave you my best material, free of charge."

"I got to go set up for lunch," I said, checking my watch.

"What are you doing at three o'clock?" he asked.

"I'll be right here."


SOMETIMES, WHEN I was listening to jazz in the hideout, Dan would drop in, grab me by the balls, and say, "You give up?" His grip and those three words still immobilized me. But I wasn't scared anymore that he was going to kill me and my family. We were friends. His version of friendship just happened to involve blow jobs. I had no idea why, but what did I know? Dan's whole life was helping people, especially kids. Everybody knew that.

Besides, the blow job took less than five minutes and when it was done, I pretended it hadn't happened. That was easy because he never said a word about it. Also, it felt good. I mean, a blow job is a blow job. I just blotted him out by covering my face with the Play-mate of the Month. When he asked "Hand or the mouth?" I didn't answer. As far as I was concerned he wasn't there, but somehow I was getting blow jobs. Not that I'd ever tell anyone. I tried hard not to think about it.

One morning, after playing my saxophone in the attic, I grabbed a Coltrane album and headed down the two flights to Dan's hideout, which was cooler than the sweltering top floor. The room was dark and the blinds drawn, as usual. I heard the shower running and Dan singing:

> Roll me over in the clover.
> Roll me over, lay me down
> And do it again.

I went right to the record player and put on *Coltrane Plays the Blues*. A minute later, the shower stopped. Dan emerged, wearing khaki shorts and a white T-shirt.

"Hey, I'm human again," he said, stretching his arms above his head. "It's like an oven out there." Then he resumed singing, over Coltrane, as if he were still in the shower. "Roll me over in the clover."

"What is that song?" I asked, annoyed.

"I learned it in the army," he said. "It's got lots of dirty verses but I can't remember them."

"It's fucking terrible."

"You know, you're starting to curse a lot," he said, frowning. "Let me tell you something else I learned in the army. It's called de-fuckinization."

"What's that?"

"After two years in the army every other word out of our mouths was fuck. *Pass the fucking bread. Pass the fucking ammo.* Before we went home we had to break the habit, so we put a tin pot on the floor in the middle of the barrack. Every time someone said fuck, he had to throw a quarter in the pot. The guy who cursed the least won all the money."

"Did you win?"

"Are you kidding me? I was the biggest contributor. It worked, though. Cost me a fortune but I stopped cursing."

"That's fucking great," I said.

Dan did that rapid head-shaking thing he did when he couldn't believe his ears.

"Give me a quarter," he growled, pushing me back on the bed.

I reached over and grabbed *Playboy* from the nightstand. It was all over in two minutes.

"Pacified!" he said. "That'll teach you who's boss."

He went into the bathroom. I figured he was going to bring me a washcloth, like he always did. My T-shirt was glued to the bedspread with sweat, and a puddle of semen was running off my belly.

I didn't hear the sink and Dan hadn't come back. I'd have to get the washcloth myself. I swiveled my legs over the edge of the bed, took my jeans off, and pulled my underwear up.

When I got to the door of the bathroom, there was Dan, standing over the white porcelain sink, in profile, jerking off. I was horrified.

His dick was enormous—a fat reddish-brown sausage that he was working back and forth. I'd never seen a grown man's hard-on before. It looked like it belonged to a different creature altogether.

I pedaled backward, unsteady on my feet. He glanced over, a blank expression on his face. Then he carried on stroking that thing and grunting. A few seconds later he groaned and loosed a torrent of semen into the basin. I wished to God I hadn't seen it.

I sat back on the bed and struggled to pull on my jeans. I couldn't have been more shocked if I'd caught Dan killing a baby. It had never occurred to me that he was turned on by what he did to me. I hadn't even thought of him as having a dick. A mouth, yes, but not a dick. I'd been way too focused on my own.

I flashed on a conversation I'd overheard only days before in the senior kitchen. Out of nowhere, one of the dishwashers announced, "Dan's a homo for sure." *That's so stupid*, I'd thought to myself. *Dan is married. Besides, he's my friend—he would have told me if he was homosexual.* But the episode had unnerved me. Was Dan a homo? Was I a homo? What the fuck was going on?

I heard the water running hard in the bathroom sink, then it stopped. A minute later, Dan appeared. He was dressed, his fly zipped, and had a sheepish look on his face.

"What? You've never seen someone jerk off before?" he asked.

"No," I said. "Not a grown-up anyway."

"Well, someone's got to do it. You never help me out that way."

"That's not going to happen," I said, shaking my head furiously. The thought of touching that thing was so gross.

"That's fine," he said. "Look, it's a cultural thing. In our society, we think there's something wrong with sex between men. In ancient Greece they thought it was normal."

I shot him a skeptical look.

"Why do you think the Greeks were obsessed with the naked male body? Every man would choose a boy as his friend and lover. They weren't homosexual. They got married and had families. But male friendship—that was the ideal."

I tried to take this in. It did explain how he could be married and still be attracted to a boy. The problem was, the boy in this Greek drama was me.

I was rowing a couple of grandmothers around the lake when I saw a pretty girl with strawberry-blond hair paddling a canoe with a friend near Turtle Island.

The next day I visited the junior dining hall toward the end of breakfast. I wanted to scope out which bunk this girl was in. She was sitting next to the same friend, along with the other fourteen- and fifteen-year-olds. In the days after, I went on more scouting missions to the junior side and observed her and her bunkmates. They were like a herd of gazelles, always moving in formation. I couldn't imagine how I'd get to her. More drastic action was called for.

"You know the redheaded girl in Bunk Thirteen?" I asked Dan one day on the mansion patio.

"Maybe, why?" he asked, suspiciously.

"'Cause I want to find out who she is."

"What do you want to know?"

"Her name, for starters."

"I don't know her name."

"Bullshit. You know every kid in camp."

"I can't help you out. You're on your own."

I got his point. But it wasn't like I was asking for top-secret information. I just wanted a lead. He bent and broke rules for me all the time.

When I mentioned the girl again a few days later, he said no way. Then he shut down the whole topic. I went on and on about her to see if I could wear him down. It drove him crazy. Finally, after a week of this, I gave up on him. I had hatched a new plan.

# 10

I DREAMED I WAS IN the basement office of the Family Service Association where my mother worked. There were soldiers lined up, awaiting inspection. To my horror, none of them had heads. A doctor described their freakish condition. The soldiers were definitely alive, and that's what terrified me. I had to turn away and leave. Once outside, I was even more confused by what I'd seen. I didn't understand how the headless soldiers could be living.

I awoke from this dream in a full-blown panic—heart racing, sweating profusely. I forced myself to sit up, pressing my wet back into the cold concrete wall of the dungeon.

As the dream played over and over, the headless soldiers still seemed real. I slowed it down and studied one of them. He didn't have a face or a brain or any way to breathe. There was no way he could be alive. Maybe these soldiers existed in some realm between life and death. Maybe that's where I'd been.

I checked my watch: four thirty. I climbed down from the top bunk, found a flashlight, and put on my clothes. Slipping out of the dungeon, I crept up the narrow stairs and headed toward the parlor.

It seemed spookier than ever: the 1920s furniture, the ancient lamps, the floor-to-ceiling drapes, the stone fireplace. I couldn't bring myself to point the flashlight at Ella and her mother.

Still, I sat on the sofa, right under their portrait. I shined the light at the three other walls. There was no other art in the room. Why were Ella and her mother still up there? I finally aimed my flashlight at the painting, half expecting the two of them to spring to life and attack me. But they were there, inside the frame. Ella's mother scowled at me, disapproving.

DAN WAS INSPECTING the meat-slicing machine when I entered the senior kitchen with a tray full of dishes.

"Who cleaned this thing last time?" he asked the kitchen boys angrily. No one answered. "I'll tell you who cleaned it. Nobody!"

He grabbed a fork, reached into the slicer, and came out with a decaying piece of turkey crawling with white maggots. I felt queasy. The other boys edged away from Dan.

"What's wrong with you mental midgets?" he yelled, threatening them with the fork. "You going to put this on a sandwich? Get this crap cleaned up and none of you leaves camp for two days." They began protesting. "Shut up ya faces before I stuff them with this," he said, aiming the writhing fork at them.

I followed Dan out of the kitchen.

"Yeah, what's your problem?" he asked gruffly when he saw me.

"You having a bad day?"

"Just the usual," he said. "That crew is so busy getting into their girlfriends' pants they can barely do their jobs. It's a miracle we haven't killed off Grandma and Grandpa."

"Yet," I added.

"Thanks. What's up with you?"

"I had a scary dream last night. It kind of freaked me out."

He stopped and turned back to me.

"Good!" he said, his mood instantly improved. "Dreams are

supposed to freak you out. Freud said they're the 'royal road to the unconscious.'"

He resumed walking but veered off the main road and followed a path down to the lake. We stopped at a pair of old Adirondack chairs on the shoreline.

"Step into my office," he said. We sat, facing the water. "Okay, tell me your dream."

As I recounted it, he looked out at the lake, nodding.

"How'd you feel when you woke up?" he asked, after I'd finished.

"Scared shitless. I was awake but the soldiers still seemed real, like it was more than a dream."

"Did you go back to sleep?"

"No. I went up to the parlor."

"Oh, great. With that creepy painting?"

"Yeah. I don't know why. Something about it."

"Did Ella talk to you?"

"No."

"Good. If she did, I'd say you really need a shrink."

I frowned.

"Hey, that was a joke," he said.

"I'm just wigged out."

"Okay, let's figure this dream out. What do you associate with soldiers?"

I hesitated. I'd never talked to anyone about this.

"My father," I finally said.

"Ken or your first father?" Dan asked.

"My first father. He was in the army."

"World War II?"

"Yeah."

"What did he die of?"

"Multiple sclerosis."

"That's a rough one, I'm sorry. Look, I don't want to say anything off the cuff. Let me think about the dream a little bit, then get back to you, okay?"

"Okay."

"Good. I got to go deal with my cooks in the junior kitchen."

I WAS HELPING two seniors out of a rowboat the next afternoon when I spotted Dan on the patio behind the mansion. He waved me over, and I climbed the grassy slope.

"I spoke to someone about your dream," he said, jumping right in. "He's a very respected psychoanalyst in New York."

I thought he was kidding, but I could see he wasn't.

"Why'd you do that?" I asked.

"Because it seemed important and I'm not an expert. This guy is."

"So what did he say?"

"Well, the soldiers in the dream definitely represent your father. The dream doesn't take place in your house in East Meadow. It takes place in your mother's office, outside the stepfamily. He said the doctor in the dream might be someone who treated your father at home. Did doctors and nurses come to your house when he was sick?"

"Yeah, they did."

"You said your father had MS. Did he lose his power of speech?"

"I have no memory of him talking," I said, "but that doesn't mean much. I was four. I only remember certain scenes, like the morning he died."

"Maybe you can ask your mother."

"Why is it so important?"

"Because in dreams, see, the head represents communication—speech. Your headless soldier can't talk. That's what's so disturbing. He's alive, but it feels to you like he's not really alive."

"So?"

"So, the shrink says the dream is your psyche's way of coping with the confusion you felt around your father."

I hadn't thought about my father in a long time. My chest ached and a lump was welling up in my throat.

"Ella Fohs," I whispered.

"What about her?" Dan asked.

"She's dead."

"She sure is."

"That's why I went to the parlor," I said.

"You lost me."

"She's dead, but it always feels like she's there, like a ghost who's visiting. Like my father."

"I don't think Freud had anything to say about that," Dan said. "You can believe whatever you want. Just don't go bananas on me."

I COULD HEAR the Supremes blaring—"Stop! In the Name of Love!"—before I got anywhere near the rec hall. I was on a mission to talk to the redhead. My cousin had tipped me off to the teen dance, and I was betting she'd be there. I'd almost asked him to go with me, so I wouldn't wind up standing alone in a corner. But if I lost my nerve I didn't want to look like a loser in front of Dave. He not only knew how to talk to girls, he'd gotten physical with them.

When we were thirteen, Dave and another tent mate snuck out one night and slipped into the thirteen-year-old girls' bunk. Hours later, he came back and told me he'd gotten into bed with Karen and "did things" with her. I didn't want to know what things. I'd had a crush on Karen since I was ten but had been too shy to talk to her. I wasn't sure I believed Dave anyway. He might have made it up to impress me. On the other hand, he had a big grin on his face whenever he talked about her.

As I approached the door of the rec hall the Supremes were cranking "You Keep Me Hangin' On" at full volume. Inside, the lights were dimmed, and it took a minute for my eyes to adjust.

The girls were bunched in tight groups along the wall, giggling and drinking bug juice out of Dixie cups. The boys were arrayed against the back, pretending they weren't looking. In between, there were two clutches of kids on the dance floor, singing along with Diana Ross.

I'd never be more prepared. I'd put on my softest, plaid flannel shirt and rolled up the sleeves to look relaxed. I'd combed my hair just right. I'd practiced lines in the mirror: *Hi, I'm Stephen, what's your name?* I wasn't leaving until I did this.

Then I saw her in the far corner, talking to the same friend. I felt a flutter in my chest. The two of them approached the dance floor, swaying together, mouthing the lyrics to "Where Did Our Love Go?" I took a deep breath and set off in their direction.

The distance was immense. I seemed to be on a conveyor belt, and it was too late to turn back. After an eternity, the conveyor dumped me in front of the two girls. They stopped dancing, curious. The music was so loud I had to move in close to be heard. The redhead's face was barely a foot away. I had daydreamed about her so often that I was surprised to see a stranger in front of me.

My mind went blank and I forgot my lines.

"Let's get out of here," I blurted. "Come take a walk with me."

Her curiosity turned to alarm. "No," she said, edging toward her friend.

"Okay," I said. Then I began the long conveyor ride back across the empty space. My head was on fire. I felt their eyes burning into me. I wanted to run but that would only make it worse. I had to be cool. This was no big deal.

Once outside, I picked up speed and rushed into the dark woods, where I'd never be found. *I'm finished,* I thought. *I'll never show my face on the junior side again. How could I do something so creepy?*


WHILE I WAS striking out with the redhead, my cousin was getting a blow job from a counselor at a Miles Davis concert—or so he said. She was a zaftig college girl who always wore a Wellesley sweatshirt, so we called her Wellesley. Dave said there hadn't been time to bring me along to the concert, a double bill with Miles and Santana. The counselors had invited Dave to jump on the back of their flatbed truck as they were leaving camp for Tanglewood. They probably figured he was eighteen. He was six feet tall with a Fu Manchu mustache.

Dave and I had been talking about this concert all summer, but getting to it had seemed hopeless. Dan would never let a couple of fifteen-year-olds go to a concert that was shaping up to be a mini-Woodstock. Sure enough, Dave said the main lawn at Tanglewood was covered with a thousand people on blankets, smoking weed and fucking. He wandered around with his mouth hanging open.

I missed it all: Miles and Santana and the sex. This was the worst day of my life for sure. I believed Dave when he said the counselors had asked him at the last minute. But the story about the blow job sounded too good to be true. It was like the Karen thing all over again.

Dan and I were sitting by the lake a few days later, watching a giant snapper haul itself up onto Turtle Island.

"I can't believe I missed Miles Davis," I said.

"That wasn't meant to happen," Dan replied. "You're not ready for that scene."

"Yeah, but my cousin went."

"He's not ready, either." He looked at me, eyebrows raised. "You jealous?"

"I guess. More about the sex than the music."

"Did he tell you he had sex there?"

"Yeah. Sort of."

"With who?"

I knew better than to answer that. It would get Wellesley in trouble.

"I don't know. I don't believe what he told me anyway."

"You shouldn't. Your cousin's a pathological liar."

He sounded pissed. "Pathological" was worse than "insecure," which is how he had described Dave before.

"So you don't believe his story?" I asked.

"I don't know what his story is. But I wouldn't believe a word he says. Any way you slice baloney, it's still baloney."

Some campers appeared on the junior shoreline, yelling and pointing at the large turtle.

"You haven't mentioned the redhead in a while," Dan said. "What gives?"

"I had my chance and I blew it. I was an idiot."

"Nah. You were probably just trying too hard. It's her loss."

But I knew it wasn't her loss. That night of the dance, when I stood close to her, our faces inches apart, she seemed so innocent, so trusting. I scared the shit out of her. After all these blow jobs there was something wrong with me. I was like a snake stalking a kitten. She was lucky to escape.

A couple of boys waded into the lake and began swimming toward Turtle Island. There was no lifeguard on duty. Dan let them swim halfway, then commanded them to turn back. They were confused, not sure where the voice of God was coming from.

"Don't make me come out there!" he bellowed, on his feet now.

They reversed course. The turtle hadn't budged. Dan returned to his chair, frowning.

"You're not worried about your attraction to girls, are you?"

"No," I said, laughing uneasily.

"Good, 'cause I don't want you to think that anything I do to you could change you in that way."

I fixed my gaze on the lake, not wanting to look at him.

"Freud said your sexuality is fully formed by age five," he went on. "That's well established. Whatever happens after that can't change who you are. You'll always be heterosexual."

I wanted to believe him. But why did I get hard-ons when he pawed me? Or did those not count?

"I've always been into girls," I said.

"Well, you're lucky then."

"What do you mean?" I asked.

"I was never sure what I was. When I was a kid I never felt normal, because I knew I wasn't. I spent a lot of years and a lot of money trying to change what I am. The shrinks made a killing off me. What a waste. Freud was right: you can't change what you are. I should have saved my money. I should have accepted who I was."

Someone who liked boys? Someone who liked women *and* boys? I was so confused.

"Do you accept yourself now?" I asked, trying to cover my bases.

"I don't know. I always held up my end on the home front. I did that much." He sighed loudly. "You know more about me than anyone on earth," he said. "You realize that? You know me better than my wife knows me."

I was only fifteen, and the head of camp just said I was his best friend. I felt so grown up.

"I'm not sure what to say."

"Well, it's true," he said. "I never told anyone what I just told you."

# 11

I DIDN'T SEE MY COUSIN for days after he told me about Tanglewood. I was spending more and more evenings in Dan's hideout. He wasn't around much. When he did show up, he'd say "Give me your best shot." I knew how these fights would end, how they always ended.

One night after dinner, I was in his room, listening to music. When he walked in and said, "Give me your best shot," I delivered a swift knee to his left thigh that made him double over in pain. It felt good.

"Holy crap," he said, bent over and shaking his head. "You're a lot stronger than you used to be. But don't forget, I'm still the boss around here." Two seconds later, I was on my back. When he was done with me, he got up and took a shower. It was unbearably hot, so I peeled off my shirt and propped myself up against the headboard.

Dan returned and sat on the corner of the bed. "Look," he said, "you know I would never do anything to hurt you, right?"

"Yeah."

"I don't want you to think that what I told you, you know, about me not being normal, has anything to do with you. It doesn't. You are who you are. Nothing that happens here is going to hurt you. You're just learning about sex. That's part of growing up. You're going to have a great sex life with girls one day, believe me."

Right then, the front door of the mansion slammed. A second later, someone was knocking on our door—hard. A jolt of fear shot up my spine as Dave walked into the room. He saw me on the bed, shirtless, and stopped in his tracks. He looked more confused than me.

"What do you want?" Dan asked him, getting to his feet.

Dave was panting, like he'd just run a wind sprint. I plastered my sweaty back against the headboard, trying to disappear.

"There was an accident," Dave blurted out. "It's bad."

"What happened?" Dan asked.

"I was walking on the road from the kitchen," Dave said, "It was dark and I saw something crawling toward me. I thought it was a bear. Then he said, 'Help me!' It was Roger, the counselor. He was bleeding, so I sat him up on the side of the road. He said Matt was driving too fast and crashed on Little Bear. I asked him if everyone was okay, and he said no. Then I ran over here to find you. I don't know why. I figured you'd be here."

Dave was talking fast but each word was crystal clear, like I was watching a slowed-down movie.

"How many?" Dan asked.

"Four counselors. Matt, Diane, Roger, and Doug."

"Does anyone know?"

"No. I came right here. You better call the police."

"Get back over there and don't leave Roger," Dan said. "I'll get help. Get going!"

Dave glanced at me, then left, slamming the door behind him. I was light-headed.

"Put your clothes on," Dan said, heading for the door. "I'll call the police, then we're getting out of here."

I didn't know why I was going with him. I figured he needed company. When we got to the junior side, Dave said someone had already taken Roger to the hospital in New Milford. Dan and I got in his wagon and drove down Little Bear Hill Road. It was real dark, except for the patches of road and trees illuminated by our headlights.

Two-thirds of the way down the mountain, we saw flashing red lights and Matt's blue Firebird. It was upside down in a ditch on the right side, its windshield shattered.

Dan pulled over, talked to the cops, then got back in the car, shaking his head.

"Matt must have been flying," he said. "Lost control, hit that rock wall, then rolled the car. He was thrown out."

I cringed.

At the hospital, we sat in the waiting room, not saying a word. Dan got up a few times and paced. I was upset about the counselors but I was more worried about my cousin. Why in the world had Dan left his room unlocked? What did Dave think when he saw me in the bed?

A nurse appeared and said that Diane, Matt's fiancée, was in critical condition but they thought she'd pull through. Roger and Doug, who'd been in the back seat, were being discharged.

Then a doctor was talking to Dan.

"Matt's in a coma," he said. "Massive head injuries."

He told Dan he could visit Matt in intensive care, and Dan turned to me.

"You want to come?" he asked. "It could be bad."

The person in the bed looked nothing like Matt. He was lying on his back under a white sheet, perfectly still—head bandaged, face swollen, tubes running every which way out of his body. He was alive, but a machine was breathing for him, making a whooshing sound every few seconds. A white ribbed tube led from the machine to a narrow black hose that plugged into a hole in Matt's neck, beneath his Adam's apple.

"What's that called?" I asked Dan, pointing at the tube.

"A tracheotomy. They cut a hole in the throat if your airway's blocked or if you need a ventilator."

I'd seen that before. Then I remembered: I was little, sitting on my father's lap, looking up at him. There was a hole in his throat.

WE ARRIVED BACK at camp after midnight. As the car neared the mansion, I saw a slender figure sitting outside on a lawn chair, waiting. It was Phyllis, the office manager. I thought she'd be upset that I was out past curfew. Then I realized it was fine—she saw me leave camp with Dan all the time. When Dan told her about Matt and Diane, she moaned and said how tragic and senseless it was.

Dan went to get his things in the mansion and I said good night to Phyllis, but she started talking to me.

"This must be difficult for you," she said.

I bobbed my head, not sure what she meant.

"I know you've had illness and death in your life," she went on. "That's a lot to handle at such a young age."

I wasn't sure what to answer, so I yawned and said good night again. As I headed down the stairs, I realized Dan must have told her my history. How else could she have known about my father? It felt like I was some kind of social-work case.

*Was* I a social-work case?

I climbed into bed but couldn't fall asleep, wondering what else Dan had said about me. Then I tried to imagine being in a coma. But mostly I worried about my cousin and what he thought when he saw me in Dan's bed.

I CAMPED OUT in Dan's hideout with the door locked for the day and night after the accident, leaving only to serve meals. Dan wasn't there at all. I didn't want to talk to anyone, especially Dave.

The following morning I woke up to a loud knock. I figured it was Dave. He gave up and went away. An hour later someone was turning the doorknob violently, trying to get in.

"Hey, open the damned door," Dan yelled. "What are you, barricading yourself in there?" I let him in.

"Bad news," he said, entering the room. "Matt died this morning."

"Shit."

"Well, it's probably a good thing. He would have been a vegetable if he lived."

"How are you doing?" I asked.

"Like I got hit by a truck. It doesn't get worse than this."

Then he changed tack.

"I saw your cousin in the kitchen this morning. I had to straighten him out a little bit."

"What do you mean?" I asked.

"His lies are getting on my nerves. I had to let him know what's what. I took care of it. His parents are coming up tomorrow. They'll take him out of here for a few days, maybe for good. He needs to get his head on straight."

I couldn't imagine what made Dan call my aunt and uncle. Did Dave say something about walking in on us? It felt as if Dan was protecting me. Dave had turned into a problem, our problem.

"Will he come back?" I asked.

"That's up to them. He's welcome back if he learns to keep his mouth shut."

Dan turned to leave. "I got to go call Matt's parents," he said. "Then I'm going to talk to the whole camp. Rumors are flying."

I waited a few minutes, then joined the crowd filing into the junior dining hall. I stood in the back, near the doors, leaning against the wall. Dave came out of the kitchen and practically ran toward me.

"Hey, man, where have you been?" he asked. "I've been looking for you. You disappeared!"

"Yeah. I went to the hospital that night, and then I didn't feel like going out."

He took me by my shoulder and led me to a quiet corner.

"Steve, Farinella went apeshit on me this morning in the kitchen."

"What?"

"Yeah, he went nuts. Like he was gonna kill me."

"What started it?" I asked.

"Oh, I got in his face. I've been looking for you since Monday night and couldn't find you. So when he came in the kitchen I went right up to him and yelled, 'Where the hell is my cousin? What was he doing in your room the other night?' The whole kitchen crew was listening."

"What did he say?"

"He goes, 'I've had it with you.' Then he pushed me into the walk-in fridge and slammed the door behind us. I'm up against one of those steel racks and he starts going off about Tanglewood and some other shit. Then he says, 'I'm gonna beat the crap out of you.'"

"He said that?"

"Yeah! So I said, 'Go ahead, hit me! I'll call my parents and let's see what happens.' He wanted to take a shot at me but I knew he wouldn't. He'd lose his job for sure if he hit a kid. I kept saying, 'Hit me. Do it!' I wanted him to, that fuck."

"So what did he do?"

"That was it. He left."

"Did he call your parents?"

"No! I called them and told them what happened. I said, 'Get me the hell out of here.' So they called to get his permission. He talked some shit to them. I don't care. They're coming up tomorrow. They're going to bring the trailer and we'll go camping somewhere."

I didn't understand any of this, but I suddenly felt bad that Dave was leaving.

"Look, there's something else I got to tell you," he said. "When we were in the fridge, Farinella said something super weird."

"What?"

"He was running all this crap about me and he says, 'Steve's mother isn't happy about him playing the saxophone. You're not a good influence on your cousin.'"

Dave's eyes got big and he was holding his head with both hands, like it might explode.

"Okay, that totally blew my mind, Steve. Your mother and Farinella have been talking, or they talked before the summer for sure. I'm really pissed at Aunt Syd. She had no right to say that, especially to someone outside the family. I'm telling you, man, Farinella had a plan for this summer and your mother was part of it. I'm telling you, she was part of it."

"That's fucked up," I said. "I mean, we both know she's freaked out that I'll become a musician."

"Exactly," Dave said. "I'm sure she talks to my mom about it all the time. That's cool. They talk about everything. But why would your mother tell Farinella? She set me up, Steve. That's not cool. That's definitely not cool."

The mess hall was filling up with campers. Dave had to get back to work in the kitchen. I stood in the corner, listening to the conversations around me. The room was hushed, not raucous the way it usually was.

When Dan walked through the double screen doors the room grew even quieter. He stood at the serving windows and faced the camp—kids, counselors, administrators, staff. For once, he didn't have to shout.

"I know you've all been hearing stories about what happened two nights ago," he said. "I wanted to tell you all at the same time. There was a car accident on Little Bear Road with four of our counselors. Two of them got cut up but were okay. Diane got banged up pretty bad and she's still in the hospital. I saw her this morning. She's going to be all right."

Diane's bunk of girls began hugging one another.

"Matt wasn't so lucky," Dan went on. "He wasn't wearing a seat belt. He got thrown from the car and suffered a bad head injury. He went into a coma." Dan paused, looking right at the boys at Matt's table. "The doctors did everything they could for Matt. I'm sorry to tell you that he died this morning."

It was silent for a second, then pandemonium.

Girls were shrieking. Boys were crying. The staff had their hands to their mouths. At the redhead's table, she and her friend were hysterical, holding on to one another. I wanted to go comfort her. Then she'd know I was a good person.

I'd never heard a hundred people cry at the same time. The strange thing was, I didn't feel that sad. Ever since I'd seen Matt in the hospital, I knew he was already gone. He would be like Ella Fohs, his ghost wandering camp forever.

When the wailing began to subside, a boy raised his hand and asked, "What do we do now? Will we still have camp?" A murmur passed through the room. Everyone had been wondering the same thing.

"Camp will go on," Dan insisted. "There's only a few days left. We're going to help each other get through this. We're like a big family. This is what family is for."

# 12

Rosh Hashanah fell on September 30 that year, along with Dave's sixteenth birthday. The Mills clan planned to celebrate the Jewish new year and my cousin's birthday at the same dinner. My mother was hosting, and she wanted the Farinellas to be there.

I knew that would be awkward. Aunt Delle and Uncle Harold had met Dan when they pulled Dave out of camp. My cousin returned to Ella Fohs for the last days of August, but I'd barely talked to him then or since, even though we went to the same school. I still didn't know if he'd told his parents about finding me in Dan's room.

Inviting the Farinellas was a nice gesture, my mother said, because they'd recently moved to Long Island and would have no place to go for the holiday. I was pretty sure Dan couldn't care less about the Jewish new year, but I knew that wasn't my mother's real reason anyway. She was catapulting Dan from acquaintance to dear friend, bypassing everything in between, and it was all about me. Wasn't it fantastic, she seemed to be saying, that Dan has taken this interest in Stephen and been such a great role model? My mother couldn't wait to introduce Dan to the rest of my aunts and uncles.

Rosh Hashanah was one of two days on the calendar, the other being Passover, when my father's clan would gather the way they had done when I was a child. In the days leading up to the new year, I was acutely aware of my father's absence. When I closed my eyes at night, I could see the headless soldiers lined up before me, ghostly and mute. I replayed questions about him I'd brought home from camp, but I hadn't yet worked up the nerve to put them to my mother.

I was in my bedroom when Dave's family arrived for the holiday dinner. He came right to my room, knocked once, and walked in. I barely said hi before he erupted.

"My mother just told me that Farinella's going to be here!" he said, incredulous. "Where does he get off showing up for Rosh Hashanah?"

"My mother invited him," I said.

"Why would she do that? I mean, I know she thinks I'm the bad guy and Farinella can do no wrong. But what the fuck is he doing at our holiday dinner?"

"I don't know, Dave. It wasn't my idea. I knew you wouldn't want to see him."

"That's the understatement of the year," he said, pacing back and forth. He picked up my desk chair, turned it around, and sat down facing me, stricken.

"Look, Steve, I don't know what happened this summer but something happened and things changed between us. What's bothering you? There's something wrong. I know something's wrong."

"There's nothing wrong, Dave. It was just a weird summer. You moved to the junior side. Then the Tanglewood thing happened. I just felt left out."

His eyes narrowed. He wasn't buying it.

"Steve, people at camp asked me why Dan was spending so much time with you."

"I don't know what that's about," I said, shaking my hea[d]
conviction.

"Look, man," my cousin said, "I'm begging you to tell me what's
wrong." His eyes were burrowing into mine, searching for clues,
cracks in my armor. I stared back, ready to deny anything. My life
depended on it.

"Nothing's wrong, Dave. I'd tell you if there was."

"You know, your mother thinks I'm jealous of Farinella," he said.
"I'm not. I just hate him."

"I know." So he *had* talked to my mother, or at least my aunt
had.

Dave sank back in the chair and I saw the fight go out of him.
The interrogation was over. Now I felt bad for him, and guilty, too.

"My parents are making me go to a shrink," he said. "I started
last week."

"Why?" I didn't know anyone who went to a psychologist.

"The usual crap," he said. "My mother and I fight too much. But
you know what? After this summer, I sort of want to see a shrink.
It's nice having someone to talk to. He actually listens to my shit."

I couldn't imagine going to a shrink. My mother said they were
for families with real problems. Besides, I already had someone who
listened to my shit: Dan.

The doorbell rang and we heard the Farinellas. Dave rolled his
eyes, vexed by what awaited him in the living room.

"Hey, happy birthday," I said, realizing I hadn't mentioned it.

"Yeah, thanks." He grimaced. "Let's just get this over with."

In the living room, I shook hands with Dan and Gary, then kissed
Betty on the cheek. Dave crossed behind us, ignoring the Farinellas.
When it was time for dinner, my mother sat at the head of the
extended holiday table, closest to the kitchen. She put Betty and
Dan, the honored guests, to her right. Ken sat to my mother's left,
and I sat to his left, opposite Dan. Dave and his parents were at the
far end, with my other aunts and uncles arrayed in the middle.

After dinner, Aunt Delle brought out a large, homemade chocolate cake, topped with sixteen candles. We dimmed the lights and sang "Happy Birthday," with the Farinellas joining in. The glow of the candles illuminated Dave's face. He was wearing that same wounded expression.

I HAD COME home from camp in a dark state of mind. At night, I hid in my room with the door closed and the lights off. Facedown in bed, I listened to Simon and Garfunkel's "Bridge over Troubled Water," crying so hard the sheets soaked through.

My body seemed possessed, as if anguish had taken up residence. I was consumed by thoughts of Matt's overturned Firebird, Ella's ghostly portrait, and always the disappearance of my father, which felt like a boulder crushing my chest. I was being punished. I didn't know for what but I was meant to suffer, and no one could know. I went to school every day and studied even harder.

My mother complained I'd had a personality transplant. It was as if one boy had gone off to camp and his sullen, sarcastic twin had returned in his place. The truth was, I'd resented my mother for years, but I'd been good at hiding it. Now, I stopped pretending. I distrusted whatever she did and felt no tenderness toward her at all. She, in turn, eyed me coldly across the table. With my siblings away at college, dinner hour became a silent affair.

The day after Rosh Hashanah, my mother and I were home by ourselves. She was in her reading chair, engrossed in the *New Yorker*, with a cup of black tea perched next to her. I sat down opposite.

"Mom, do you have a few minutes?"

She laid down the magazine and peered at me suspiciously. I'd barely said anything to her for a month.

"I want to ask you some things about my father." I was trying to sound casual, as if talking about him was something we did, as opposed to the thing we had never done. But her body stiffened and her mouth clamped shut.

"It would help me," I added, and she seemed to let down her guard a bit.

"All right," she said. "What would you like to know?"

"I was wondering if he was able to talk in his last years. You know, after I was born."

"Is there some reason you're wondering about that?" she asked. Did I need reasons to ask about my own father?

"Yeah," I said, trying to stay calm. "I had a very intense dream this summer. I think it was about my father. It made me wonder whether he was able to talk." I worried that she'd ask me to tell her the dream. But she got quiet, struggling with what to say.

"Well," she began, "Si pretty much stopped speaking around the time you started. You were talking early, around eighteen or twenty months. He'd been having trouble speaking, and swallowing, too. He could still talk a little bit, but it was hard to understand. Uncle Harold and I could make it out, but no one else."

"So how did he and I communicate?"

"Oh, you two communicated plenty. It just wasn't talking. You'd come home from nursery school and run straight to our bedroom. Si would be there, reading in his wheelchair, and you'd climb on his lap. He always lit up when he saw you."

Her face softened, and I didn't move a muscle for fear of breaking the spell. But she had stopped.

"Do you think I was troubled that he couldn't speak?" I asked.

"No. It's just how things were. It didn't seem to bother you at all. You two were very connected, almost inseparable. Whenever I went out, to shop or run errands, I'd have the grandmother come over from next door to babysit. But you only wanted to be with your father."

*Your father.* She hadn't said those words since I was six.

"This may be a strange question," I said, "but did he ever have a tracheotomy?"

The softness in her face vanished, replaced by a mask of pain.

"Yes, it was terrible. He had a bad pneumonia. I thought he was going to die. I got him in the car and took him to the hospital. They did a tracheotomy on the spot. It saved his life. He was in there a couple of weeks and I stayed with him the whole time. You were two, maybe three. Our friends took care of you, mostly Pauline Klein. She was a nurse."

"I remember that," I said. "I had a fever, and I was throwing up in a metal bucket."

"You had German measles. Pauline stayed with you, then she'd come to the hospital and check on Si. She was the only one I trusted completely about his care." I saw a memory cross her face. "That was the first time Pauline said to me, 'Syd, you do know he's terminal.' I did know, but I'd never admitted it before."

"Did he know?"

"We never discussed it, that was our code. Anyway, when you got over the measles, Pauline brought you to the hospital every day so you could wave to your father through the window. His room was on the ground floor. He was so happy to see you."

"I don't remember that."

"Well, that's not surprising. You were a toddler. I'm amazed you remember the tracheotomy."

"It came back to me this summer when I saw Matt in the hospital."

"Why do you think these questions are coming up now?" she asked.

"I don't know. Does it matter? I just want to know my father better. That seems pretty normal, right?"

She didn't answer.

"Is there something else you want to know?" she asked.

"What happened after the pneumonia?"

"He pulled through, but it was rough. I drove him home from the hospital. He had an ulcerated wound on his spine, because they hadn't turned him enough. He was in agony from the pain and the spasms. He screamed all the way home. I got him into bed, but he woke up in the middle of the night with a fever of 105. It was a urinary infection. I took him back to the hospital. He recovered after another week, but it was downhill from there. That's when we got that sling contraption. It had a jack and a crank. That's how I got him in and out of bed. His body was dead weight." She shook her head. "Do you remember that thing?"

"I do. I used to wake up when I heard you cranking it at night."

"The nights were the worst. He'd get these spasms where his legs would go up in the air, completely rigid. He couldn't move them at all, but he'd have to go to the bathroom something awful. I took him to the VA doctor at Fort Hamilton. The doctor took me outside and said, 'You've got to admit him right now, Sydell. You can't do this at home anymore.' I said, 'No, I can't do that. He'll die. He needs to be with his family.'"

She gave a little snort. "So he went on. Those last two years were bad. The second pneumonia killed him. I had the flu and was feeding him. I'm sure he caught it from me. As awful as that was, I was okay with it." Her voice was choking. "No one should have to go through what he went through. No one."

I thought she was going to cry, but no tears came. She was quiet for a long time.

Then she said, "I have some of your father's things. Would you like to see them?"

I was stunned.

"Yes, of course. I didn't know you had anything."

"I was waiting to give them to you."

"Waiting for what?" I asked.

"I guess for you to be old enough. You know, this isn't easy for me, Stephen."

"I know, Mom. I can see that."

She led me into her bedroom, opened the closet door, and pointed to a couple of boxes on the top shelf in the back. I got a step stool and took the boxes down. They were heavy. I carried them, one at a time, into the living room, where I set them on the floor. Each box was labeled "Si" in black Magic Marker.

With a knife, I sliced the brown packing tape on the first box, opened it, and peered inside. There were hundreds of letters, rubber banded together in bundles of twenty or thirty. The airmail envelopes were fringed with red and blue bars, and the upper left-hand corner of each one named the sender: S/SGT SEYMOUR MILLS, 58TH FIGHTER SQUADRON, 33RD FIGHTER GROUP.

I fanned through a couple of bundles. Most of the letters were addressed to Mrs. S. Mills—Sadie, the grandmother I never knew—in flowing block-letter style, with the first letter of each word larger than the others. It reminded me of Uncle Harold's handwriting, which always seemed like calligraphy.

"That's a lot of letters," I said.

"Si was devoted to his mother. All three brothers were, tied at the apron strings. I don't think he went a day during the war without writing her."

I took all the bundles from the box, two fistfuls at a time. Beneath them, I found a trove of personal possessions. Some were from the war: dog tags, medals, a gold Army Air Corps ring, a knife bayonet, a copy of *Prayer Book for Jews in the Armed Forces of the United States*. There was a Boy Scout sash, an NYU diploma, and a small travel chess set. I unzipped a blue velvet pouch and removed two small black leather boxes with straps.

"What are these?" I asked my mother.

"Those are tefillin. Orthodox Jews wrap them around their forehead and right arm when they pray in the morning. My father wrapped tefillin every day. Your father got these on his bar mitzvah. I doubt he ever put them on. He was agnostic."

In the second box an American flag sat on top, folded in perfectly creased triangles. My mother, who hadn't touched a thing in the first box, reached over and lifted the flag out with both hands.

"I forgot about this," she said. "It covered your father's casket. It was a military funeral."

"I didn't know that," I said. I suddenly realized I had no idea where my father was buried.

"Where was the funeral?" I asked.

"Long Island National. It's a military cemetery in Farmingdale. The funeral was delayed because of the blizzard. It was freezing cold, and you were sick. Aunt Gwen stayed with you."

"What was the funeral like?"

"It was rough. I kept it together until they played 'Taps' and fired the guns. That did me in." Her eyes welled up, and she handed me back the flag, which I set down carefully on the coffee table.

When I reached back into the box I came out with a photo album, the largest and heaviest I'd ever seen—about sixteen inches wide, a foot high, and three inches thick. It was bound by a white cord and two fat metal bolts. Beneath it was a second photo album as big as the first.

"Those albums were your father's record of the war," my mother said. "He took photos and kept a diary everywhere he went. When he was hospitalized, at the end of the war, he spent months putting those together."

I was speechless. These two treasure chests had been sitting up there in the closet for years, gathering dust, unmentioned and unopened. My mother slumped against the side of her chair, staring vacantly at the boxes.

"Thanks, Mom," I said.

"They're yours now, Stephen," she said softly. "You take them."

I went to her chair and she grasped my hand, getting to her feet. Then we hugged. For a moment, I had my mother back.

Part Two

FLIGHT

# 13

REB NOTA LEANED BACK IN his tall leather chair, peered across his gunmetal gray desk, and observed me for several seconds without saying a word. He was a handsome man of forty or so, with chiseled features, a neatly trimmed goatee, silver wire-frame glasses, and a large black velvet yarmulke that covered half his head. The other half was starting to show a bit of salt with the pepper.

Ohr Somayach yeshiva was filled with rabbis whose mastery of Talmud impressed me. But Reb Nota was the only one who intimidated me. He was not some shtetl Jew, the kind who looked askance at American college students like me, young men who'd been raised on sex, drugs, and rock 'n' roll only to find themselves on the doorstep of an Orthodox yeshiva in Jerusalem. He was an all-American boy who loved baseball and had dreamed of playing for the Brooklyn Dodgers. He'd attended university and was well read in literature, philosophy, history—you name it. And he was just as happy discussing the US presidential campaign as the upcoming Israeli election. Reb Nota could pass, no questions asked, as a college professor or a Washington lobbyist.

As if his commanding presence weren't enough, Reb Nota had a killer gaze that burrowed deep into your soul. Or so we yeshiva students believed. He seemed to read not just our minds but our hearts. On this particular morning, my twenty-first birthday, I had news to share with him and I was dreading it.

"*Nu*, Shlomo?" he finally asked, after getting a good read on my soul. He called me by my Hebrew name, which I'd been given at birth in memory of my mother's father, a rabbi from Poland. In yeshiva, we all went by our Hebrew names.

"You've been wrestling with something," he said. "Tell me."

"Reb Nota, I've thought a lot about this. I've decided to go back to the States for a year. I need to finish college."

He took a long, audible breath and nodded. I fiddled with the dangling straps of my tefillin, which I was wearing because I'd come directly from morning prayers. The two small leather boxes, bound to my forehead and upper arm, were a daily reminder commanded by Torah of the Exodus from Egypt. They were my father's tefillin, the ones I'd found inside the boxes my mother had given me.

I began absentmindedly stroking my beard, a habit I'd picked up while parsing Talmud with my study partner. I'd grown the beard over the previous eight months, and it had come in uneven and bristly, like a hunk of reddish Brillo. I had cut my burgeoning Jew-fro, leaving my hair as short as it had been in junior high, and I was now wearing large tortoise-shell glasses with thick lenses. I sported a black knit yarmulke, edged with sky blue. Under my shirt I wore tzitzis, the white-fringed garment that reminds one of God at all times.

But I'd gone no further. I hadn't gotten the full yeshiva makeover, which would have meant black jacket, black hat, and black shoes. I was still wearing jeans and sneakers. There would be plenty of time to go *shtarker*—hard-core religious—when I returned after graduating college.

"How strong are you, Shlomo?" Reb Nota finally asked. "Do you have the strength to maintain your Yiddishkeit while attending college in America? That's easy to do here. You're surrounded by dozens of other yeshiva students, studying Torah sixteen hours a day. Back at college, you'll be alone, with your girlfriend and Friedrich Nietzsche and all that *trayfe* food. What will happen to your Yiddishkeit then, hmm?"

How did he know about my girlfriend? Was he hazarding a wild guess, trying to smoke me out? No. He definitely knew. Someone must have told him. He couldn't have been surprised. Pangs for the girlfriend left behind was a common ailment afflicting the *ba'al teshuvah*—a returner, someone like me from a secular background who had taken up religious study and observance as an adult.

"Real world, Shlomo. Are you *shtarker* enough?" Was my intention strong enough to steer me through secular America without succumbing?

"Yes," I assured him. "I'll be back in a year—less than a year."

"Why go? You studied with their best minds. You had the college girlfriend. What's left to experience?"

Good question. Did I need a piece of paper that told the world I'd graduated? I had no plans for using it.

"I promised my parents," I said, going with what I thought might fly. "They freaked out when I transferred here from Hebrew University. I made a commitment to finish college next year."

"This is a good reason." He dipped his head to one side, acknowledging my case.

"But?"

"But you're not ready, Shlomo. If you were a pitching prospect I wouldn't send you straight from Class A ball to the majors. You'd get eaten alive by the hitters and the pressure. You need more time here. Another year. Then you'll be ready to walk out on the mound and face down the secular world. We're talking about your *nefesh*, Shlomo, your Jewish soul."

Reb Nota was leaning forward now, eyes narrowed, jaw clenched. This was it. I had to take a stand right here, right now, or next thing I knew, instead of finishing college I'd be married and circumcising my firstborn.

"That's why you're here, Shlomo—your *nefesh*. Never forget that. Never forget what brought you here."

IF MY JEWISH soul had brought me to yeshiva, something else had made me stay: for the first time in years, I wasn't longing to die. When the sun went down, I didn't find myself alone in my room, spiraling into despair, surrendering to the misery that had been my near-constant companion throughout high school and the first years of college. Instead, I lost myself in evening prayer, wrestled with medieval commentaries on the Talmud, and talked late into the night with my dorm mates, marveling at how radically our lives had changed in Jerusalem.

Before yeshiva, if I'd found refuge at all it had been in the arms of girls. It began the summer after the car crash at camp. It was 1971, and I'd just turned sixteen. My parents sent me on a youth group tour of Israel for eight weeks. We were twenty-five teenagers overseen by three adult chaperones. Along the way, one of them, a young rabbi, had a nervous breakdown and had to be shipped back to the States. Then, one morning in Haifa, our other minders, a couple, went AWOL. Half our teen group headed right to the *shuk* to score some Lebanese blond hash. Others bought a bottle of whiskey, found a tape player, and started a dance party. I was too antisocial for any of that.

I crossed paths in the lobby with a girl from another group. I'd met her the week before at a hostel in the Galilee. She was tall and skinny with a blond shag haircut and super sad eyes. In no time at all we were up in her room, entangled on her twin bed, which we dragged outside onto the cramped fourth-floor balcony.

We stayed there for three days, leaving only to eat, always return- ing to the narrow bed overlooking the street below. Sometimes, she would climb on the ledge and traverse it from end to end like a tightrope walker. I shut my eyes and begged her to come down. When I opened my eyes I could see right up her denim cutoffs that she wasn't wearing underwear. I wanted to get those little shorts off her body and her embroidered white peasant blouse, too. But she insisted that wouldn't happen.

"I've had sex," she said. "I want you to wait for someone innocent." I pictured the redhead at camp and knew I wasn't innocent—or normal.

This girl didn't have to tell me that a man had done bad things to her. I could see it in her eyes and hear it in her voice. I held her tight, wanting to take the pain from her. In return, she heard about my father's death and my own sense of doom. I'd been like the walking dead since the last summer at camp, just waiting to be extinguished.

I called her Girl of the Sea. She called me Boy of the Sky. We cut each other's thumbs with a razor and mixed our blood, smudging a piece of paper deep red and pledging our love. We promised each other a world beyond this one, a place free of fear. We slept together beneath a bowl of stars, glued to each other like terrified children. One night, when the moon was high and we were falling into each other's eyes, I wanted to tell her about Dan Farinella. Maybe she could explain what that had been about. But I was too ashamed and couldn't find the words.

The next morning, a new chaperone appeared, paid our hotel bill, and shuttled our group off to a kibbutz. The Girl of the Sea went to an archeological dig. We never crossed paths again.

WHILE I WAS on the youth tour, Dan was running a camp in western Massachusetts called Wim-o-Weh. He still worked at Oyster Bay High School, but he had left Camp Ella Fohs. He stopped taking me with him to camp in the off-season, or anywhere else, for that matter. He never touched me again or said another word about it.

Once in a while, he'd call me up—he only lived a few minutes away—and we'd go to a movie. Then we'd talk about it over dinner at some Italian place he deemed acceptable. I thought of him as a mentor, giving me advice and job references. I'd just finished tenth grade and was counting on him for a college recommendation when the time came. He always remembered my birthday, handing me an envelope with cash or a gift certificate. My mother continued having the Farinellas to our house for the Jewish holidays. Once, he invited my parents and me to an "antidrug night" that he hosted at Oyster Bay High School.

Then, out of the blue, the Farinellas announced they were moving to Illinois. Dan had taken a job running Camp Henry Horner, operated by the Jewish Council for Youth Services, about an hour north of Chicago. He had complained that Camp Ella Fohs didn't support his agenda of interracial camping. Henry Horner would be fertile ground for his pioneering ideas, he said. My mother approved. She arranged for my sister, who was a design student at Cornell University, to be director of arts and crafts at the camp in Illinois that first summer.

In the spring of eleventh grade, my two best friends found girlfriends and couldn't stop grinning or talking about anything but sex. I fell for a svelte Jewish girl of Turkish ancestry, with jet-black hair and dreamy eyes. Ronnie and I made out a few times but hadn't gone further than that. When a friend's parents went out of town, he said we could stay over in his wood-paneled basement.

That night, I waited in my pinstripe pajamas next to the pullout sofa while Ronnie prepared in the bathroom. She emerged wearing a blue silk kimono. I could barely believe my eyes. I drew her to me, running my right hand down her back. She took my face in her hands and kissed me. I tasted her lips and inhaled her hair. She smelled like Boone's Farm apple wine and Herbal Essence Shampoo. She giggled and pulled away, opening her kimono to show me she was naked. I hesitated, but she took my hand and placed it on her right breast. After a few seconds I trailed my hand down her smooth stomach to her navel, then down farther still. We moved onto the sofa bed, which creaked loudly. I entered her slowly but could only penetrate so far before I could go no farther. I was scared I'd hurt her. We kept trying then stopped, reassuring each other that it would be okay.

We tried again two days later in her bedroom after school, with her wire-haired terrier looking on. This time I felt something give way and there was a rush of blood onto the sheets, catching us both by surprise. Ronnie shut her eyes and I kept going.

Later that week we were lying on her bedroom floor when she proposed giving me a blow job. I winced. She had a mouthful of braces. All that wire looked scary, but I wasn't going to say no. It hurt at first. I couldn't tell if it was the braces or her teeth. I got hard, but I kept seeing Farinella's fat slobbering lips. I opened my eyes to make sure it was a girl's mouth on me. I came, but it felt like someone else was there, watching.

I told Ronnie it was my first blow job, which was how I saw it, or wanted to see it anyway. The others hadn't counted. Besides, whatever Dan had done to me may have been weird, but it hadn't changed me. I had a girlfriend now, just like he said I would.

My dark moods receded that summer. They couldn't compete with the novelty of fucking Ronnie on the white shag carpet in her parents' living room on hot and humid afternoons. Even the dog seemed to be smiling. But that fall, my senior year of high school, I began withdrawing from her. I hated myself for doing it. She was terrific: smart, funny, affectionate. Her only flaw, as far as I could tell, was that she loved me, and the more she loved me the more I pulled away. My silences grew longer, more obvious.

Over the winter, I broke up with her. I said it was because I'd be leaving soon for college and it would be better for us to separate in advance. We both cried. I lay in bed that night wondering how love had turned into misery.

I'd been accepted to Haverford, a small, Quaker liberal arts school outside Philadelphia and, thanks to my father's benefits as a disabled veteran, my tuition was largely covered. Almost immediately, I isolated myself at college, lying in a fetal position for hours each night, fixated on the puke-green cinder block walls of my room, fantasizing about death. Late one night I picked up the phone to call the college counseling service. But what would I tell them? I had no reason to be in agony. The session would be over as soon as it started. I hung up, and propelled my body to the desk and cranked out my work.

The despair lifted momentarily during sophomore year when I met Claire, a tall girl from the Midwest with tawny curls and a kind, radiant face. She was studying modern dance and seemed to vibrate with enthusiasm for life. She laughed easily and, unlike me, wasn't cynical at all. A Quaker pacifist, Claire had grown up overseas, where her parents were medical workers in the Peace Corps. She introduced me to baking bread, backpacking, and carrying a pocket guide to identify trees. We began sleeping together almost every night, taking turns in each other's room. I got a bad case of the flu that fall and lay in her bed, my feverish head in her lap. She stroked my hair and read me German love poems.

I sensed Claire was drawn to my dark side. One of her sisters had committed suicide. Our grief seemed to bind us, but still I worried. Why would this life-affirming nature girl want to be with me? At night, after we made love and Claire fell asleep, I'd lie there, hollow and heavy, caught in my familiar prison of solitary suffering. Something had gone terribly wrong with me, and there was nothing that I, much less Claire, could do. It was better to surrender, to die. I never shared this—I was too scared of losing her.

"You know, you feel like a stranger when we make love," she said one night, not a minute after we'd finished.

"What do you mean?"

"I'm not sure. It's like you disappear and someone else is there but I don't know him."

I replayed what had happened. I was inside her, my body thrumming with pleasure and yet . . . I felt far away, numb and guilty, as if I didn't want to know her or let her know me. Maybe that's just how I was. I began feeling less and less worthy of her and didn't want to spend the next year at Haverford in agony. Going to Hebrew University in Jerusalem for my junior year was a welcome way out.

The separation was excruciating. After class each day I'd rush back to my tiny apartment and check the wrought iron mailbox. If I found a light-blue envelope with Claire's name in the corner, I'd make myself a cup of chai Adani tea, place it next to my ancient wicker chair by the window, and give myself over to her declarations of love, written in beautiful, densely packed script. I would immediately write back, sometimes one page, sometimes ten.

That ended when I transferred from Hebrew University to yeshiva. At the time, I'd been studying medieval philosophy and Talmud, but the university lecture hall made the texts seem desiccated and lifeless. I was in Israel, so why not go directly to the living, breathing source?

I visited a friend who was studying at Ohr Somayach, and after one day there I realized that the Reform Judaism I had brushed off as a teenager was a heavily diluted concoction. I had known that intellectually, of course, but now I saw how it paled beside the depth and intensity of Orthodox practice.

I also noticed that my Jewish Yemeni neighbors in Jerusalem were chanting similar prayers and studying the same texts as the Ashkenazi rabbis at Ohr Somayach. These two far-flung communities, which had precious little contact over the previous two thousand years, were swimming in the same ancient, spiritual river, and I'd never even dipped a toe in it. I may have been steeped in Plato, Descartes, and Kant, but I couldn't tell you the first thing about Jewish law, theology, or mysticism. If I was going to learn, or reject, my own people's religion, then I wanted it to be the genuine article.

I began going to the yeshiva every day to study Gemara—the Rabbinic analysis and commentary that runs through the Talmud. I loved the dialectical style of learning, the mental tennis match of challenge and response, driven by logical deduction and spirited debate. My college classes seemed dull by comparison. When the semester ended at Hebrew University, I gave up my apartment and moved into the yeshiva.

My mother was horrified. Her Orthodox father had sent her at age four to heder, a traditional Jewish school, to learn Hebrew and Torah in the afternoons. She hated it, quit when her father fell ill, and reinvented herself as a progressive, secular Jew. She couldn't believe I'd embrace the Old World religion she had rejected.

THE YESHIVA HOUSED some fifty students, mostly college-age Americans, with a smattering from Canada, Europe, Russia, and South Africa. Many had been recruited at the Western Wall, where a charismatic American rabbi from the yeshiva would strike up conversations with young Jewish men visiting on vacation or studying. Some were on their way home after spending months in Indian ashrams or Thai monasteries. I recognized these fellow travelers. Shaped by the sixties and disaffected by American materialism, we were spiritually starved. Reb Nota thought such lost souls should be brought home to their own heritage.

Ohr Somayach was more austere than Haverford or Hebrew University. The quarters were Spartan, the meals simple. There were no lawns for Frisbee, no television for entertainment, and there were definitely no girls. Every minute of the day was jammed with Talmud, study groups, and prayer, as if law school were crossed with monastic training.

I was temperamentally suited to this life. Poring over an obscure ancient text for hours at a time came easily. I knew how to read and write Hebrew, which gave me a head start over fellow newcomers who were starting from scratch. I made fast progress learning Aramaic, the Roman-era language of the Talmud. Reb Nota thought I had the makings of a serious student, the kind who might, after years of devoted study, be a candidate for rabbinic ordination and the life of a teacher. I saw a path stretching out before me and knew I was capable.

Cultivating faith was tougher. I had never believed in God, especially one who would keep busy intervening in human affairs. But I made a deal with myself: I would suspend disbelief. I'd pray as if

I believed in God. I would take Kierkegaard's leap of faith—the Jewish version—and see what happened.

What happened was I landed in my body. To my surprise, prayer was an intensely physical act. I began each day wrapping my right arm and forehead in the binding leather straps of tefillin. I chanted Hebrew verses at my own pace while bowing, swaying, twisting, turning, and writhing. The yeshiva style of prayer seemed more like the ecstatic shaking of the seventeenth-century Quakers, far from the polite, all-rise-and-recite Judaism I'd grown up with.

The opening to God was passionate and cathartic. A roomful of davening yeshiva students was a raucous, high-energy event, a barely contained chaos of discordant voices and flailing bodies. It felt good. Kierkegaard was onto something: faith was a welcome way out of the hall of mirrors we call thinking. After morning prayers I was purified, emptied of the grief and despair that had once stalked me after dark. Since high school, I'd known that girls could suspend my pain, but yeshiva was better—it obliterated pain. Gone was the miasma of doom that had enveloped me.

I committed myself to following the 613 commandments dictated by the holy Torah, which cover everything from how to cut your beard (don't) to what to do with the mother bird taken from its nest (release her) to when to spill your seed (never). The latter prohibition seemed the most daunting. No sex was one thing. No sex and no jerking off seemed out of the question. But as with everything else, I suspended disbelief and set about retraining my mind and body. For a couple of months I got up too early, went to bed too late, and took too many cold showers to indulge myself. Then I discovered a copy of *Playboy* hidden in the side pocket of my roommate's suitcase. He'd been there longer than me, so I'd figured he had emergency relief stashed somewhere. That night, I felt deeply unworthy.

Dating was strictly forbidden except as prelude to marriage. Judaism is a religion of householders, not monks. The celibate regimen of yeshiva study has an expiration date. If sexual energy is distracting your focus from Gemara, then it's time to get married. The morning after the wedding you go back to studying. I watched, amazed, as some of my friends who had been in yeshiva only a year longer than me went out on arranged dates with young women, ideally the daughter of a respected rabbi, and immediately began making wedding plans. "She's a good girl," one guy reported after a date. He meant she was scrupulously religious.

A few who had been in yeshiva two or three years longer than me had received ordination and were beginning to teach. I wanted what they had: the esoteric wisdom, the imposing beard, the festive Shabbas meal set out by the serene, radiant wife. But more than any of that, I wanted their certainty. I craved certainty.

But doubt kept creeping in. How could we really know Torah was the word of God? How could I reconcile that word with evolution and science? Was there any room for creativity and dissent in a community that vested absolute authority in a bunch of old guys with limited life experience?

I questioned my motives. Sure, I loved to pray and study, but maybe I just needed the approval of father figures. A few of my fellow yeshiva students had lost their fathers. We knew who we were, and some of us joked darkly about our acute hunger to belong.

Mostly, though, I doubted my doubting. Why was I still questioning revealed truth? Why wasn't I ready to buy a black hat? Why did I panic at the thought of dating a "good girl"? Why couldn't I get with the program?

Reb Nota was right. My Jewish soul—Shlomo's soul—had found its way home. But Stephen kept checking the doors for escape routes.

It was May 1976. My junior year abroad was coming to an end. I had to decide if I would return to Haverford as I'd promised my parents, or if this stint would become a lifetime in Jerusalem. On my twenty-first birthday, my head and arm bound in tefillin, I made the decision to return to the States and finish the academic path I'd begun. I wasn't ready to stop being Stephen yet.

Besides, it would be a welcome test. I would keep kosher,

guard the Sabbath, and study Gemara. Perhaps this trial by fire would purify my heart. Certainty would emerge. After graduation, I'd return to Jerusalem, don a black hat, and embrace the Rabbinic path.

I LOCKED EYES with Reb Nota.

"I'll guard my *nefesh*, Reb Nota," I said. I didn't blink and, after a few seconds, he nodded.

"Okay, Shlomo. Let's talk about the world you're going back to."

"Good."

"Your girlfriend. Is she Jewish?" he asked.

"No. Quaker."

"How serious is it?"

"Well, it was serious. Now I'm just scared."

"Of what?"

"She's talking about converting." Claire's recent letters had revealed she was studying Hebrew and reading deeply in Jewish history and religion.

He arched one eyebrow.

"I told her: 'Don't do this for me.' I said we can't be together now. That's the only way to be sure she's doing this for herself."

"And?"

"She's planning to come here to study Torah."

"So . . . she's coming here, and you want to go there?"

No one had put it like that before. It sounded crazy. Maybe it wasn't the prospect of Claire's converting that scared me. It was that this amazing girl was ready to follow me anywhere.

"Yes, she's coming to Israel and I want to go back to the States."

Reb Nota looked pleased. "What college are you attending?"

"Haverford."

"Good school. What are you studying?"

"I'm a religion major with a minor in philosophy. I need to write a senior thesis. I'm thinking about contrasting the political philosophies of Rambam and Spinoza."

Reb Nota frowned. Spinoza had been expelled from Amsterdam's Jewish community at age twenty-three for "abominable heresies." I had a thing for him.

"Spinoza had a brilliant mind, Shlomo. But that's not enough. For a Jew, brilliance without Torah is hollow, even dangerous. So, go ahead, read Spinoza. But cling to the Rambam."

"I understand."

"And where will you find Torah in Pennsylvania?" he asked.

"I'm not sure."

"The Philadelphia yeshiva," he said, answering his own question. "It's only a few miles from Haverford." I should have known he'd already mapped out my life.

He stood up, and I got to my feet, too. He shook my right hand and placed his left hand on my shoulder. I felt relieved to be leaving with his blessing.

"Thank you, Reb Nota."

"Go. Get your diploma, Shlomo," he said, smiling. A second later, his grip on my right hand tightened. "But remember, you're not one of them. You belong to us."

# 14

Shlomo's observance survived barely one semester back at college. At first, I prayed with intensity three times a day. On Friday afternoons I walked five miles to the Talmudical Yeshiva of Philadelphia, where I studied Gemara for a night and day with black-hatted young men who'd never heard of Haverford College. When the Sabbath was over, I secluded myself in a basement carrel of the college library, decoding the arcane speculations of Spinoza, who reportedly didn't go out for days at a time and abstained from sex entirely. I wondered if he found the life of the mind as depressing as I did.

Reb Nota had been right. My spiritual resolve withered from the daily temptations, nagging doubts, and grinding isolation. In my small, one-room apartment I consoled myself by listening to Springsteen's *Born to Run* album or reading Nietzsche on the cowardice of religion. I fantasized about buying a one-way ticket to Jerusalem but couldn't seem to muster such a dramatic leap.

My preoccupation with death was back, and I found no refuge

in my rickety belief in God. Each morning, I went through the motions of prayer while fixated on the void of life beyond graduation. Two thesis advisers suggested I pursue a doctorate in comparative religion or medieval philosophy and become an academic like them. The prospect seemed grim. It was like yeshiva without the spiritual intensity and sense of belonging, which were the best parts.

On the other hand, I had an economics professor, a columnist for the *New York Times*, who encouraged me to think of economics as a lever for social change. I loved the mathematical certainty of it, all those equations that could be applied to real-world problems. He recommended a graduate school like the University of Wisconsin that had a more progressive bent. Getting a doctorate and working for a labor union or international development group sounded more appealing than slaving over medieval texts for the rest of my life. But I'd have to get up to speed on calculus, statistics, and econometrics before applying to grad school. He suggested Columbia University for that, and I decided to enroll there in the summer, after I graduated.

As soon as I made the decision, I stopped wearing a yarmulke, gave up praying, and dispensed with the weekly trek to the yeshiva. Coping with one world instead of two was a huge relief. Claire stopped off at Haverford to visit me and other friends on her way to Israel, perhaps looking for a sign that we could still be together. But her Jewish faith was waxing and mine was waning. I hugged her goodbye and wished her well.

Then, on a beautiful spring day in 1977, hours before my graduation ceremony, things turned romantic with a friend I'd known since freshman year. Aviva was the perfect partner to help me cross back to the realm of the secular. The daughter of Holocaust survivors, she'd grown up in an Orthodox household but had thrown over most of its strictures. She read Hebrew and spoke Yiddish but also did yoga and danced to rock 'n' roll. She was heading to New

York to work at a publishing house, and we moved in together, along with another couple, on the Upper West Side.

THE VETERANS ADMINISTRATION would pay most of my tuition at Columbia, but I was down to my last few dollars for living expenses when I walked into the university's employment office that summer and studied the white strips of paper thumbtacked to the bulletin board. One caught my eye: part-time administrative assistant needed, Institute for Intercultural Studies.

I'd read enough anthropology to know the institute was Margaret Mead's office inside the American Museum of Natural History. I jumped on the C train, raced down to the museum, climbed several flights in one of the turrets, and found myself facing Joan Gordan, a German Jewish refugee with short gray hair and librarian glasses around her neck.

"You will find this work very boring, but I want perfection, yes?" she said in a heavy German accent. I swore there was nothing I loved more than mathematical precision and well-organized lists. She hired me on the spot, but I sensed reluctance. I understood better the next day when I met the rest of the staff: the Institute for Intercultural Studies was a women-only brain trust.

Mead was the matriarch of this tribe. Rhoda Métraux, an esteemed anthropologist, was Mead's right hand and life partner. Then there was Marie Eichelberger, in her early eighties, who was the executive director as well as Mead's close friend and gatekeeper for fifty years. Joan Gordan, my boss, was the archivist and bibliographer. Three younger women, dynamos all, rounded out the staff and made the institute run. I felt like a bit of a mascot.

The archival work, tracking Mead's publications and citations, was rote and dull, as Gordan had promised. But on those mornings when Mead appeared in the office, things got more interesting. She was in her midseventies, an elfin woman in a cape clasped at the neck, leaning on a wooden walking stick. Her face was quite square, set off by clear-framed glasses and silvery gray hair cut in a short bob. She reminded me of a character out of *Ivanhoe*, so it seemed fitting that she presided over anthropology from a castle turret. I was too much in awe of her to introduce myself, but she sought me out and made me feel like part of the family.

Gordan told me our job was to help Mead finish cataloging her collection. I thought she might be kidding, since Mead had already had a half century to do that. She had joined the museum in 1926, the year she returned from her first trip to Samoa, unpacked her steamer trunks, wrote *Coming of Age in Samoa*, and changed anthropology forever.

In the decades after, her floor's enormous storeroom had become one of the world's most renowned attics. It housed a treasure trove of artifacts from her expeditions to Samoa, Papua New Guinea, Manus, and other South Seas realms. Hundreds of the artifacts were already on display in the museum's Peoples of the Pacific Hall, but Gordan told me there were more steamer trunks sitting back there.

The first day I met her, Mead and Rhoda Métraux spent a couple of hours in the storeroom. Then Métraux called in Gordan and me. She pointed to a metal and wood steamer trunk, one of several crowding the center of the large, high-ceilinged room lined with tall metal shelves, and told me to open it. "That should be Samoa," she said, checking her list.

I pulled up hard on the latch and lifted a lid that was a lot heavier than it looked. The three of us peered into it and were transported back to the 1920s. The top layer was packed with neatly arranged books, coconut shells, and masks. Métraux began carefully removing them, one at a time, identifying each item so I could record it on a piece of ledger paper. Gordan watched over my shoulder.

I endeared myself to Joan Gordan, partly because of my fastidious note-taking and partly because I painted her apartment over a weekend. When Marie Eichelberger heard about Joan's apartment makeover, she asked me to paint *her* apartment. Eichelberger was pleased with the result, and when she was happy, Mead was happy.

Mead invited me to a dinner party at her apartment in the Dakota, attended by the head of the museum and luminaries of anthropology. I said barely a word. I was too busy studying her, the way she controlled a room, even when she wasn't speaking. After any topic was discussed, the half dozen men arrayed around the table fell silent and awaited her verdict. She was merciless in cutting down specious ideas, and I almost felt sorry for those on the receiving end. This was a different Mead than the one I'd grown to know in the office: the mother hen, fretting over the well-being of her team.

In May 1978, when I told her I'd be leaving to study at the University of Wisconsin, she pulled me into her office and asked if I had the tuition covered. I said no.

"How much are you short?" she asked.

"A thousand."

"Joan will write you a check."

I was astonished. I'd never experienced such generosity and thanked her profusely. She waved me off, saying she had confidence in me. Her words were strong medicine. Ever since returning from yeshiva, I'd struggled to find my way. At Columbia I'd become painfully aware I'd be competing with econ and math nerds who were better prepared. If Margaret Mead thought I was a horse worth betting on, who was I to disagree?

The job with Mead had been part-time. I needed to find something else that summer to save up money, and I had an idea about who might provide it.

Dan Farinella had been offering me jobs at Camp Henry Horner ever since he moved to Illinois six years earlier. I'd turned him down each time. After the summer of the car crash, I never wanted to work in a camp again. Sometimes, when I was walking down the

street, I'd see a blue Pontiac Firebird like Matt's and my mind was
yanked backward with a sickening rush: I was getting a blow job
in Dan's secret room or gazing at the ghostly portrait of Ella Fohs.
Then the memory was gone and I was left numb.

In my senior year of high school, I had asked Dan to write a
college recommendation for me. He replied immediately, saying his
secretary was typing it up and would mail me a copy. Then he wrote:

> When I read it over I felt sad because you are no longer the young-
> ster that I enjoyed knowing at camp and seeing around for those
> few years. You are a young man now on your way and I suppose I
> feel like the father seeing the son go off. It is kind of sad but what
> has to be will be.

A few days later, his recommendation arrived. It began, "This
young man is one of the finest persons I have ever met," and it
made me uneasy. We both knew I had never been just a camper and
employee.

During my sophomore year of college, Claire and I were going
to spend winter break with her family in the Midwest. I decided we
should visit Dan at Camp Henry Horner, which was on the way. I
wanted Dan to meet Claire. I was sure he'd be impressed, and I told
her that he had been an important person in my life.

When we arrived at camp Dan greeted us with a gruff hello, then
ignored Claire completely. He talked to me for a couple of minutes
as if we'd never met before, and showed us to a cabin. I thought I
must have done or said something to offend him, but I didn't want
to ask and make a scene. If his surliness bothered Claire, she didn't
show it.

The next morning, while she tested a bread recipe in the camp's
kitchen, Dan gave me a tour of the grounds in the bitter cold. After
twenty minutes, we needed to warm up and he showed me to a
small cabin near the center of camp. "This is my place," he said.
It was sparsely furnished: bed, desk, chest of drawers. There was a

small coffee table at the foot of the bed with a movie projector on it and, opposite that, one of those portable, pull-down screens I'd last seen at Camp Ella Fohs.

Dan walked over to the projector. "I've got some porn here," he said. "You want to watch something?"

My legs went shaky and my hands clenched the pockets of my down jacket. He was looking right at me, his face impassive and blank. It was the same dead expression he'd had that first night in the infirmary when I was thirteen.

"No, that's okay," I said, forcing a smile.

"What do you want to do?" he asked.

"Let's go finish the tour," I replied, edging toward the door.

Outside, I came to when the frigid air hit my lungs. *That didn't happen*, I thought. Claire was fifty yards away in the kitchen. What had I been thinking to bring her here?

Dan and I walked down to the lake, not saying a word. We stood on the dock, hands in our pockets, the wind whipping off the water and stinging our faces. Canadian geese gathered on the opposite shore.

"It's freezing here," I said, just to break the silence.

"Yeah, welcome to the Midwest. It's a long damn winter in the cornfields."

"What do you do all winter?" I asked.

"I stay busy. If I don't, it gets lonely and depressing. I've got groups here almost every weekend. Board meetings, committees, group therapy sessions. You name it. I go down to Highland Park and do social work there."

"Like what?"

"Oh, they called me in because the Italian gangs are beating up the nice Jewish boys. I've been running sensitivity sessions for them. I get the two groups in the same room. It's fun. The Italian kids remind me of myself at that age. They could do anything but they're trapped by how they think they're supposed to be. They pick up all their values on the street. What a waste."

"How's your health?"

"Not too bad. High cholesterol. I split logs for firewood. That's how I stay in shape. I never seem to lose any weight. It's just packed tighter." He grabbed his midsection to demonstrate.

"And camp?"

"The first year was rough. I had to rebuild. I couldn't get any outside support to do what I wanted."

"Which was what?"

"To get white kids and Black kids in the same bunk and measure how it changes their lives. No one was doing that. I would go to these conferences on intergroup camping and ethnicity. They weren't talking about the melting pot anymore. That's out. They're all saying ethnicity comes first. It's all bullshit. I keep telling them every kid is a person first. They've all got the same basic needs. After that, maybe they're ethnic. Anyway, that first year, I went to the big conference at Grossinger's and the Jewish Welfare Board ignored me. But I met a smart lady at the American Jewish Committee. She put up some money to fund a pilot project. It's going great. I'm getting old and tired, Steve, but I'm not giving up yet."

"I'm not surprised."

We fell silent again. He said he had to go into town, so I went looking for Claire. I found her in the camp kitchen, taking two steaming loaves of oatmeal bread out of the oven. They smelled amazing.

"I love this oven," she said, beaming at her handiwork.

"I love *you*," I said, pulling her to me. "I think we should get out of here and head to your parents'."

"Are you sure? I thought we were staying till tomorrow. Is everything okay?"

"Yeah, everything's great. I had a long talk with Dan. I saw the camp in winter. What's left?"

I wrote Dan a two-line note before we drove off. I didn't talk to him or see him for the next three years. We exchanged a few letters, and he reminded me that I had a standing job offer at the camp. I never bothered to turn down his offer. I didn't think he expected a response.

THE IDEA OF working for Dan came to me during my final week in Margaret Mead's office. My friend Josh and I were hanging out in his apartment in the East Village. He was graduating from NYU Film School and, like me, needed work. We were drinking beers and racking our brains for some magical way to make money off photography that summer when I blurted out Dan's name.

"He's the director of a summer camp in Illinois. I worked for him in Connecticut as a teenager. He has this cool program where he brings kids together from every neighborhood in Chicago— white, Black, Latino. They share a bunk and learn how to get along. We could document it with a slide show."

"Video would be better," Josh chimed in. "That way we could interview the kids. We could even shoot video in their neighbor-hoods."

"That's brilliant."

"Tell me about Dan. What's his deal?" Josh asked.

"He's half Italian, half Jewish. Grew up in the Bronx. Kind of a tough guy with a heart of gold. He was a social worker in schools— you know, helping kids with problems—and he ran my camp in the summertime. It was mostly Jewish, but even back then he was talking about interracial camping. He was a rebel."

It was no accident I hatched this idea while working for Marga-ret Mead. It would be like an anthropological field study of Camp Henry Horner. Josh didn't need convincing. The prospect of get-ting paid to spend the summer working together was too good to pass up.

I felt a twinge of uneasiness about our plan, the same way I'd felt when reading Dan's college recommendation. I was somehow caught in a lie, but giving Josh the full story was unthinkable. I wouldn't even know what to say. It was better to pretend those things had never happened and just move on. I was an adult now, and I was fine.

Dan loved our documentary idea. The timing was great, he said. He'd been looking for some way to promote his program, and he'd pay us a good fee. Even better, Josh and I would get to bank our wages since we'd be living at camp and have no expenses. It was the perfect short-term gig.

When Aviva asked me for the backstory on Dan, I told her how he'd been a positive influence in my childhood. *He's a real visionary*, I said.

## 15

CAMP HENRY HORNER WAS FOUNDED by the Jewish Council for Youth Services in the early 1900s with the mission of serving "young, impoverished Jewish boys from the City of Chicago." It was the Illinois version of Ella Fohs.

The camp sat in the northeastern corner of the state, just an hour's drive from Chicago. Most of its prairie flatland had long ago been carved into corn and dairy farms, but by the late 1970s those farms were disappearing under the onslaught of suburban development. Henry Horner was one of the last rustic outposts: 175 acres of woods and grassy fields that ran down to a small sandy beach and a big U-shaped dock on Wooster Lake. There were enough bunks to house some 140 boys and girls. Another 200 day campers piled out of buses each morning from the nearby northern suburbs of Chicago.

In late June 1978, Josh and I arrived at the camp after a fourteen-hour drive from New York in his pale green Pontiac LeMans. We passed under a Camp Henry Horner sign, suspended from a log that hung above the dirt road. Right away I noticed that Dan and Betty had built a large suburban ranch home just inside the entrance. They were now living at camp year-round.

We pulled up to the house and knocked on the door. I heard a dog bark, then Dan appeared, a small mutt beside him.

"Hey, it's my two New York filmmakers," he said. "This is Bagel," he added, pointing to the dog.

Betty appeared, beaming. I hadn't seen her in six years. She seemed older, not the girlish woman I had first met when I was thirteen.

"How are your parents?" she asked me.

"They're good. They send their best."

"I miss them," she said with obvious sincerity. "They're the only ones in New York we stay in touch with."

I scanned the spacious living room. "Nice house," I said to her.

"If I was going to live in the middle of nowhere, Steve, I had to design the house I wanted."

"And she did," Dan said, shaking his head as if it was all beyond him.

"How's camp going?" I asked him.

"The usual disasters before opening day, but we've got a good group this year." He paused to size up Josh. "Are you guys going to make us famous?"

"I don't know about that," Josh replied, "but we'll put together a good show."

"That's what I want to hear," Dan said.

I'd been so anxious that Josh and Dan like each other. I could relax now.

We moved into a cabin on the far side of camp that stood in a thick stand of oak trees. It was dilapidated on the outside, but we made the large, wood-paneled room feel like home, or at least like a rustic dorm room. I had packed my stuff for grad school into the trunk of Josh's car. Now we moved it all into the cabin, including my collection of two hundred vinyl LPs and the books on economic history I'd sworn to read over the summer.

That night, we sat on the screened-in porch, Josh smoking Camels, the two of us passing a pint of Jim Beam, and discussed how to go about documenting the camp. We had brought 35-millimeter cameras and a lot of slide film, but we had no video equipment—it was too expensive. Getting our hands on some would be the first order of business.

We attended Dan's counselor orientation the next morning. It was an eclectic group of white and Black college-age kids, mostly from Chicago but some from as far afield as Europe. Many had gone to Henry Horner as campers and were fervent about Dan's mission.

He stood at the front of the circle, arms folded, wearing his trademark khaki shorts and a tight blue T-shirt that showcased his belly and biceps. "Every kid in your bunk will be carrying around stereotypes about the other kids," he opened. "On day one, they'll be thinking, 'Mexicans are lazy. Blacks are criminals. Jews love money.' Stereotypes happen when you live behind walls and walls lead to ignorance. Your job is breaking down walls and building bridges."

To accomplish that, he suggested they hang back and do nothing. "When you put nine kids together in a bunk, the stereotypes will disappear faster than you can talk. They'll figure out for themselves that the other kid is a person just like them."

Dan briefed the counselors on our documentary project. When the session was over, I broke the news to him that we needed video equipment. He grimaced, then asked us to write up a short proposal. He had a donor in mind. Three days later, an officer at Continental Bank in Chicago cut us a check for two thousand dollars. Ecstatic, Josh and I went right out and bought ourselves a broadcast-quality video rig.

In short order we found four kids—a Black boy, a Mexican American girl, a Jewish boy, and a white girl—who were eager to talk about their camp experience. We visited their homes in Chicago, met their families, toured their neighborhoods, and heard their life stories. We trailed them at camp, shooting photos and video of their activities. Within a month, we had assembled hundreds of images and dozens of hours of videotape. We would spend the next few weeks assembling it into a slide and video presentation to screen at the end of the summer.

In early August, the *Chicago Tribune* ran a story about Camp Henry Horner. The headline could have been the title of our project: "Multi-racial Summer Camp [Makes] World of Difference to Kids." The article featured two boys from opposite sides of the city, who had little experience with people of other races until coming to Henry Horner. It quoted Dan on combating racial stereotypes.

After a decade of fighting naysayers in the Jewish camping world, Dan's moment had finally arrived. Intergroup camping was now hot, or at least grabbing the attention of one of the nation's leading newspapers. In the dining hall, a hundred boys and girls crowded around copies of the article. Their camp was suddenly famous and they were giddy.

After lunch, I thought I'd take out a canoe and enjoy some solitude. I headed toward the waterfront, planning to walk through the woods. But when I reached the trees, something caught my attention.

Thirty yards to my left, Dan was at the back door of his cabin, the one he'd taken me to four years earlier, the one where he kept his porn and projector. I'd been avoiding this cabin all summer. Now, he was working a key in the lock, a boy of thirteen standing behind him. I recognized the boy: Jake, a sweet, dark-haired kid I'd spoken to many times. His eyes were cast down at the ground.

I watched Jake follow Dan into the cabin and the door close behind them. My brain flashed back a decade, and I was walking through the door of Dan's hideout in the mansion at Camp Ella Fohs. With a sharp intake of breath, I doubled over, like I'd been punched in the gut. Horrified by the sight of that large man with the small boy, I was flooded with revulsion and hatred. My mind tried to push the scene away, to make it not be happening. But I knew Jake was trapped. He couldn't escape, not till Dan was done with him.

I raced toward our cabin with my head pounding and my eyes fixed on the path. I had to start packing and get out. At the cabin, I found Josh sitting on the porch, writing a letter. I stopped, my brain caught in a spin cycle of memories from Ella Fohs. I thought I might be going crazy.

"We need to talk," I said.

"Okay, let's talk." He put down his pen.

"Not here. Let's go to town."

At a coffee shop in Round Lake I chose the farthest booth in the back corner. There was no one else in the place. We ordered coffee. Josh sat patiently, quietly, which was unlike him.

What the hell could I say? Where would I even start? It felt as if I'd been dreaming this other shameful, hideous life with Dan but now I'd discovered it had actually happened. What if Josh didn't believe me? What if he believed me but thought it was my fault?

The waitress set down our cups of coffee. I inched closer to the edge of a mental cliff and peered down into the void below.

"There's something I didn't tell you about Dan," I began.

"All right. Tell me now."

My fingernails dug into my thighs beneath the table.

"When I was a kid, he did things to me. Sexual things."

Josh's eyes narrowed.

"He molested you?"

"I guess. I never knew what it was."

"How old were you?"

"Thirteen. He took me to camp in the off-season. That's when it started. It went on till I was fifteen."

"What did he do to you?"

"Hand jobs, blow jobs. I didn't understand what was going on. I've never told anyone."

"Well, now you have."

My body began unwinding, like I'd been tightened to the point of snapping.

"You don't seem shocked," I said. "I didn't know what you'd think, but I was sure you'd be shocked."

"I went to an all-boys prep school till sixth grade," Josh said. "This shit happened—not to me, but it happened, believe me."

I felt a little better. I wasn't the only one. I wasn't a complete freak.

"So why'd you decide to tell me now?" he asked.

"Because a half hour ago I saw Dan go into a cabin with Jake. He looked like me when I was thirteen. I'm sure Dan is molesting him."

"Oh, shit."

"There are probably others," I said. "I mean, how could there not be, right?"

I thought about this, recalling the other boys in Jake's bunk.

"Oh, my God!" I blurted out.

"What?"

"I am such an idiot."

"*What?*"

"There must have been others at Ella Fohs. All those years. There had to be other boys. It never occurred to me. Never. I was sure I was the only one. I was Dan's special friend."

"Yeah. I'm sure they were all special," Josh said with disgust.

"I can't believe any of this, man. I'm in shock."

"You know, I got to say, it was weird the way you built up Dan to me before the summer. You made him out to be this giant among men, saving kids and all that."

"I know. I thought he was God's gift. Like what he did to me never happened. But it did happen—and it's happening now."

"What do you want to do?" Josh asked.

"I can't stay here. It's like I'm in a nightmare and I can't wake up. I mean, it was bad before, but I didn't know the truth. Now I know, and it's happening right in front of me. He's evil."

I couldn't sleep that night. I lay on my back, eyes glued to the ceiling, my hands cradling a skinny white cat on my chest that had adopted us the week before. I was thinking about Jake, how small he looked next to Dan. I had been that small, that helpless.

I'd never grasped it until I saw Jake playing my part. I remembered the first weekend Dan took me to camp—the way he handed my mother the box of cannoli, then trapped me in the infirmary, then let me eat all the sugar cereal I wanted, then grabbed my dick, then took me to the nice Italian restaurant. He went from friendly to menacing and back again. I was always on guard, always terrified.

The moment I saw Jake's body engulfed by Dan's, I understood what I couldn't fathom as a child: good Dan and bad Dan worked together. Good Dan had known what I needed—attention, friendship, protection—and he provided that to get what bad Dan wanted: control of my body. They shared the same plan.

I sat up in bed, still holding the cat. For the first time, I saw how the thing actually worked. Dan had taken me on those walks in the woods and made me feel special. He'd visited our house and earned my mother's trust with happy talk. It was all a con. If he picked the right kid, a needy one like me, success was practically guaranteed. It was diabolical. He probably peeled off the weak, the fatherless, the "scared rabbits," as he had labeled me at thirteen. Jake was just one more. There had to be others.

Before falling asleep I made a decision: I wasn't leaving camp. I was going to stay and find out what Dan was doing and to whom.


I TRIED TO think like a detective. If Dan had been spending time with certain boys, then someone at camp would have noticed, the same way the kitchen crew at Ella Fohs had registered how much time he spent with me. I could start with the kitchen boys at Henry Horner, but I didn't know them very well. The counselors might be helpful, but most of them seemed to worship Dan. If I approached them, they might tip him off.

What I needed were longtime staff who were independent

thinkers, not lackeys. I could only think of two: Ray and Vinny. Ray ran the waterfront. Vinny was the maintenance man. Talking to them would be risky. What if they went right to Dan and told him I was asking questions? I'd have to take that chance.

After lunch I went down to the boathouse. Ray and Vinny were sitting outside on the ramp. Ray sported a Mohawk haircut, a Fu Manchu mustache, and his usual blue Speedos. Vinny was bearlike, with tightly curled hair, a fat mustache, and a flavor-saver beard. They were the Cheech and Chong of Henry Horner, good at their jobs but just as good at chilling.

I joined them on the ramp. My throat felt tight, my hands clammy. I considered aborting the mission.

"Hey, Steve, what's up?" Vinny asked.

"I want to talk to you guys about something. I'm not sure how to ask this . . ."

"That's cool," Ray said. "Just ask."

"Right. Have you ever suspected that Dan is molesting boys in camp?"

The second the words left my lips, I wanted to take them back. They sounded bat-shit crazy.

Ray and Vinny exchanged a look, then both nodded, yes.

"Why, did you see something?" Ray asked.

"Yeah, I saw Dan go into a cabin with Jake yesterday after lunch."

"His hideout?" Vinny asked.

"Is that what you guys call it?"

"Yeah. That's where he takes them," Vinny said.

I could barely believe what I was hearing.

"Jake is definitely one of Danny's boys," Ray added.

*Danny's boys.*

"How long have you known about this?" I heard myself ask.

"Two years." Vinny said. "There was a different guy doing maintenance that summer. He thought it was strange how the kitchen boys were with Danny all the time, especially the ones with family problems. Kids started saying stuff to him. They told him that Danny was showing them dirty movies. He talked to me at the end of that summer."

"I wasn't there that year," Ray interjected. "Vinny filled me in when I came back. Two female counselors suspected, too. Oh, we were all onto him."

"Jesus. Did you say anything?" I asked.

"No," Ray answered. "We didn't have to. He knew we knew. We called it the 'summer of the sunglasses.' He wore these big shades all the time. He would hang out in the animal pen with the shades on, just staring at the animals. It was weird, man. He avoided us all summer. I was so upset about the whole thing, I left camp for two days."

I was trying to wrap my head around this, all the people who knew and how routine it was.

"Did you ever talk about doing anything? You know, to stop him?"

"Yeah, we did," Vinny answered. "We thought about going to the cops or the Jewish Council. But they'd just say we were a bunch of dope-smoking crazies."

"No doubt," Ray chimed in. "No one's going to believe us over Danny."

I wanted to tell them about my own abuse. I hadn't planned on it, but we were in this together now, coconspirators.

"He did it to me," I said. "At Camp Ella Fohs in Connecticut."

They both gaped at me.

"Whoa," Vinny said.

"Jesus Christ," Ray said.

"I'm willing to talk to anyone if it'll help stop him."

"When was this, Steve?" Ray asked.

"It ended eight years ago. I was fifteen."

"I'm really sorry, man," Ray said, "but that's ancient history. I don't think that'll help here."

"How can you stand it?" I asked. "Just being around him, knowing what he's doing."

"It's fucked up, but this is his camp," Vinny said. "We just work here."

# 16

I THOUGHT ABOUT GOING TO the police. But what would I tell them? That Dan had molested me years earlier in a different state? Why would they believe me? He was a local hero and I was a nobody. In the process, the whole world would find out I'd been sexually molested, or claimed to be, and I'd be left to face the public shaming.

Besides, I was sure it had been my fault, at least in part. I'd never fought back or said stop. Even more damning: I had felt pleasure, gotten a hard-on, had an orgasm. I was guilty as hell and hated myself for it. Why had I worked for him as a teenager at Ella Fohs? Why in God's name was I working for him now? How bad could the abuse have been?

As for Jake, all I could tell the police was that I'd seen him go into a cabin with Dan. So what? I wasn't even sure I wanted to expose Jake by reporting my suspicions. I couldn't know how that would end for him. One thing was for sure: if anyone had done that when I was thirteen, I would have denied everything because Dan had godlike power over me.

As I agonized over this, the local newspaper ran a story about a school teacher convicted for molesting a girl in his class. I had never read a story like it. Suddenly what I'd been contemplating was real: a child molester going to prison.

I couldn't see putting Dan behind bars. The teacher was a pedophile, a criminal who preyed on children. The newspaper said so. Dan Farinella wasn't that. He had bettered the lives of thousands of kids. Sure, he'd hurt a bunch of others, including me. He was a good person with a bad problem.

I felt like I was holding a stick of dynamite. If I lit the fuse there was no telling who or what would get blown up. Odds were, Camp Henry Horner would be finished, whether or not Dan was convicted. The story would run on the front page of the *Chicago Tribune*. Hundreds of campers, counselors, and parents would be lined up pointing a finger at me for destroying their beloved camp. I couldn't handle that.

But I couldn't stay quiet, either. So I came up with a new idea: confront Dan directly. I'd tell him I was onto him, let him know he was cornered. No one else had to be involved.

Dan was as restless as ever but he'd slowed down a bit since Ella Fohs. Instead of patrolling camp on foot, he'd cruise around on an all-terrain vehicle, a red three-wheeler with balloon tires. I knew his routine. In midafternoon, he'd roar up to the waterfront and dismount in his plaid bathing suit, carrying a towel. Watching him play-fight with the boys in the lake, I had a knot in my stomach—disgust and helplessness—as I imagined what his hands were doing beneath the water line. In the mess hall, I kept an eye on his interactions with the kitchen crew. I monitored his hideout, noting which boys came and went.

When Dan and I crossed paths, I tried to act normal, but I had a hard time remembering what that was. How had I pretended all these years that what he'd done to me had never happened? That kind of acting was no longer possible. I was jittery and trying too hard. He was scowling more than usual, or was I just imagining it? Did he know that I knew, the way he had with Ray and Vinny?

Dan was getting in my head, and I began looking for him

everywhere: behind trees, inside doorways, outside my cabin. I kept putting off the confrontation.

JOSH HAD BEEN enamored of a counselor from Bavaria since the first day of camp. With her corn silk hair, blue eyes, and freckled round face, she could have passed as a local farmer's daughter. We called her Miss Peanuts Butter because that's how she referred to her favorite American food. Josh had been turning the charm on her full blast and making some headway.

But in early August, his younger brother, Tony, appeared at camp on the first leg of a summer road trip. Miss Peanuts Butter took an instant liking to Tony and the next morning announced she'd join him hitchhiking. Josh was not pleased, but he swallowed his pride and ferried the two of them to Interstate 94.

When he returned to the cabin he began pacing furiously. I knew a brainstorm was imminent.

"We've got to get our hands on some acid," he finally said.

"What the hell are you talking about? Why?"

"Because you've never done it and I need to change my head."

I was scared of LSD. I'd barely even smoked weed. I didn't like anything that made me feel out of control. He called a friend in New York and asked him to find us some acid. The whole thing sounded like a long shot. In the meantime, Josh was busy giving me a hard time about my "just-dropped-out-of-yeshiva" look.

"All you're missing is the yarmulke," he said, grimacing. "You can't go to Madison looking like that. Trust me, you just can't."

I shaved off my beard, but he was undeterred. "We've got to do something about those glasses. They make you look uptight. And stop plastering down your hair," he carped. "You need to get back to your Israel-summer-of-'71-look: long wavy locks."

An hour later we were scanning the shelves of an eyewear store in Round Lake. Josh picked out three frames and laid them on the counter. I chose a sleek, gold-rimmed pair and put them on.

"Wow, you've got a face!" he cried in mock amazement.

I tilted the mirror on the counter and squinted. Someone much cooler than me was squinting back.

JUST BEFORE CAMP ended, Josh and I presented our eagerly awaited slide and video show in the dining hall. It was a huge hit. As the images of the kids flashed across the screen, Dan was hooting and applauding along with everyone else. I felt no pleasure at all, knowing what I had to do the next day.

It was raining heavily the following morning. By midafternoon, camp was a sodden mess and everyone was in their bunks. I knew I'd find Dan at his house or in his hideout. I told Josh where I was going, just in case, and headed toward the clearing in the center of camp.

I spotted Dan standing alone in front of the administration building, with Bagel sitting next to him. He wasn't wearing a raincoat and he was soaked. I was used to seeing him in motion but he was stock-still, almost as if he were waiting for me.

*Do it*, I said to myself. When I reached him, he eyed me warily and swiped the water off his face with the palm of his hand.

"I need to talk to you," I said.

His face tightened. *He knows*, I thought.

"Let's get in my car," he replied.

I had prepared myself for possible responses, but that wasn't one of them. He turned and began walking toward his blue wagon, followed by the dog.

A voice in my head was saying, *Do not get in the fucking car!* I'd seen *The Godfather*, Dan's favorite movie, enough times to know what happens on sudden car trips. I didn't want to end up like Pauli or Carlo, with a bullet in the brain or strangled to death. Dan was capable of anything now that he knew it was over. Otherwise we'd be going to his office or cabin. This was a setup. *Do not get in the fucking car!*

When we reached his wagon it was raining even harder. Dan opened the driver-side back door for Bagel. Then he opened the front door and got in. I peered through the rear window, checking to see if anyone was back there. Only the dog. I stood with my hand on the front door handle, rain pelting my face.

*Don't run now. It's okay if he kills you. It's okay to die doing this.*

I got in but didn't put on my seat belt, not wanting to be restrained. There was a clap of thunder, followed by an intense downpour, the rain hammering on the hood and roof. Dan started the engine, backed up the car, and followed the dirt road toward the camp entrance. I was gaming out scenarios, thinking where he might take us. Just then, the car veered off the road to the right and began careening across the grass and mud of the ball field. Sheets of rain swamped the windshield wipers, which couldn't keep up. The waterfall on the roof was deafening. My feet were jammed against the floorboard.

We were headed for the woods, and he seemed to be picking up speed. *Is he going to kill both of us?* I got ready to jump but a few yards shy of the tree line the car slowed. He steered into the woods, stopped abruptly, and cut the engine. The rain was billowing down every window, encasing us in a noisy bubble.

"So?" he asked, staring straight ahead.

"I know what you're doing," I said. My body was shaking from the adrenaline and fear.

"Yeah?"

"You've got to stop."

No response.

"You're hurting kids. You need to stop."

Still nothing.

Then he said, "I know."

His face was drained, defeated.

"I'm going to get out of camping," he said softly.

"And do what?"

"I'll get a desk job. Look, I'm fifty. My heart's not good. I'm too old for this shit. It's time."

I hadn't been expecting total surrender. I wanted so badly to believe him.

"I'm going to be watching, Dan. I want you out of camping." My words came from some deep place, and the bravado surprised me.

"I'm out," he said. "I'm out."

I wanted to tell him what he had done to me, but I couldn't put the words together. Besides, he had just owned up to all of it.

We stayed there in silence for a minute, inside the bubble, with the rain pelting down.

"Okay," he said. Then he started the car and put it in reverse.

I felt like I'd jumped from a plane and survived.


ON THE LAST day of camp an envelope arrived from New York with a small white capsule.

"What kind of acid is this?" Josh asked, perturbed. Then he turned to me: "Whatever it is, this is one hit. You're up, my friend. You are this cabin's top priority."

I eyed the capsule skeptically.

"I won't let you out of my sight," he said. "I promise."

I had survived the confrontation with Dan. Was I scared of a little white pill? Well, yeah. But I saw poetic justice in taking acid for the first time right under the nose of the lying, child-abusing, antidrug crusader.

"When?" I asked.

"Tomorrow. We'll need to get out of here. The vibes are too heavy. We'll go to the nature preserve."

"Okay," I said, "but remember, Aviva gets in at eight tomorrow night." I had to pick her up at O'Hare, then bring her back to camp. The following day, she and I would be driving to Madison, where she'd help me find a place to live.

"No problem, Captain," Josh said. "Launch time is ten. You'll be down by six."

At the nature preserve we waited a full hour after I swallowed the pill but I felt nothing. Josh said to wait another half hour, so we did. When he stood up to leave I burst out laughing.

"What?" he asked.

"My hands," I said. "They're alive." I was holding my palms a foot away from my face. They were two pulsating topographic maps of the Amazon basin: steep, flesh-toned gorges cut through by raging blue rivers.

"Mission control, we have liftoff," Josh said, now in a cheerier mood.

I wandered into a grove of trees, where I had the creeping sensation my mind was less and less tethered to my body.

"I want to go back to camp," I said.

Those were the last words I'd speak for eight hours.

Henry Horner was empty of campers and staff. As Josh led us down to the lake, my body magically did what had to be done, traversing a field of vibratory chaos. I poured myself onto the wooden dock and Wooster Lake began emanating from my head in a beautiful blue wave before rolling back on itself.

Nonsense words were drifting in, riding that wave: "Two Responses to the Theologico-Politico Dilemma: A Study of Maimonides and Spinoza." I turned to Josh, wondering if he'd heard it, too. He was holding an orange binder and reciting the words, insisting I had written them. "Wow, this is heady stuff, man," he said. "Where are the emotions?"

*Yes, where were they?* I wondered. I dropped the question in the lake and it sank.

Dan appeared on the dock, standing over me. From my vantage point, flat on my back, he looked like a gigantic inflated balloon in the Thanksgiving Day parade. His head and torso were five times too big for his legs.

"Hey, I need to talk to you," he barked.

"Stephen's taken a vow of silence," Josh explained.

"What are you talking about?" Dan asked, irritated.

"He's not speaking today," Josh replied, shrugging. "We're on hold till tomorrow."

Dan frowned. *I'm supposed to fear him*, I thought. *I should feel fear*. But his glowering face, puffed-out chest, and tough-guy talk seemed comical. I grinned at his performance. It was quite good. Dead-on, really. He turned and left.

Hours later, I was lying on my bed in the cabin, communing with the cat. Josh disappeared to the porch and I heard other voices: Tony and Miss Peanuts Butter. But that was impossible.

"The hitchhikers are back," Josh said, now kneeling beside me. "How are you feeling?"

I was trying to remember what hitchhiking was.

"Still mute, huh? Look, I don't want to disturb your blissful state," he said, gesturing to the cat on my chest, "but you're due at O'Hare in two hours. That means you need to need to start initiating touch-down. I recommend a hot shower." My body followed him to the bathroom, where he turned on the water. I stepped in and he was gone. I heard him arguing with his brother over a baseball bet.

I closed my eyes and retreated into the warm, watery realm. After a few moments I sensed a presence and opened my eyes. Miss Peanuts Butter was in the shower with me, naked.

"I'm tired of those two," she whispered.

I pulled her toward me until she was under the waterfall. She had been sent by the universe to guide me back into my body. Miss Peanuts Butter wrapped herself around me, like a warm, pulsating octopus. A pleasurable current passed through her tentacles, and there was a subtle tingling at ten thousand points of contact.

Consciousness, which had been floating unencumbered since morning, began seeping into those vibrating nodes, like a gas condensing to liquid, then filling the cracks and crevices of the organism. The body I had observed all day with curiosity but no sense of ownership was morphing into *my* body. *This is what it's like to live inside skin*, I thought.

I stroked the flanks of the octopus, and it shape-shifted back to blond-haired water nymph. The word *sex* flashed in my brain. But the mechanics of it were hopelessly complicated—impenetrable. Why did sex usually seem so important?

"What is LSD like?" Miss Peanuts Butter asked, her eyes wide. "Tell me."

"We're just pure consciousness," I said. "Nothing else."

She smiled. Then I directed my hand to turn off the water. My hand responded. I was down.

Aviva almost didn't recognize me at the airport. I'd forgotten to warn her that I'd shaved my beard, grown my hair, and gotten new glasses. Once we left camp, on the drive to Madison, she wanted to hear about the summer. Josh and I had done great work, I said, but Dan turned out to be a real asshole. She was taken aback. I didn't say a word about Jake, or Ray and Vinny's bombshell, or my white-knuckled ride in Dan's station wagon. My own childhood abuse never came up.

I'd solved the Dan problem. No one needed to know.

17

Something was wrong.

My econometrics professor was standing at the front of the room, chalk in hand, gesturing at the ribbon of math symbols he'd unfurled on the blackboard. He was speaking fast, about multiple linear regression and unbiased estimators. The guy sitting to my right was scribbling furiously. The girl to my left was writing even faster. My own notebook was blank.

For three weeks I'd listened intently as the professor's voice wafted through my skull like a spring breeze through an open window. At first I figured it was the challenge of new, intimidating material. I'd hang in there and my math brain was sure to kick into gear. By week two, though, there was nothing in gear beyond a grinding cog of anxiety. The equations beckoned to me, just out of reach. Now it was week three, and time to panic.

I'd never had a problem in school. My powers of concentration were extreme. In yeshiva, I often got so immersed in Talmud I'd miss meals. At Columbia, I'd taken four economics and math courses, worked for Margaret Mead, and motored through reams of graduate-level assignments at night. I may have been antisocial and suicidal, but I sure as hell knew how to focus. That was my superpower. Now, when I needed that power most, it was gone.

Desperate, I talked to my adviser, got a study partner, and shut myself away in the stacks of the economics library. It didn't help. By week six, each lecture was an ordeal of confusion, frustration, and shame. I began to think the unthinkable: I might have to drop out. In late October I stopped going to classes. But I didn't have the courage to face my professors or the dean.

Then, one day in November, I picked up the *New York Times* and saw the headline: "Margaret Mead Is Dead of Cancer at 76." It didn't seem possible. She'd appeared fine six months earlier. I stood on the sidewalk reading the obituary. There had been "a yearlong battle with cancer," it said. Now I understood why she had felt such urgency to get her collection in order.

I walked down to Lake Mendota and sat on a rock, buffeted by an icy wind. I shielded my face with both hands to lessen the sting and hide my shame. Mead had believed in me, supported me. She was hardly alone. There were economics professors who'd encouraged me, and my parents, who thought I'd come to my senses by committing to an academic path. But looming largest was my father, who would have wanted his veteran's benefits to underwrite success, not failure.

I met with the dean and told him I was withdrawing. He was sorry to hear it, he said, but made no attempt to dissuade me. I broke the news to my parents on the phone. I could tell they were in shock because they didn't ask what I planned to do next.

FOR MONTHS AFTER leaving grad school I felt I was being stalked. I wasn't sure by whom or what, but my nervous system was crackling, on high alert. I had to keep moving. I wandered the streets alone at night in the dead of Wisconsin winter, consumed with self-loathing. I was cycling through pursuits on a weekly basis:

saxophone, carpentry, photography, welding, mandolin. I worked the four a.m. shift at the bakery in the student union. But I got too agitated to stick with it and had to bolt.

I hitchhiked to the Pacific Northwest in a blizzard, sleeping in barns with cows along the way. I had a two-day affair in Seattle with the girlfriend of a friend from college. When she confessed it to him, I hitchhiked to his house in Michigan and he pummeled me with his fists, which made me feel better for a few hours. I fled to Wyoming, where I hung drywall in an oil boomtown, caught a ride to Montana to see a total solar eclipse, then joined a protest against uranium mining in the Black Hills. Along the way, I carried a paper bag full of psilocybin mushrooms and chewed on the desiccated caps and stems when I craved release from the relentless fear that gripped my body.

So I wasn't surprised when I got busted for shoplifting. A security guard grabbed me as I exited the University Book Store in Madison without paying for the Polaroid camera I'd stuffed in my backpack. I'd been expecting him somehow.

At the time, I was living in a housing cooperative, which was less a house than a way of life—punk rock–driven, LSD-fueled, anarchistic. Most of the thirty residents were kind of, sort of enrolled at the university. But first, they were poets, Maoists, antinuke activists, slam dancers, macrobiotic warriors, feminist strippers, witches, and psychonauts. I'd seen an ad—"Housing co-op with room for rent"—and had shown up at the weekly meeting and persuaded a quorum of residents that I was tolerant of drugs and willing to cook one meal a month for thirty people.

The house itself was gigantic: a four-story Mediterranean Revival with brick walls and a couple dozen rooms. I had only been in the house a few weeks when I fell hard for Melissa, a girl who lived three doors down. She was nineteen, a soft-spoken fine arts student from Kansas with a crooked smile and dark brown eyes. She wore Wrangler jeans and hand-tooled cowboy boots so pointy I couldn't imagine how she got her feet in them.

I would sit on her floor, propped against a Japanese mattress folded up in the corner, and watch, rapt, as she drew in a sketch-book, her pencil conjuring vibrant, abstract landscapes of swirls and spikes and spirals. With her other hand, she smoked Newports. On the cassette deck, Patti Smith wailed, "Outside of society, that's where I want to be."

Petty theft was part of the house's punk ethos. I'd never stolen a thing in my life, but I took to it with alarming speed. I stole bags of groceries, all manner of house supplies, endless rolls of camera film. But mostly I stole acrylic paint. Melissa coveted tubes of the stuff. They were crazy expensive. The first time I set eyes on the University Book Store's towering display rack—row upon row of exotic cobalts and vermilions and magentas—I was spellbound. I lifted a couple dozen tubes right there, hundreds of dollars' worth. I loaded them into my backpack by the fistful, ran to the painting studio, and dumped them on Melissa's workbench with a flourish. She was ecstatic, oohing and aahing over each one like a kid open-ing gifts on Christmas morning. I'd never delivered such happiness. I was hooked.

After my arrest, I signed a Deferred Prosecution Agreement. It promised my record would be wiped clean if I attended First Offenders School, worked at a "lawful occupation," and stayed out of trouble for a year. It also stipulated that I "associate only with law-abiding persons"—an impossibility unless I cut ties to everyone I knew in Madison. I decided to skate by on that one.

My life was increasingly unmoored from my past. I received a wedding invitation from my cousin Dave, who was getting married in New York. It should have been an automatic yes, but I declined, saying I had too much going on to make it. It was hard to imagine anyone who had less going on than me. I knew my absence would hurt him, but what did it matter? Our childhood bond had broken that summer when we were fifteen and had never been repaired. Besides, there was no way I was going to face fifty relatives and try to explain why I'd dropped out of grad school.

Then I got a "fuck you" letter from Aviva, who was furious that I'd never mustered the courage to tell her about Melissa. She'd found out from someone else. An aerogram from Claire arrived soon after. She was living in Jerusalem as an Orthodox Jew, tutoring in a religious girls' school. I had ignored a friendly letter from her the previous fall. Now she took a more confrontational approach: it was inconceivable to her that the power of my religious experience could have dwindled into nothingness. "But what difference do my words make to you," she wrote, "you who are such a contradictory bundle of caring and indifference, of running to and running away, of truth and lies."

I tried to locate the person she was talking to. That would be Shlomo, the one who had prayed to God three times a day and studied Gemara late into the night. Where was he? *Road to Ruin* by the Ramones was blaring outside in the hallway and a fragrant cloud of weed was curling beneath my door. There was no sign of Shlomo anywhere.

I bristled at Claire for saying I'd lost my way spiritually, but her charge of cruel indifference hurt more because I knew it was true.

I set her letter aside. I knew I'd never answer it.

WHEN I CLOCKED in to work at the classy French restaurant where I waited tables, the pots were piling up fast and the chef was cursing. He ordered me to hunt down Tommy, the dishwasher. I found him in the men's changing room, a syringe in his arm.

"Tommy, sorry to interrupt," I said. "The pots?"

"Sure, sure. You want some of this coke?" he asked, withdrawing the needle and waving it in my direction.

"No, thanks," I said. "I've snorted it. That's plenty." There was no way I'd put a needle in my arm. That shit was for junkies.

"This is a whole other thing, man," Tommy said. "Trust me."

Why *not* trust this kid I barely knew? My life was wrecked already.

I rolled up my sleeve, and Tommy cooked some coke in a spoon.

After sucking it into the syringe, he tapped the fat vein in the crook of my right arm and slid the needle in ever so slowly. It was still in there when a tidal wave of euphoria surged through my body, like a head-to-toe orgasm that wouldn't quit. I was melting, my heart opening, all barriers between me and the world dissolving. I felt overcome with gratitude. This washer of pots with whom I'd never exchanged more than three words had morphed into my personal savior, the bringer of good news.

I threw my arms around him.

"I love you, Tommy. This is so beautiful."

"I know, man, I love you, too," he said, hugging me tightly.

I suited up and got to work, floating through ether. I talked to each person I waited on, spontaneously and deeply. Is this what it's like to be happy? I wondered. Do people feel like this *without* intravenous drugs? I didn't need to escape my body. I didn't need to kill it.

Tommy and I went back to his dingy town house apartment at midnight to shoot up again, this time at his kitchen table, which was cluttered with dirty dishes and empty beer cans. The high wasn't as powerful as the first go-round and it wore off faster. Still. I rode my bike home.

At two a.m. I was back at Tommy's. Then I rode home again. At four a.m. I was in his living room, sharing the love and paying dearly in cash. I knew he was jacking up my price to subsidize his habit. I didn't care. I felt squeamish about shooting up and he was like a nurse on call. That had to be worth something. But I was out of money and there would be no six a.m. session. I got back on my bike and pedaled home.

I'D DONE MY best to put Dan Farinella out of my mind. When he did bubble up into consciousness, I pushed him aside: *I dealt with that. Time to move on.*

There came a morning, though, as the warm glow of another

coke high receded and the sunrise intruded, when I had to admit the days were counting down toward summer, the dreaded summer. I wasn't naïve—Dan had to be molesting boys year-round, the way he'd done to me. But he always targeted his new victims in summertime, and camp would be opening in less than two months. If he was still running things, still hurting kids, I'd feel responsible.

*I should call him immediately, go down to Illinois, confront him again.* But why was I the enforcer? No one else at Henry Horner had ever confronted him. Maybe they knew that trying to stop him was futile. Maybe his behavior wasn't as awful as I thought. Maybe they were sane and I was crazy.

What I really wanted, what I craved, was never to see or talk to Dan Farinella again. Just thinking about him made me want to visit my favorite dishwasher.

IN THE EARLY fall, my parents stopped in Madison on their way home from a visit to Chicago. I took them to a local diner and picked at my blueberry pancakes while my mother interrogated me across a red Formica booth.

"Tell me what you're doing here that you couldn't do in New York," she opened.

"I'm living, Mom."

"*Nu?* You can do that in New York. Millions of people do."

She changed the topic, moving from the difficult to the hellish.

"We saw Dan and Betty," she reported. "Dan said it was a terrific year at camp, the best ever." She looked pleased to deliver this news.

I wasn't surprised. I knew Dan had lied to me, but I was too busy imploding to do anything about it. He'd called my bluff and I'd folded. My mother went on about the media show that Josh and I had produced, how Dan was so thrilled and screening it everywhere. She beamed over this signal achievement of her drop-out son.

"I haven't had time to call Dan," I said. "I'm just too busy."

ON A SPARKLING autumn day, I did some LSD with a friend at the house. How he'd wound up there I have no idea. As a college freshman, he'd been the Nordic golden boy—a blond-haired, hard-bodied soccer player from small-town Wisconsin. Within a few months at the housing co-op, he was out of the closet, wearing pink dresses, and gobbling hallucinogens for breakfast. He was an excellent tripping partner, exquisitely sensitive to everything around him, always in the moment, never in a hurry.

We walked a few miles to the university arboretum—a thousand pristine acres of prairie, forest, and wetland. As we wandered through the dense woods, a strong breeze was modulating the vibrant colors of falling leaves. Mother Nature had turned herself inside out and spilled her viscera across the forest floor in a flood of reds, oranges, and golds. We threw ourselves into the river of color and swam in it for hours.

With the sun setting, we left Eden and ran smack into civilization: a hundred-car freight train passing through the Mills Street crossing. We sat in the grass and waited. Over the next couple of minutes I didn't so much see a freight train as witness the entire history of the American railroad: the Native American tribes vanquished by the iron horse, the Chinese laborers who died building it, the Black men chain-ganged by the railroad companies to drive their expansion southward. Car by car I saw the great American enterprise get built atop human blood and misery, thousands of spectral beings in a nightmarish hologram.

My body seemed no more real to me than the ghostly captives in the freight cars. *I belong with them*, I thought. As far back as I could remember, I had a pair of hands at my throat. I was always on the verge of being strangled, never knowing who my executioner was.

*Who was the executioner?* The question had dogged me for years. There was some inexorable force dragging me toward oblivion. I was powerless against my killer, whoever or whatever it was.

Now the answer came to me: I was the executioner. It had always been me, but I wasn't meant to know until this moment and this freight train. I'd been waiting for this train since I realized I was doomed. I'd been staving off the inevitable, and the inevitable was now here.

I began writhing on my belly, like a lizard, toward the tracks. I wasn't scared. My life and death were unspooling before me. I was generating this movie, but there was an element of surprise, the promise of revelation. That's what I was after: I needed to see the end, I needed the suffering to be over. I was only five or six feet from the train. The roar of the freight cars was deafening as I lunged toward the tracks.

A large hand clamped down hard on my arm. My friend crouched over me in his soft pink dress, his baby face and blond hair framed by an expanse of sky. I tried yanking my arm away to escape his grip, but he was too strong. He smiled down at me, like a parent restraining a toddler. Then the train was gone.

# 18

I KNOW THE EXACT MOMENT when I suspected I was a zombie. It was early December 1979, my second winter in Madison.

I needed to steal another Polaroid camera. Not wanting to tempt fate at the University Book Store, I took the bus to JCPenney in a mall on the outskirts of town. I found the camera I wanted, shoved it in my bulky down jacket, and walked out through the heavy glass doors.

I had taken only five or six steps when I heard the alarm blare and saw a security guard give chase. I dropped the camera and headed for the farm behind the mall. I was too fast for the guard, but he called in a dragnet of cops and a police chopper that whirred overhead. I was pinned down for two hours beneath a piece of farm equipment in a sea of corn before the sun finally set, night fell, and I was able to escape for home.

"Stephen, it seems like you *want* to go to jail," a friend said, laughing uneasily, when I told him what had happened. "Are you looking to get punished?"

I must have been in some kind of trance. I didn't want to go to jail, but I seemed to have no control over my criminal behavior. I was like one of those mindless undead creatures in *White Zombie*, a movie I'd just seen, whose robotic actions were directed by an evil master. That night, I dreamed the FBI arrested me for my camera theft. They also dredged Lake Mendota and found a black-handled knife from the restaurant where I worked, tying me to a crime I couldn't recall committing.

When I awoke it took me a couple of seconds to realize I wasn't under arrest at all. I was a free man and made up my mind to stop stealing. Still, the dream unsettled me. I couldn't be sure the police hadn't identified me at the mall the day before. They might be looking for me at that very minute. I'd have to be on guard, take some basic precautions.

Two seconds later came a knock at the front door. My heart leapt to my throat and I froze, petrified. Another knock. I tiptoed into the living room and peered between the curtains. There was a car parked downstairs, maybe an unmarked police car. I threw on some clothes, climbed out the back window, and sprinted down the block to a friend's house—the same friend who'd warned me the day before about going to jail.

"That was me knocking on your door just now," he said. "No one is following you, man, except for me, because you're acting crazy."

I ditched him, walked downtown, and drifted into the University Book Store. I picked up a paperback called *The Kapetanios*, the story of the anti-fascist partisans in the Greek civil war of the 1940s. I was on a reading binge of European revolutionary movements.

I stuffed the book in my jacket and walked through the turnstile, but I didn't make it to the entrance. A security guard was waiting, and the police arrived moments later. I was calm, watching impassively as this dream unfolded. I felt the same as I had crawling on my belly toward the freight train.

I was arraigned, posted bail, and a pretrial hearing was scheduled. The theft had violated my Deferred Prosecution Agreement. I understood that this body—my body—could be going to jail, zombie or not. A lawyer at a legal clinic offered to represent me at pretrial for two hundred fifty dollars. I calculated how much cocaine that would buy and said no. Then the court assigned me a public defender whose fifty-dollar fee sounded better. At the hearing, he engineered a plea deal. I paid a fine, no jail time.

Just like that, I had a criminal record. More tangible than the conviction was the new, more visceral current of fear. I couldn't walk into a store, any store, without getting the jittery sensation that my body would try to steal something. I was always cowering, just waiting for my thieving, zombie hand to make a move.

I decided to leave the country. I was on the run anyway, fleeing from real and spectral authorities almost since the day I'd arrived in Madison. If I stayed put I'd only get busted again. I'd tried going west but it hadn't ended well. Besides, it wasn't far enough. I had to get so far away there would be nothing to remind me of my past: nobody from grad school, no happy reports about Dan Farinella, no brightly lit stores that made me want to steal shit.

I had to believe that with that kind of distance, I'd gain a bird's-eye view on the catastrophe that was my life. I'd see where it all went wrong, find some long-buried clue, and crack the case of my unraveling psyche.

Leaving Melissa would be hard. Our love was the one constant in my frenetic days and nights. She encouraged my escape plan, seeing I needed a do-over, and we promised to reunite somewhere overseas the following spring.

The only question left was: Where would I go?

My MOTHER AND Ken were moving from East Meadow to a rent-stabilized apartment in Manhattan. I flew home to clear out my bedroom in the house where I'd grown up. On opening my closet, there were the two boxes of my father's things on the floor, where I'd left them nine years earlier.

I sat cross-legged on the carpet and opened the box with the two bulky photo albums. Until this moment I'd been more keen to possess these albums than explore them. Now I took one out and ran my hand over its rich brown leather cover.

There was a note on the second page, written in white ink on black mounting paper in gorgeous script:

This book is intended to be a chronological, graphic portrayal of my life overseas. Unfortunately, there are several deficiencies. In the first place, there was a combined lack of camera, film & opportunity. It is not possible, then, to show you all the places we "visited." But, more important, it is beyond the capability of writer or photographer, however expert, to convey the gamut of emotions thru which a G.I. passes, or to reproduce any of the odors with which he comes in contact: from rotting bodies, to Arab hovels, to destroyed Italian cities, Indian streets, Chinese rice paddies in the still of early morning, the disinfectant odor of a hospital.

How can anyone re-create the scream of a wounded man? The swishing noise of big shells? The whine of a bomb? The sigh of comfort when a guy takes off his shoes? No, this attempt is a feeble one, albeit my best.

The page was signed with a flourish in white ink: *Si.* I leafed through page after page of photos—rugged mountain passes, bustling casbahs, crewmates in P-38s—all accompanied by my father's running narrative. His squadron were "military migrants" who moved like nomads across the African desert. His friends were "unkempt, unshaven, befouled and dirty." Former friends, he wrote, had been stripped of their dog tags before being dumped in a common grave, killed by gunshot, land mine, shell, or drowning.

His journey progressed across North Africa: Morocco, Algeria, Tunisia. His squadron provided air cover for the invasion of Sicily, then pushed north to Naples. After that, they were deployed to an air base in India, then China, where they joined forces with the Nationalist Chinese against the Japanese occupiers.

On July 8, 1944, he wrote: "Heading back to India, medically." There were a few snapshots of his fellow patients at the 263rd General Hospital in Calcutta, but no explanation of why he was there. Two months later, he was transferred to the Army Air Forces Convalescent Hospital in Pawling, New York. It was all very mysterious.

My father had been twenty-four when he went ashore in North Africa, the same age as me. He'd been chosen by fate and the US Armed Forces to fight at the front. My life had devolved into drugs, petty crime, and paranoia. Was he just a natural-born leader of men and I just a natural-born fuckup? I decided now that my own travels would begin in North Africa, where he had set out on his.

There was one more thing to do before leaving my childhood home for the last time. I crawled underneath my desk to see, on the pegboard behind it, the name, Stephen Mills, that I'd scrawled there in second grade. My father had never come back, and here I was, twenty years later, still adrift.

IN THEIR NEW apartment, with my parents in their reading chairs, I decided to break the news of my travel plans. I figured that telling them would force my hand. There could be no turning back.

"I'm stunned," Ken said.

"I'm not," my mother chimed in. "Nothing you do would surprise me anymore."

This announcement was just one more indulgence in a string of them, she complained. She recited the girlfriends who had come and gone, the foray into yeshiva, the dive into and out of grad school. It all happened without warning and then vanished without explanation. They could only imagine what was going through my astoundingly selfish head at any given time.

The real problem, she said, working up a good head of steam, was that I was a dilettante—shallow, self-centered, and immature—who looked down on a simple life of work, love, and commitment.

How was I going to pay for this lark? my mother asked. I would use my father's VA benefits, I told her, the thousands she had banked for me after he died. That did it. I had kicked them in the head, dishonored the family.

Then Ken piled on. In my vapid search for self, I had walked all over many good people, he said. But the proof of my selfishness was the way I'd treated Dan Farinella. They'd heard that I wasn't in touch with him anymore.

"How could you be so insensitive after all that Dan has done for you and for our family?" he asked angrily. "How could you treat such a good man so shabbily?"

*If you only knew who Dan was*, I thought. *If you only knew what he did to me, what he's still doing to other boys.* But I said nothing.

My head was throbbing, my body braced with the same dread I'd felt at age thirteen when Dan dropped me at home after molesting me for the first time. They must never find out what I'd done with him, I'd sworn, or my life would be over.

Twelve years later, I still hated myself for it. But I hated them even more.

BACK IN MADISON, I bought a set of vinyl records called *You Can Learn Arabic* and listened to a lesson each morning. I told my friends I'd be leaving for North Africa soon. Weeks passed, and Melissa worried I'd never leave, that I'd just keep talking about it.

Then one night, Tommy wasn't at his dishwashing station or in the changing room. The chef said he had overdosed but was alive, in St. Mary's Hospital. His family would be sending him to rehab. This was a giant, flashing exit sign if I ever saw one. But I still didn't book a flight.

Months before, Josh and I had talked about traveling together, but I figured it was a fantasy since he was ensconced with his girlfriend. Now he called from New York. "I'm ready," he said. "Let's go to Southeast Asia."

"I'm ready, too," I answered, "but I'm going to North Africa, where my father was during the war."

"I get the father thing. But North Africa? The women wear veils and the drugs are illegal. You're the only person I know who would find that appealing."

"Look, I'm studying Arabic. I've got all the records."

"You bought records? Jesus. Listen to me. Asia's the place. Bali, Bangkok, Kathmandu. Besides, didn't you tell me your father wound up in China and India?"

"Yeah, but—"

"We'll do his odyssey in reverse and start in Asia. After we finish, you can go on to North Africa."

As soon as Josh called I realized why I hadn't left yet: I was scared, not of intestinal parasites or armed bandits or any of the other hazards I'd read about in third-world travel guides. No, I was afraid, petrified, really, of myself. I was scared of my lunge toward the train, of the tracks in the crook of my arm, of my panic around security guards. I was horrified by my dreams, which were increasingly blood-drenched. I may have been a mindless zombie, but I knew I needed someone to watch my back.

A month later, at a bar in New York, Josh and I drank shots of bourbon as we mapped out a route through Southeast Asia.

"I've got to figure out my life," I said. "This is my chance to purge the past, all the psychic pain. I don't know where that shit came from but I've got to purge it this year. If I don't, I can't face coming back. I just can't."

Josh took a slug of bourbon and eyed me with disbelief.

"Are you planning to have any fun on this trip?" he asked.

"No," I answered.

# 19

By the time we got to Nepal, I was ready to give up on my psychic purge. For six months, Josh and I had followed a well-worn trail, beginning in Bali, that catered to hippie tastes in cut-rate hostels, banana pancakes, cotton genie pants, and ganja. This low-rent nomadic life seemed tailor-made for an internal reckoning.

I did ample magic mushrooms on empty, moonlit beaches in Bali, the better to ponder my personal history. In northern Sumatra, we stayed for a week in a traditional Batak house jutting out over Lake Toba, atop a submerged supervolcano. I took a psychological deep dive, filling a notebook with words, arrows, and drawings that traced the people and events of my life going back to my father. The takeaway wasn't news: I'd been in a downward spiral for a long time.

I began questioning whether it made sense to excavate my life. Maybe if I just lived in the present and kept moving, all the old pain would burn up of its own accord. There were more than enough volcanoes to climb, trance dances to see, nasi goreng to eat. When memory intruded, it was time to catch another train. I thought hedonism might help. During monsoon season in the northern Thai jungle, I tried opiated sex with a henna-haired German. She cut me loose after a week, saying I was too serious and didn't understand pleasure for pleasure's sake.

In Nepal, I reverted to near-constant anxiety: time was running out to solve the mystery of my drive to self-destruct. We trekked around the Annapurna massif, crossing the Thorong La pass at nearly 18,000 feet during the first snowfall of the season. When we descended, there was a letter waiting from Melissa. She'd fallen in love with a friend of ours, she wrote.

Her confession followed me like a dark cloud on our next trek through Langtang National Park, near the Tibetan border. On the advice of our guide, I plunged with him into Gosaikunda, a glacial lake ringed by high peaks, one of the divine abodes in Hindu mythology. I hit the freezing azure surface and, for a moment, thought my lungs had collapsed. When I emerged from the icy water I felt weightless, untethered. I realized Melissa had cut my last tie to America. I didn't need to ever go back.

What the hell would I do in Asia, though? Our money, which I kept track of, was almost gone. I broke the news to Josh as we sat across a table in Le Petit Prince Pie Shop on Freak Street in Kathmandu. We had enough cash left to fly to India and spend six weeks before we'd need to part ways. Josh said he'd reunite with his girlfriend in New York and hunt for work.

At this, he reached into the pocket of his yak wool vest, removed a small sphere of bright green hashish the size of a grape, and placed it between us on the rough-hewn tabletop. It had been a gift from Ang, our intrepid guide. Apart from shepherding us for six weeks over high-altitude passes, cooking us pumpkin ten different ways, and leading us in rounds of Tibetan song, Ang was also a connoisseur of charas—hand-pressed sativa resin so pure and transcendent that the god Shiva himself was said to smoke it before meditating.

"If we're flying to India we won't have time to smoke this," Josh said ruefully. "And we can't risk taking it through customs."

We stared at the temple ball of hash, which seemed to stare back at us like a disembodied eyeball.

"We could eat it," Josh mused.

Two pulls on the hash pipe had always gotten me plenty high. God only knew how much mind-scrambling THC was sitting there on the table. But what did I have to lose? Life had me cornered. I couldn't return to my past and I couldn't afford a future. I nodded my assent. Josh cut the marble in half and dissolved it in the two bowls of curry rice soup we'd ordered for lunch. Thirty minutes later, we exited onto Freak Street.

I had achieved perfect forgetfulness about the hash in my stomach when I began laughing at the unlikely carnival surrounding us: street vendors hawking cheap Hindu deities; Europeans clad in orange, green, and red genie garb; Tibetan mothers, papooses slung over their muscular backs, flaunting enormous chunks of turquoise and coral around their necks. And where did all those cows come from?

I leaned on a windowsill as my laughs turned to gasps for air between short exhalations. Jabbing pains in my stomach were radiating up into my chest cavity, compressing my ribs in wave after wave of boat-rocking nausea. I wasn't getting off, I was blasting off, like a rocket.

My feet were wet. A little girl, squatting next to me, was relieving herself. Rivulets of urine ran between the cobblestones and pooled around my flip-flops. She smiled up at me sweetly, and I smiled back. Freak Street collapsed into two dimensions like a balloon stuck by a pin. The entire circus with all its ancient props, rainbow-colored acrobats, and lumbering animals was no more real than a mile of busy wallpaper.

Then my visual field shifted to a more primitive cubism, as if a giant hand had dumped a pile of puzzle pieces and dared me to make sense of them. Soon, there were only colors and faces and emotional energies. I knew this phase well from past bad trips. The drug had hijacked my brain and was piloting the rocket with the giddy delight of an escaped lunatic.

I needed to lie down, I told Josh, and he got us into a taxi. Back at our guesthouse, an English-speaking doctor took my pulse and ordered us to the hospital. Josh dragged him out the front door with us. Once at the hospital, I lay on a gurney as our doctor and their doctor argued in Nepali.

I was trying to locate my body, consciously willing each breath. An ocean of blackness lapped at my visual field, shrinking it, slowly but surely. *Just stay conscious*, I thought. *Just stay conscious.* I struggled to recall a name or a place, anything to orient me and stop the dissolution of my mind. Josh's face floated above me. I recognized him: he and I had come to Asia. I couldn't remember why.

His face dissolved and I was staring down at a boy's naked body, stretched out on the gurney. *That's me.* I had to get into that body, but the more I tried, the farther away it got. I was a cyclone of fear—heart pounding, breath racing—thrashing about for something to cling to. The world was flying apart. A white light flickered at the center of the chaos. If that last bit of light was extinguished, I was done for. It blinked on and off, on and off. I didn't want to die.

Someone forced me to sitting. I was in a dark, dank room with a low ceiling and no windows, just a squalid concrete floor with a drain in the middle. A girl held an orange plastic cup to my mouth and made me drink. I wondered where the liquid was going. In the far corner stood a boy, mop in hand. Josh, kneeling, held my head as the girl refilled the cup from a large bucket, then lifted it to my mouth again.

I heard the first eruption before realizing the source. The expulsion of vomit knocked me forward, convulsing my body. The boy pushed his mop, steering a wide, brown stream toward the drain in the floor. I felt searing pain in my balls, as if they were being jolted by an electrical current. I bore down on Josh's shoulder and doubled over, trying to ride out the shocks.

Tremendous pressure was building in my pelvis, like a column of steam needing to escape. It surged through my midsection and chest, then erupted out of my face in a prolonged waterfall, which pooled on the floor. *There's my life*, I thought. Again the boy attacked the mess with his mop, shunting it toward the black hole.

Then I fell into a coma-like state.

I slept for sixteen hours. My dreams were riotous. I woke up in a room with open windows. A breeze caressed my face and a songbird warbled outside. Loud sounds and bright lights were painful, as if my nervous system had blown out and then been reset for life in the womb.

Josh was standing over me, clearly happy to see me alive.

"I don't get it," I said.

"What?"

"We both ate the same hash. What happened?"

"You needed to purge," he said. "I didn't."

"That was the bottom, man. That was definitely the bottom."

"What was there?" he asked.

"Death. It tore me to shreds. But something in me wanted to live. I definitely wanted to live."

BEFORE WE LEFT for India, I wrote to Uncle Milt, my father's older brother. He had lived with their mother in the Bronx during the war and worked to support her while his two younger brothers were in the service. He and my father had written each other every few days. I asked him why my father had been transferred to the army hospital in Calcutta. Three weeks later, my uncle's reply was waiting for me at a post office in New Delhi:

> Your father came undone in Asia. They diagnosed him as emotionally disturbed and transferred him to the psychoneurotic ward of the Army Air Forces Convalescent Hospital in Pawling. That ward was the garbage can of army medicine. They dumped all the nutjobs and undiagnosed cases there. He was sure he was going crazy, forsaken by his body and his mind.

I felt like a nutjob myself. My brain, still reeling from the hashish death trip, couldn't filter the sensory riot of India. I was in a kind of dream state, and the kaleidoscopic drama around me seemed weightless and empty.

When I slept, my zombie self, taking orders from a psychic power, was blowing up my family or the entire Earth. These dreams left me drained and anxious. I had the eerie feeling I was mirroring my father's undoing, like a ghost stalking another ghost. I couldn't get to sleep without taking one or two methaqualone tablets, a sedative-hypnotic I'd started buying over the counter in Indian pharmacies. Better known as Quaaludes, they were perfect for the ordeal of long-haul train travel.

As Josh and I crisscrossed India, the aftermath of the Vietnam War was front-page news. America's role had ended in 1975 with the fall of Saigon and the evacuation of US troops, but the war was still reverberating in 1980. Vietnam's invasion of Cambodia and the toppling of the Khmer Rouge government had pushed hundreds of thousands of Cambodians to the Thai border, where they were sub-sisting in makeshift camps. Farther south, waves of boat people, as they were called, were fleeing Communist Vietnam, most of them crammed into refugee camps on the Thai and Malaysian coasts.

I decided what to do when my money ran out: volunteer with one of the relief groups in Thailand. I'd be able to stay in Asia and maybe turn the volunteering into something long-term. But I needed to regain my strength. In the Rajasthan desert, I did nothing but rest. After a few weeks, my body felt better. I was more embedded in my experience, not outside of it.

Josh and I ended our journey together in Calcutta, where my father had been hospitalized. I looked for the army's 263rd General Hospital, but no one had heard of it. We walked the streets of the teeming city, admiring its colonial architecture and flinching at its notorious poverty. Josh bought his plane ticket to New York, and I got mine to Bangkok.

After ditching my sorry-looking backpack and buying a hard-shell suitcase, I packed my meager wardrobe, a few journals, a dozen rolls of film, a small bag of Tibetan turquoise, and a lot of Quaaludes. The suitcase was still half-empty. I was exiting the Hippie Trail a lot lighter than when I'd started.

## 20

FINDING A VOLUNTEER POSITION IN Thailand was harder than I'd expected. I made the rounds of the big agencies in Bangkok—Save the Children, International Rescue Committee, Red Cross—but they didn't know what to make of me, some guy showing up on their doorstep. It wasn't done, they said.

A few of the administrators were sympathetic and told me, in hushed tones, about a person who might help. His name was Jerry. Each of them scribbled his phone number on a scrap of paper and slipped it to me as I was leaving.

I called Jerry, and we met at a bar. He was in his forties, a fair-haired farm boy from Nebraska.

"You called me at the perfect time," he said, smiling broadly.

Jerry was a Seventh-day Adventist minister who ran the church's relief operations in Thailand. He needed volunteers badly down in Songkhla, near the border with Malaysia. It was one of the largest camps holding Vietnamese boat people.

I asked when I could start. Jerry fished a train ticket out of his pocket and handed it to me.

After an eighteen-hour journey to the coastal town of Songkhla, I met my new housemates: a wholesome crew of young Adventist men and women. They explained their rules: no meat, no alcohol, no tobacco, no movies, no premarital sex. One of them, a teenager, told me she'd never read a novel. I tried to interest her in my copy of *Crime and Punishment*, and she declined politely.

I'd be sharing a room with the three guys and sleeping on a twin mattress covered by mosquito netting. A Thai woman cooked the meals, did the laundry, and made sure everyone wore their raincoats. After seven months on the Hippie Trail, this Adventist pad seemed like the Ritz. Over dinner my new friends said I'd be teaching English and preparing refugees for resettlement in the States.

The next morning, I checked myself in the mirror, something I hadn't done for a while. I'd been too scared after the hash meltdown in Kathmandu. My face, neck, and arms were tan but my jawline was pale. I'd shaved off my Himalayan beard. Bleached-out brown curls spilled over my forehead and ears. I pushed them back and was alarmed to see how far my hairline had receded. On my right wrist I wore a Casio watch I'd picked up for five bucks in a Bangkok market. I figured I'd need to know what time it was.

I looked presentable enough, but the more I studied the person in the mirror, the less real he seemed. For weeks, I'd been taking the Quaaludes to fall asleep, leaving me strung out. Savage dreams jangled my nerves at night. It had been unsettling to wake up that morning next to strangers, not Josh. I was on my own now.

WE DROVE TO Songkhla Refugee Camp in a small, open-air truck. It was monsoon season, and the dirt roads were rutted and muddy. We took a hard left at the shoreline and ahead of us loomed a wooden guard tower, the entrance to the camp. A small market of makeshift stalls, where Thai women sold produce and fish, slowed our path to a white metal gate. Two Thai military police, wearing aviator shades and leaning on semiautomatics, waved us through.

The camp's main square was surrounded on three sides by wooden barracks, the largest of them flying the flag of the United Nations High Commissioner for Refugees. A group of officials from various embassies were holding an impromptu meeting outside, comparing notes on applicants. Long lines of Vietnamese refugees, dog-eared documents in hand, clogged the doorways, waiting for the interview that might send them to the States or another Western country.

One of the Adventists handed me a tattered, brown English-Vietnamese phrase book and said I'd be teaching in the Baptist church. "Look for the big open building in the middle of camp," she said.

I started walking along a dirt road that separated the beach on my right from the metal-roofed barracks on my left. Giant waves were crashing thirty yards away, and hundreds of people jammed the road. There were pairs of men shouldering bamboo and other building supplies. Women wearing every possible color and floral design were toting plastic bags overflowing with fruits and vegetables. Barefoot children lugged empty tin cans to the water hydrants at the front of each barrack. The throng parted for a girl selling breakfast from a steaming cauldron of noodle soup. I inhaled a fragrant cloud of lemongrass and ginger.

Each metal-roofed barrack looked like a small shantytown: a jumble of hanging laundry, corrugated metal, green oil drums, and piles of woven baskets atop tables made of driftwood. Tattered blue and white tarps shaded the barbers, seamstresses, and other artisans from the rain and sun.

The Baptist church was a large, open-air bamboo structure with a thatched roof, right next to the Catholic church. I stood in the mud for a second, wondering what I'd gotten myself into, then climbed the steps. There were a dozen rows of backless benches full to capacity with a hundred people. Many more were standing in the side aisles, and still others outside the church, craning their necks through the open framing. At the front, two girls were hanging a blackboard from a bamboo rail, and I put my hands together, Thai-style, to thank them.

Most of my students looked to be in their teens and twenties, but there were also mothers cradling infants, wizened old men with wispy beards, and gap-toothed grandmothers. Grade-school-age children sat cross-legged on the floor right in front of me. There were three or four students to each brown phrase book—not ideal but manageable. More challenging was the thunderous roar of crashing surf.

"Good morning, class!" I shouted.

"Good morning, teacher!" they yelled back even louder.

The Adventists had warned me that following a lesson plan was pointless. Hundreds of people entered and left Songkhla every week, so class turnover was constant. The rapt faces staring up at me appeared starved for the sounds of English, as if a single word might determine their fate in America. I chose a page at random.

On the blackboard I scrawled *Shopping at the Supermarket* and next to it the Vietnamese equivalent. There was a flurry of activity as everyone wrote in their pink-covered notebooks. Vietnamese is one of the few Asian languages written in the Roman alphabet, a project begun by sixteenth-century Jesuit missionaries and made mandatory by French colonizers in the early twentieth century. Everyone in the class could read what I'd written in both languages.

*How much is the rice?* I wrote beneath the topic of the day, before reciting the phrase two times, slowly and loudly.

"How much is the rice?" they chorused.

"Please give me two pounds," I screamed.

The teens and younger adults were fearless at contorting their mouths to produce the strange new sounds. The elders barely moved their lips at all. They looked at me forlornly, perhaps divining the yawning cultural divide that lay ahead. Up front, the kids were parroting each phrase like they were born in the USA.

When the class ended, I taught two more. After the third class, I was starving. A boy of thirteen or fourteen took me by the hand and led me to the food ration window, where I was handed a paper bowl containing a ball of rice and a small tin of sardines. I followed my new friend to the beach and we sat down next to a thirty-foot-long junk, a sturdy weather-beaten vessel that had delivered 110 people to the camp's front door six months earlier.

IF YOU DIDN'T know Songkhla Refugee Camp existed, you'd have never found it. A strip of beach two hundred yards long, it was bordered at either end by wire fence and Thai guard towers, at the back by dense jungle, and along the front by the Gulf of Thailand. Given the sea currents, there was no point in Thailand closer to the South Vietnamese fishing villages that were the main departure points for an exodus by sea that was unprecedented in human history.

Since the fall of South Vietnam to the Communist North, some one million men, women, and children had boarded mostly unseaworthy boats and set out to traverse a watery ring of hell filled with Vietnamese gunboats, murderous pirates, howling typhoons, and impossibly large sharks. What should have been a voyage of three days usually turned into a week or more, most of it without food or water. More than two hundred thousand desperate pilgrims never made it to the other shore. The survivors made landfall up and down the coast near Songkhla.

I cringed to imagine five thousand traumatized New Yorkers squeezed into a holding camp the size of a football field, lining up to share twenty port-a-potties. The Vietnamese managed to transform these wretched conditions into a well-ordered village with an unlikely aura of normalcy. Children romped on the beach with homemade pull-toys; teenagers played soccer and volleyball; women squatted in their barracks, sewing clothes or cooking over small iron braziers; the men drank tea and chain-smoked at mini cafés on the beach, trading the latest rumor of a guerrilla force preparing to liberate Vietnam. At sunset, small groups of homesick souls would gather on the sand, gazing across the gulf toward the motherland.

The geniality and hospitality of these survivors was astonishing. I couldn't walk twenty yards in camp without getting big smiles, words of genuine thanks, random questions about America—the Freedom Land, they called it—or an invitation to lunch or dinner. I acccpted one or two such offers each day, then sat cross-legged for hours on the plywood floor of a family's cramped quarters, devouring homemade food and riveting stories shared with disarming honesty: tales of war and near starvation, heartbreaking separations and ecstatic reunions, tragedies on the high seas and hand-of-God rescues.

I'd been at Songkhla for two full weeks before realizing I hadn't written a word in my journal, thought about Melissa once, or agonized over my past at all. I didn't need Quaaludes to get to sleep and my nightmares were gone. When I did remember my dreams, they were filled with faces and happenings in the camp, as if I'd lived there forever. I hadn't been so immersed in the ceaseless flow of life since my yeshiva days, and the sheer intensity seemed to blot out memory. I was energized and happy.

But within two months, my psyche reverted to form, and once again I was dreaming of zombies rampaging through my childhood home. The nightmares left me so wrung out that I feared going to sleep, leaving me dependent again on the white pills. Anxiety followed close behind, and I developed severe stomach pain that came and went.

My friend Minh worried about me. He was a novelist and professor of philosophy who gave me daily lessons in Vietnamese. Forty years old with crinkled-up eyes, he had a thin mustache and a sinewy build. As a leader of the Buddhist peace movement, Minh had been jailed by the South Vietnamese government during the war, then jailed again by the Communists after it ended. I advocated for him with the US immigration authorities, who had rejected his application.

"Oh, Stephen, my American savior!" he always greeted me, sardonically.

"I'm no one's savior."

"What do you mean? You Americans are experts at saving

everybody," he laughed. "But you won't be able to help me if you get any skinnier."

More than my weight, Minh was worried about my dreams and insisted I get my fortune read. It surprised me that a philosophy professor would consult a fortune-teller.

"I'm Vietnamese first, professor second," he explained. "You need to see Mrs. Pham right away."

We found Mrs. Pham in her quarters, washing vegetables with rough, weathered hands. She was in her fifties, I guessed. Her long black hair was parted in the middle and pulled back in a tight bun. I kicked off my flip-flops and sat down on her bamboo mat. She knelt in front of me, took my hands in hers, and studied the palms. She spoke softly and Minh translated.

"You are very sad and lonely, and it is affecting your work. There is a girl. She doesn't love you anymore. It's best to forget her."

"I'm trying," I said.

Mrs. Pham turned her attention to the heel of my right palm, running her fingers over a jagged patch of raised skin: scar tissue from a motorcycle spill I'd taken in Bali. The wound had festered for weeks, turning into jungle rot before I could find antibiotics.

"An accident," I volunteered. Minh translated, and Mrs. Pham grew more animated.

"No, not an accident," Minh relayed. "This place on the hand is your heart. You were wounded in the heart very badly."

"Yeah, I know. My girlfriend."

"Not your girlfriend," Minh insisted. "Mrs. Pham says this scar is much older. It has been on your heart since you were a boy, but now it is so big you can see it on the hand." Mrs. Pham continued, and Minh's face creased with worry.

"What?" I asked.

"She says an evil spirit is chasing you. You are trying to escape. That's why you fell off the motorcycle." Minh saw my confusion. "We Vietnamese believe in ghosts and evil spirits," he said. "You need to keep this evil spirit away, my friend."

"All right," I said. "Ask her how." Mrs. Pham peered at the lines crisscrossing both palms, then spoke.

"It is good news," Minh reported. "She says your father will save you."

I was amazed. I'd never mentioned my father to Minh, much less to Mrs. Pham. "What does she say about him?" I asked.

"She says your father is dead. He is protecting you from misfortune. That's what our ancestors do."


ON MY FIRST day in Songkhla I noticed that many girls and young women had closely cropped hair. "Thai pirates," I was told matter-of-factly when I asked about this. Vietnamese girls prepared for the voyage by getting their hair shorn and wearing boys' clothes—a ploy to deceive attackers. These raids were not the exception; they were the rule. The month I arrived, more than eighty percent of boats had been attacked, most of them several times, by large fishing vessels freelancing as buccaneers, which was an age-old tradition in the Gulf of Thailand.

Marauding pirates would storm a boat, throw the men overboard or kill them outright, gang-rape the women and girls, take anything of value, and then depart, sometimes ramming the frail craft and sinking it. Tens of thousands of Vietnamese died in this way. More than once I met someone who was the sole survivor of a boat that had set out with fifty or a hundred people. The camp's orphanage was full.

Then there was Kra. I first heard that awful name when I inquired after Mai, a teenage girl in my class. Mai would sit in the back looking dazed, mouthing the English robotically. I never saw her speak with other girls, and one day I asked an older woman about her.

"Kra," she said. "She was in hell."

Ko Kra, I learned, was a small island off the coast that Thai pirates had turned into a jungle prison where they tortured and raped Vietnamese women. Hundreds perished on Kra, many of them raped to death. Countless others were sold to fishing boats or directly into prostitution. Mai was one of those who had been rescued by a courageous UN field officer.

Pretty soon, Mai stopped coming to class entirely. I ran into her leaving Minh's barrack one day as I was arriving. He and his girl-friend, Thuy, had been counseling Mai, he explained. She had fallen into despair. The next time I saw her she was alone on the beach, staring into the distance.

I was eating lunch with Minh and Thuy a few days later when the barrack loudspeaker delivered some news in Vietnamese. Thuy buried her face in her hands, and Minh hung his head.

"They say Mai took her own life," he reported.

"I'm so sorry," I said.

"This is my fault," Minh moaned. "She asked for our help. I failed her."

"No, no, don't say that," I said. "You tried your best."

I bought a few large bottles of beer at the Thai market, and the three of us drank and smoked for hours. Minh, who was inconsol-able, recounted the friends he'd lost during the war and the voyage. Night fell and I missed my ride back to the Adventist house. Minh insisted I sleep in his hammock, and he lay down on the floor near me. I slept fitfully, haunted by Mai.

Just before dawn, I had a nightmare about Dan Farinella, my first. He was half man, half beast. Instead of hands, he had the paws of a bear, with long, razor-sharp claws. He had kidnapped several babies and was tearing the flesh off their bodies. I was his forced accomplice, wanting to stop him but standing by instead, petrified and helpless.

When I awoke from the dream, I was coiled tight inside the hammock and struggled to get my bearings. *I'm in Songkhla Refugee Camp, in Minh's hammock.* My body shuddered from the memory of Dan torturing children.

I pried myself out of the webbing and stepped over Minh. The first rays of light were painting the horizon pink and the camp was perfectly still. I staggered barefoot to the beach and fell into the sand near the tide line.

EACH MORNING ON my arrival in camp I'd see a monk about my age standing motionless in the dirt path, eyes closed, cradling a begging bowl with both hands. Streams of people flowed around him, as if he were a statue. His robes wrapped a small, wiry frame in a saffron cocoon, exposing a copper-colored right shoulder and a lean, muscular bicep. His face, with its high cheekbones, almond eyes, and slightly elongated ears, was unlined and boyish.

Every so often, someone would approach and offer alms—a mother, say, with her children in tow, all bowing before they placed cooked rice or other food, wrapped in banana leaves, into the wooden bowl. Then he would take one small step down the path and stop. Then another. And another.

The monk, Thich Huyen Viet, asked me to join him in teaching an English class one day in the Buddhist temple. Afterward, he invited me to tea in his bamboo hut, next door. It was the last stop in camp before the guard tower.

The monk's living quarters were small, perhaps eight feet by ten feet, with a wooden sleeping platform, a white rope hammock slung between two bamboo posts, and a small table and chairs. A blackboard hung from one of the walls, filled with writing in Vietnamese. There was no floor, just sand. A window without glass framed a picture-postcard view of the shimmering blue ocean.

All in all, it was what you'd expect of a monastic's cell save for one thing: there were two large dogs and seven cats in residence, making the hut feel like a kennel at full occupancy. When I came in, all nine of the boarders were lined up, waiting for their afternoon gruel of rice and tofu.

"They are strict vegetarians," the monk said, laughing.

Like reclusive deer in hunting season, the cats and dogs had figured out that the monk's hut was a demilitarized zone, a refuge within a refuge. From their point of view, the rest of camp must have seemed like a giant wok in search of meat. He doted on the animals as if they were his children or monastic novitiates. I watched, puzzled, as he gently tapped a cat's rear end with a small stick.

"I am a cat teacher," he said.

"What are you teaching them?"

"To stay inside," he replied, patiently.

He lit a fire with four lumps of charcoal and brewed some Lapsang Souchong tea. I sat at the table and a cat jumped on my lap. Two others sprawled in front of me, and the dogs lay down at my feet.

"My dear friend," the monk said, "do you know the most important ingredient in making tea?"

I knew it couldn't be tea or water. That was too obvious.

"No, what?"

"Time. You need enough time to prepare the tea and drink it with a calm, clear mind," he said, tapping the right side of his forehead with a slender index finger. "Let's enjoy this wonderful tea together, empty of all thought and worry."

He poured two cups and sat opposite me. We sipped slowly for several moments, while the cats lounged between us. It was good, strong tea.

Then the monk spoke. "Please tell me, my friend, why did you come to Songkhla?"

"What do you mean?"

"People tell me you are a good teacher, and you listen to their troubles. This is wonderful. But you are not getting paid. And you are not a missionary. Why then?"

"I don't know. I feel at home here. Maybe I'm just drawn to suffering."

"Oh, then maybe you are a monk?" he asked, smiling mischievously.

"Yes, I may be. A Jewish monk."

"Jewish?" he said with delighted surprise. "I have read about your people but I have never met a Jew. You have wandered for thousands of years, yes?"

"That's right."

"Then I think you have a lot to teach us. We Vietnamese are beginning our exile. We must learn from the Jews so we can keep our traditions in America. Please teach me Jewish history, so I can know how you survived."

"All right," I said, "but only if you teach me about Buddhism."

"Oh, so simple!" he said, smiling. "My dear friend, the Buddha taught two things only: the cause of suffering and the end of suffering. That is all." He gestured toward the window. "Suffering is all around. It is like the sand, very easy to find here in Songkhla. But the end of suffering, oh, that is much more precious. That takes practice."

"I'm good at the suffering part," I said. "Not so good at ending it."

"Then we will practice together, Buddhist monk and Jewish monk. This hut will be our monastery."

After my last class each day I would retreat to Huyen Viet's hut, receive meditation instruction, and share the story of Jewish survival. Quite often, we were interrupted by a knock on the door: a grief-stricken parent, a distressed teenager, a traumatized new arrival. The monk would receive the supplicant at his small table, serve tea, and listen intently as they poured out their hearts.

I understood none of it, but I could tell from the visitors' expressions of thanks and their grateful bows that some burden was always left behind. I was amazed that a monastic so young, much less one who had been cloistered since age thirteen, could minister so naturally under these extreme conditions.

I had my own visitors in the hut: ex-government officials, Buddhist lay leaders, human rights activists. They came with notebooks and pens, wishing to speak with "the Jew" about resisting assimilation in America.

How could they make sure their children would keep their Vietnamese language and customs? Why was there so much divorce in America? Did boys and girls really hold hands in public? Sometimes they worried aloud that their ghosts would be doomed to wander forever, far from the sacred ground of their ancestors.

HUYEN VIET AND I were teaching a class together at the temple when my voice suddenly grew weak and I felt dizzy. Scared I might pass out, I asked him to take over. Next door, I poured my body into the monk's hammock and relived an echo of the Kathmandu episode: my visual field was wavering, as if I were receding from the world. I focused my meditative attention on the pounding surf.

When class was over, Huyen Viet suggested I spend the night in his hut. I stretched out on the wooden platform and was soon immersed in terrifying dreams of combat. When daylight broke, I heard a Vietnamese love song blaring from the PA system and saw the monk guiding a dozen students, ages fifteen to seventy, through tai chi forms on the beach.

I paid a visit to one of the French physicians in the Doctors Without Borders clinic. She suspected I had a virus and gave me some pills. But the dizzy spells persisted, accompanied by intestinal pain and nausea. I stopped sleeping in the Adventist house and moved into Huyen Viet's hut. My body was growing weaker, but I kept teaching several classes a day.

The UN announced it was giving the Adventists four thousand dollars to build a library in camp. Jerry called from Bangkok and asked if I'd give up teaching the following month to oversee the construction and running of the library. I agreed, not divulging my weakened condition. The offer was exactly what I'd hoped for: a longer-term, paid position.

But my body wouldn't cooperate. Once a week or so, dizziness would overtake me in the middle of class and I'd dismiss the students early. Cocooned in the monk's hammock, my hands and feet would go numb, and a fluid pain coursed through my eyes and ears. More disturbing, I felt a visceral aversion to other people, fearful of contact or seeing faces, with the exception of Huyen Viet, whom I trusted completely. The world seemed to be melting, and me along with it.

I returned to the French doctor, who put me on drugs for parasites, but there was no improvement. My condition—"the teacher's stomach," usually pronounced with a soft "ch" sound—became a topic of concern in camp. Mrs. Pham, the fortune-teller, insisted on treating me. I lay down on her bamboo mat, shirtless. She detected the evil spirit, painted my chest with brown mud, and chanted over me.

I was grateful but embarrassed by the attention. Just before seeing her, I'd learned that two of my students—sisters, seventeen and twenty-one years old—were carrying the babies of pirates. The older sister planned to get an abortion; the younger one had decided to keep her baby. Back in our hut, Huyen Viet was sharing tea with someone he called "the man with no mind"— he had tried to drown himself after the loss of his wife and children at sea.

In the midst of this rolling catastrophe, the teacher's stomach seemed like a bad joke. But the Vietnamese, connoisseurs of suffering, made no such distinctions. A student would stop me in the road to relay some new horror, then inquire about my stomach without changing expression, as if compassion, once summoned, would keep flowing until it had filled all vessels.

At night, I agonized over my condition as the cats stalked rats outside the hut. Did I have some rare tropical illness? Cancer?

"How is your mind, brother?" Huyen Viet asked, taking a break from studying Buddhist sutras in Pali.

"I think I may be going insane," I said.

"Oh, the brain is too big! Too many thoughts. Please be more stupid."

I recalled what my uncle had written about my father: *He was sure he was going crazy, forsaken by his body and his mind.*

I'D BEEN IN Songkhla several months, and my Thai visa was about to expire. I'd need to get it renewed in Penang, an island off the coast of Malaysia. It was a three-hour trip by train and ferry. While there, I would grab a few days of badly needed R&R at the Yeng Keng, a super-cheap, Chinese hotel that Josh and I had discovered a year earlier. After filling a small backpack with a few clothes, a journal, and some Quaaludes, I stashed the rest of my things under Huyen Viet's sleeping platform and said goodbye.

Two hours later I reached the jumping-off point for Penang and joined a crush of people streaming toward the ferry. As I stepped onto the boat, I had to steady myself on the rail. A shooting pain in my bowels radiated up into my chest. Hot flashes scorched my face. I tried to focus on the harbor front of Penang but its wooden piers and colorful junks were fading away. I wrestled my journal out of my pack, tore off a blank sheet of paper, and wrote in large block letters: I FEEL ILL. I HAVE TAKEN NO DRUGS. I DON'T KNOW WHAT'S WRONG.

The ferry's horn blew one piercing blast, and suddenly we were churning through choppy seas. A gust of wind blew my note overboard. I swooned and dry heaved over the rail, then sank to the deck.

In Penang I stumbled off the ferry and climbed into a rickshaw, pedaled by a small, barefoot man. "Yeng Keng," I whispered, then slumped against the cushioned seat. When we stopped at a light, the driver eyed me warily.

"Please no dying," he said.

"Take me to the hospital," I replied.

Once there, a nurse took my vitals and a doctor appeared. Dr. Koo was a studious-looking young man with silver-framed glasses, trained in America. He reviewed the nurse's notes, then asked what drugs I'd taken. None, I insisted. He asked what I was doing in Malaysia, and I told him about Songkhla.

"The dizziness, numbness, heaves, and hot flashes are secondary symptoms of panic," Dr. Koo said. "We'll put you on Valium and run some tests to see if there's an underlying problem causing the intestinal distress."

I relaxed on the Valium and took in the room for the first time. There were four other beds, filled with old men. A ceiling fan turned at a hypnotically slow pace. The clickity-clack of dice tumbling in a cup wafted up from the alley below, along with the mournful wail of Chinese love songs. I fell into a deep sleep, punctuated by nightmares.

Dr. Koo came to see me in the morning.

"The blood and urine tests came back normal," he said, holding the lab results. "That doesn't mean there isn't something wrong, but finding it will require more tests."

He pulled up a chair.

"I'm glad the Valium helped," he continued. "That confirms my hunch. You were experiencing panic. How long have you been having that?"

"A couple of years. But it's getting worse."

"Have you noticed what triggers these episodes?"

"No. I just suddenly feel like I'm outside my body, floating away. I get scared of people and terrified of dying."

"Bad dreams?" he asked.

"Horrible."

"What are they about?"

"I'm being chased by zombies, or I'm in a war."

"Are you a combat veteran by any chance?"

"No, why?"

"Because your symptoms sound a lot like post-traumatic stress disorder.

He could tell I'd never heard of it.

"It's the reexperiencing of a catastrophic event," he explained. "We usually see it in soldiers. It was just added to the diagnostic manual."

"I've never been in the army," I said.

"All right. Just thought I'd check. You should get a gastrointestinal workup. We could do it here, but I suggest you get it done at home. A refugee camp is probably not the best place for you right now."

When he left, I took stock of my situation. A tropical disease didn't worry me. I was more scared that whatever I had vomited out in Kathmandu was back in my body. I knew this was preposterous, medically speaking, but it felt like some kind of psychological venom—the evil spirit, as Mrs. Pham had called it—had taken hold of me. It was getting stronger and I was getting weaker. What gastrointestinal test would find *that*?

I called Josh in New York. Alarmed, he urged me to fly home but not before speaking to his father, a neurosurgeon. Dr. Horwitz asked me a few questions, then said I needed to see the "best tropical disease man in New York." He'd arrange it.

For a moment, I considered taking the next train back to Songkhla and holing up in Huyen Viet's hut. I knew that was the Valium talking, though. I needed to get treated in the States, then return to the camp as soon as I was able. My friends there would understand, although I couldn't shake the feeling I was abandoning them. No one else had the luxury of walking out, not without official papers anyway.

After reserving a one-way flight, I checked out of the hospital in Penang and caught a plane to Tokyo, then another to New York. The second flight stopped in Anchorage, Alaska, where the plane refueled and we passed through US Customs. As I approached the customs officer, I was taken aback to see a framed portrait of President Ronald Reagan hanging on the wall. It was March 1981. There had been changes in my absence.

The officer welcomed me home. *Please don't take my Quaaludes*, I silently implored him. He eyed my daypack and cocked his head as if to say, *Is that it?*, then waved me through. I went to the men's room and took one of the white pills.

Twelve hours later, I walked through the door of my parents' apartment and hugged each of them. Then I climbed onto the pullout sofa bed in their guest room, took the last two white pills, and slept for most of a day. I awoke disoriented, and it took a second to realize where I was. The bookshelf next to the sofa was filled with my father's Modern Library of classics. I picked out E. M. Forster's *A Passage to India* and opened it to find a sticker that read PROPERTY OF SEYMOUR MILLS. Like my father, I'd been shipped home from Asia with a mysterious illness at age twenty-five.

There was a daily calendar atop the bookshelf, and I tore off the previous day's page to reveal the correct date: Tuesday, March 3. I blinked a few times to be sure I was reading the numbers right. It was the anniversary of my father's death. His two boxes were in the closet, just a few feet away. There was something I wanted in those boxes.

I found them on the top shelf where I'd left them the year before and pulled them out, rooting around inside until I found my father's Army Air Corps ring. I placed it, with the raised five-pointed star and outstretched wings, on the ring finger of my right hand. The ring fit perfectly.

Part Three

RECKONING

# 21

DURING MY FIRST WEEKS BACK in New York I was too sick to get out of bed. I suffered episodes of acute intestinal pain that sent me to the emergency room twice. After sleeping poorly, if at all, I'd awake to headache, nausea, and dizziness, as if I'd spent the night drinking heavily. The violence of my dreams was so terrifying that I'd find myself sweating profusely and gasping for air.

I knew there was a psychosomatic component. Dr. Koo had told me as much in Penang. But the primary problem was my gastrointestinal tract, that was clear. All I had to do was identify the tropical disease, cancer, or God-knows-what, start treating it, and return my body to a state of good health that I could only dimly remember.

My first stop was the dean of tropical disease experts, recommended by Josh's father. After studying my jaundiced eyes and poking around my swollen midsection, he suspected hepatitis or perhaps an amoeba in my liver. When the lab work revealed neither, he sent me on to a gastroenterologist, who scoped my upper GI tract and diagnosed me with a duodenal ulcer.

The ulcer resolved with medication but my symptoms did not. Another round of testing turned up giardia, which had invaded my small intestine. I went on atropine, a nasty drug used to combat intestinal infections and, disconcertingly, pesticide poisonings.

A month later, the giardia was gone, but I was still suffering. My next stop was a lower GI specialist. He scoped my large intestine and found colitis. "Probably triggered by a bacterial infection you picked up in Asia," he said. He treated me with a sulfa drug that kept me pinned to my bed for days with blinding headaches and punishing body aches. One morning I couldn't bear it anymore and flushed the pills down the toilet.

At this point, I'd been home for months and felt sicker than ever. Even worse was the never-ending and predictable cycle: new doctor, new diagnosis, raised hopes, harsh drug treatment, dashed hopes, despair. I felt like I had some kind of werewolf syndrome for which there was no antidote. Meanwhile, the intestinal pain was now accompanied by blurred vision and vertigo.

"You need to get tested for MS," my mother said, grimly. I suspected she'd been harboring this fear for a while. Multiple sclerosis is not an inherited disease but the genetic risk is heritable, so I was somewhat more likely to have it than the average person. MS seemed unlikely, far-fetched even. But I had unraveled in Asia, physically and mentally, just as my father had, in an echo of his life that was, itself, far-fetched.


WITH MY LIFE mirroring my father's, I found myself yearning for him, to know him more deeply. I clung to my few indelible memories: sitting on his lap, his arms around me, as my uncles bantered in the backyard; watching my mother feed him from the yellow tray on his wheelchair; peering through a cloud of menthol vapor as she hoisted him off the bed during the night. I could picture a handful of idyllic scenes from my father's Bronx boyhood that Uncle Harold had shared when I was little. I returned over and over to the photos of him at war that filled the albums he had carefully compiled. But I couldn't assemble these fragments into any kind of whole, into flesh and blood.

The heavy box of his wartime letters called to me. I pulled the carton out of the closet, set it on the sofa bed, and tilted it sideways. Dozens of bundles tumbled out. After removing the decaying green rubber bands that had bound the letters for four decades, I sorted them, first by year, then by month, week, and day.

Starting at the beginning, I quickly discovered that my father was not the robust, outdoorsy type I'd imagined ever since Uncle Harold told me that he had led their Boy Scout troop. In his letters, he liked to remind his mother of his childhood ailments—anemia, lung spots, and chronic earaches—and how needlessly she had worried. When the Army Air Corps made him a staff sergeant, he wrote as if he'd redeemed himself:

> I am terribly proud of you being proud of me. I am able to stand before you with all my stripes—four on each arm—and say: "Look, Mother, this is your victory. This is the sick little kid you nursed for 21 years; the kid you believed would fail an army physical; the kid you let go reluctantly eighteen months and two days ago. Well, today I feel healthier than ever and have gained a greater degree of self-confidence. What more could I ask?

I'd known that my father and his brothers were devoted to their mother, but the depth of love revealed in the letters was something foreign to my ear. He addressed her with ardor and honesty: "This letter is being sent only to you because it says things I have wanted so long to say, only to you." For Mother's Day he confessed his gratitude: it was her strength of heart, "rock and gold," that would get him and his brothers through "the whole bloody mess of war." When he learned his squadron would be shipping out—"the imminent move is spelled Africa"—he fretted to his brother Milt that the news would "damn near kill" her.

The adoration of his mother was equaled by his anger at his father. I knew from my uncles that my grandfather had been in vaudeville, and that he left the family to move in with another woman. The abandonment cut my father to the core, and he wrote about his own father with rage and derision: "He's as full of shit as a Christmas turkey—a case of exaggerated self-pity and ego. Tell him to take a good deep breath and blow it out his foot locker."

His two brothers, on the other hand, were as cherished as his mother was, and he expressed his feelings for them just as freely. Harold was younger than him by five years. Uncle Harold had often played old records for Dave and me—popular songs he'd written and recorded after the war when he dreamed of a singing career. My father, it turned out, had shared this passion. His letters to Harold, or Hesh as he was known in the family, were filled with lyrics he'd picked up in the army, accompanied by his own longings:

> You'll never know, kid, how frequently I think of you. Someone sings and I remember that Hesh could run circles around him. We get into a sing-fest and your help is missing. But it ain't just singing I mean. How swell it would be having you as my assistant crew chief. I never believed in absence making the heart grow fonder, especially where females were concerned. But being away from you and Milt has brought the three of us closer together. I have thought frequently of the time when we choose wives. My hope is that my wife will love you guys as much as I do.

My father's letters to Milt, no less loving, evoked a different kind of longing: they were an unburdening to a confidant, a mentor. Milt, five years older, was my father's north star in literature, music, politics, and Freudian psychology:

> Milt, you cannot appreciate what your letters have meant to me. Yes, you await my missives anxiously but there is still some degree of solace and sanity in your surroundings. Here it is different.

There is little consolation, no sanity. Mail is a vibrant link with
my old world and old living.

These letters were filled with impassioned critiques of Tenny-
son's poems, Forster's novels, and Mahler's symphonies. It was an
unending conversation about books and religion, as well as a frank,
unvarnished account of army life. My father had been overseas only
a couple of months when he encountered vitriolic anti-Semitism,
far beyond anything he'd ever experienced in the Bronx:

> I've often gotten into periods of moodiness, uncontrollable tem-
> per, lack of patience. Reading of homegrown fascists has been
> contributory to this recent depression of mine. One of my tent
> mates made the classic statement: "Sometimes I think the wrong
> people are being killed." More than once, Milt, I have felt the fin-
> gers of racism. More than once my anger has risen to the boiling
> point and I have gone as far as possible as a result. Now I should
> like to kick my behind for not having gone further, lots further.
> A guy becomes so damned confused; he wonders why he should
> be risking his life, living in filth, away from his loved ones, only
> to hear others call it a Jewish war.

As my father's counselor, Milt also found him female pen pals,
prospective love interests for the day he returned home. Milt had
interviewed a young woman, Eleanor Gallant, for a secretarial job at
the Harlem Book Company where he worked, and he gave her my
father's address. She wrote to him often, but when she got romantically involved with a different GI, Eleanor turned the assignment
over to her best friend, my mother. She was barely eighteen years
old. "You'll like him," she was told. "He's a very good writer."

The letters made clear that writing was not his only gift. He
was never happier than in a crowd—an easygoing talker who
befriended everyone in his realm. When the 100th Infantry Battalion, composed of Japanese Americans and Hawaiians, made camp

in the North African desert next to my father's unit, he immediately got to know them, despite his squadron's reflexive suspicion of the "Japs." He was so taken with the battalion's music, and especially its singing, he helped them procure a violin, mandolin, and guitars, then produced and emceed a performance they put on for his unit's officers.

This outgoing, sociable man was contemplative by nature, writing frequently about the precariousness of life, which struck him in unlikely moments:

> In the evening, we went to an open-air camp movie. A pleasant evening was brought to a stinging finish since getting back meant passing a row of Italian graves. The white crosses stood luminous in the dark, making sudden establishment to the realism in which we live. Three graves were marked in Italian, "Unknown."

My father was quick to fess up to his fear. Describing the nightly punishment his unit took from the Luftwaffe, he wrote:

> In 25 days we were bombed and strafed 36 times, but Lady Luck favored us. "Your hero" was scared—no fanciness like frightened, just plain damn scared. Seeing those black crosses on silver wings, swearing that each one sought you, hearing the whistle of bombs while you hug the ground and pray. Then it's all over and you laugh at yourself, till you see the bomb craters and pieces of shrapnel, or till the next attack. One realizes how tight every muscle has become, how gradually one's sense of humor has disappeared.

In May 1943 his mother happily informed him that he had been voted "The Most Popular G.I. from the Bronx" in a contest sponsored by the landmark Prospect Theater. There was a photo of her and my uncles accepting the award from an officer in his absence. But the award did not buoy my father's spirits—the opposite in fact:

This is going to be difficult to word because I don't wish to hurt your feelings or be misconstrued. My first reaction to the news clipping, of course, was a swelling egotism, but I am not ego-maniac enough to fall for it. Rather, it caused a kind of mental recession. What hurt most was the use of the word "hero." That made me a bit angry. Here are a bunch of civilians voting for the bravery of soldiers they don't know. Sometime ago, I attended a memorial service. There before us were ninety-some-odd crosses in a straight row—an extremely small price to pay for an import-ant position. But back your way there are ninety mothers, fathers, wives, children bemoaning the loss of ninety heroes. But those kids didn't want to die, no more than I do, no more than any of us do.

It was only four months after this letter that Milt wrote with the news that their mother was dying of lymphoma. "I am frantic," my father responded to his brother and mother:

Believe me, I shall leave no stone unturned, no channel unex-plored. This is the eve of Rosh Hashanah and services have been planned. My determination to attend has been bolstered immea-surably. In time of dire need, a man must turn to something greater than himself. I not only turn, but humbly. Please, Mom, wait for me, please.

His mother's decline was a painful ordeal, made worse by a lack of morphine. I learned from my uncles that she tried to kill herself twice during her illness. Milt spared my father the worst, but he could read between the lines:

Milt, when your letter came today, I wept—without shame. And my tears were as much for you as for Mother. I realize what sort of hell must have been yours in this past year, how you must have suffered for and with all of us. To the fact that Mother will soon leave us I am quite resigned. I wish only to be home before the appointed time—to see Mother, whatever her physical condition, to ease her mind just a little. Secondly, it is my desire to make up to you as much of this as possible. We'll all wear campaign ribbons when this is over—for fights not half as hard as yours.

My father requested an urgent furlough but in the midst of the invasion of Italy, the army rejected it. Two months later, while stationed outside Naples, he received word of his mother's death:

I didn't cry, Milt. I couldn't. But my heart wept till it ached. Truthfully, my thoughts became morbid and melodramatic and self-pitying. How would "home" seem to me now without that friend we conventionally called "Mother"?

In this same letter my father hinted at his illness for the first time, revealing to Milt that he'd been hospitalized after the invasion of Italy:

Life has been nothing short of hellish in the past months, despite some easy periods. I spent Dec 1–5 in a hospital with what the doc ambiguously called "psychoneurosis." The boys will never let me forget that I spent five days in a "nut ward." No violence, however, nor armed guards. Just a bunch of war-weary G.I.s.

The bad news kept coming: my father learned the navy had laid claim to Milt, after having drafted Harold a year earlier. He wrote of "the complete fall of our home" in five short steps: their father's departure, their mother's death, each of the three sons pressed into service of country. Perhaps it was this dark frame of mind that made him come clean about his own condition:

Something has happened. Our squadron doc sums it up very nicely: "Increased inability to maintain equilibrium." That explains why

I spent five days in a hospital. At that time, they ran me through a few "psycho" tests and maintained it was hypersensitivity, the news of Mom's illness, etc. But whatever shock came from that quarter is certainly dissipated now. I saw the doc again and have appointments for the hospital: complete neurological exam and eye refraction. There is good cause to believe that the trouble may be in my eyes, correctible by glasses. Meanwhile, don't worry. I'm not. My greatest fear is that a move might come up, leaving me behind.

My father's body had turned on him, and the doctors had no clue why. His eye and neurological tests came back normal. "It was decided organic disturbances were out of the question," he wrote. His symptoms pointed toward a disorder "of a definitely non-dangerous character." But he was hospitalized again in Karachi, where his squadron was now stationed, and put under observation. "So, here I am in the neuro-ward, taking life easy with a vengeance."

Milt must not have been reassured, because he wrote to one of my father's friends in the squadron, and I found the friend's reply:

All the trouble seemed to be in Si's eyes. They were bothering him. He also complained of headaches and losing his sense of balance. I've often watched him when he was standing still, he'd just weave backward and forward, to and fro. He's perfectly OK now. Nothing to worry about.

The squadron was transferred from India to Chengdu in China, where my father was exhausted each morning after walking a half mile from the mess hall to the hangar. He would need to lie down and rest. His superior officer accused him of malingering, of looking to get shipped home because his "mommy" had died. My father hauled off and decked him.

A court-martial seemed certain. Instead, the base commander

kept insisting, above my father's objections, that he was "a psycho-neurotic":

> I finally quit fighting and went along with him. I was given a "hypnosis test" about which I can divulge little, since I was told to remember nothing. Two days later they told me to prepare for removal to India. Here I am, stuck for several days at an Indian way station, pending removal to a general hospital. What this means is beyond me. It may forebode rest camps, hospitalization or even a return to the States. A man was immediately assigned to watch me. If I were not so damned tired I'd revel in this hidden power of mine. The tragedy is humorous.

He was sent to the army's 263rd hospital in Calcutta, the one that Josh and I had tried in vain to find. "I am making the most of a sorry situation," he wrote to Milt. "No hospitalization is pleasant—too much restraint." On the other hand, there was plenty of diversion, including his new roommates. "With your psychological background, I could see deeper into the varieties of neurotics, dementias, paranoias, chronic alcoholics. But then, a guy like you would not wind up in a place like this."

The hospital's psychiatrist concluded that he was having a delayed reaction to sixteen months of combat and that he had developed an "intense, self-consuming hatred" for the two officers who had refused him a furlough to see his dying mother. He also resented his father's new married life, the doctor said, and had a hard time accepting that "this world is inhabited by people who blindly, spitefully dislike others"—Jim Crowism, my father called it. "I'm facing a future unequipped, even frightened," he confided to Milt.

> It is a peculiarly vicious cycle: my mental cares lead to physical impairment, which, receiving my attention, worsens my mental attitude. These problems are not without solution but thinking of them has not helped—it has aggravated me.

It was heartbreaking, really: while he was hiding in foxholes and evading Luftwaffe dive bombers, his real killer, multiple sclerosis, was stalking him silently. By 1943, his immune system had launched a sneak attack on his nervous system, eroding the myelin sheath that protects nerve fibers. Those newly damaged fibers were playing havoc with the flow of signals between his brain and body, producing the blurred vision, dizziness, and fatigue that are the early hallmarks of the disease. Oblivious to this neurological war within, his army doctors went on a Freudian wild-goose chase.

My father began signing off his letters, "Psychoneurotically yours." With the end of hospitalization in sight, he was longing for home and his messages to Milt dwelled on the reunion at hand:

> You know how unbounded are my devotion and love for you—only their existence makes a letter like this possible. I have complied with the promise to tell you everything, but never indulged in possibilities. Now, because of your questions, the line must deviate. . . . The doc has spoken to me to complete my charts. The decision will undoubtedly be a return ticket to the States. The gears are in motion. Chin up, fella. The kid'll be along eventually.

A month later his transfer papers came through, putting him under the full control of an army medical board. "After three and a half years, my relations with the squadron are completely severed," he wrote with brutal finality.

His last letter to Milt, dated October 26, 1944, was sent from the Army Air Forces Convalescent Hospital in Pawling, New York. They had decided to ship my father home.

AT PAWLING, HE was placed in a psychiatric ward "with the mental cases and the emotionally disturbed," I learned from Gerry Reyman, a good friend he had made there. My father had plenty of physical symptoms that came and went—leg spasms, limping, double vision, spastic bladder—but the psychiatrists were focused on "stabilizing" his mind. Gerry found that ironic: "Your father was the most stable guy I knew. But even he believed it was all in his head."

Uncle Milt filled in the rest of the story. After five months in Pawling my father wasn't getting better. In March 1945, he was eligible for discharge and deeply worried about getting classified as Section 8—mentally unfit—which meant he'd get no veteran's benefits.

On his last day there, he went for his discharge physical. The head psychiatrist was out that day, so he was seen by a young neurologist, who examined his eyes and asked him to walk across the room and back. It took all of five minutes before the doctor yelled at the psychiatric staff, "Get this man out of here! He has multiple sclerosis."

"That doctor was an angel," Uncle Milt told me. "Our lives would have been very different if he hadn't appeared that morning. In fact, you might not be here. The army changed his status to total disability, which meant he'd get financial support for the rest of his life."

My father returned to the family's Bronx apartment to live with his brothers. He no longer wanted to study engineering, which was the reason he'd chosen the Army Air Corps. Instead, he decided to major in English and become a writer. He enrolled at New York University, despite his creeping disability, which required Uncle Harold to carry him on his back up four flights of stairs each day after school. For the brothers, their reunion was a joy. Recalling it to me, Uncle Milt wept openly.

As for Uncle Harold, he told me he'd been depressed on and off for a decade while I was growing up. After going to therapy, he came to realize it was seasonal. The gloom would overtake him every year during the first week of March, the week his older brother died.

Through my father's writing, I had stumbled on the origins of some fraternal paradise from which we had all been banished. His loss had left a gaping hole in the family and now I understood why. Milt and Harold were born ten years apart and the eldest was more father than brother to the youngest. It was Si, the man in the middle, who had bound the three of them together and, beyond the brothers, the entire tribe. That was why they had all gathered around him during my first years.

Dozens of family and friends kept visiting, my uncles said, not out of obligation but because they had such a great time. My father, the social ambassador, had brought them there: guys in his squadron, invalids at Pawling, nurses who tended him after the war. Even when paralyzed, he needed to connect, to laugh, to love, and his generosity of spirit made him beloved. All this familial warmth had swaddled me from the day I was born. Until he died, I'd known an abundance of affection and the comfort of belonging.

But I'd never had the chance to hear my father's voice. Now, having read hundreds of his letters, sometimes staying up all night to do so, I not only heard him—I had come to know him and feel his presence.

The person I found was, like my uncles, warm, decent, funny, and compassionate—a mensch. But he commingled his brothers' traits in unique and unlikely ways: he was a pensive extrovert, a man who viewed humankind darkly but was irresistibly drawn to humans; he had a real temper, triggered by outrage, whether at racists or at his own father; he was passionate about culture, high or low, familiar or foreign. What's more, he channeled all of these contradictions, all of who he was, into crystalline prose that was brutally honest, even when it hurt.

I loved and admired this man, and for the first time, at age twenty-seven, I glimpsed the bond that might have been and never was. This felt like a different kind of loss, not the singular calamity of death but an unabating, lifelong absence. Still, I consoled myself that I had been held and treasured by this remarkable person. I was his son and carried his spirit within me.

It had always been thus—I'd just forgotten. When I was seven, my father's presence had been as real to me as my own heartbeat. That was the year I saw the movie *Carousel* and learned from it that my father was quite literally watching over me. I'd sit on my bedroom floor and sing "You'll Never Walk Alone"—the movie's anthem of comfort, hope, and resilience in a very dark time. Now, twenty years later, I found myself singing it again.

# 22

I DIDN'T HAVE MULTIPLE SCLEROSIS, the doctors told me. With that, my path diverged from my father's, medically speaking, but I was still debilitated and had no idea what ailed me. I called Josh's father again and recapped the merry-go-round of tests, procedures, and treatments.

"Based on what you're telling me, Stephen, you sound like a head case," the neurosurgeon said.

"What do you mean?"

"Your symptoms are real enough, but if there's no disease present then we need to treat the panic and try to make you feel better."

"All right. How?"

"I want you to see Ken Greenspan. He's a psychiatrist—the best. His specialty is biofeedback. If anyone can help you it's him." It was the last thing I wanted to hear. He was banishing me to the realm of the psychoneurotic, where my father had languished.

With a bit of homework, I learned that Dr. Greenspan, director of the Center for Stress-Related Disorders at Columbia-Presbyterian Medical Center, was one of the pioneers of biofeedback who had brought it into the medical mainstream. He'd had success treating everything from hypertension to migraines, chronic anxiety to spastic colons. Still, he was a psychiatrist.

I put off calling him until desperation trumped despair and I made an appointment. Riding the subway to his practice on the Upper West Side, my body slumped against the rock-hard bench and my head rattled on the graffiti-covered glass.

Greenspan greeted me in his spacious Riverside Drive apartment overlooking the 79th Street Boat Basin. A towering bald man in his forties, he loped toward me with a wide grin, hand extended, exuding confidence. After introductions, he directed me into his office, a small room with a desk, two leather easy chairs, and a tall bank of electronic equipment that bristled with flashing lights and a tangle of colored wires.

I related the past couple of years, described my symptoms, and, since he was a psychiatrist, shared a few scenes from the nonstop horror film that was my dream world. Then I paused, awaiting the doctor's verdict.

"You've come to the right place," he said. "I'm glad you saw all those doctors. It's important to rule out any underlying disease or condition. But I can tell you right now, you've got shell shock."

"I don't understand," I said. "Isn't shell shock from war? I've never been in a war."

"That may be, but you're sleeping in one."

"What do you mean?"

"You're flashing back to some overwhelming death experience. It's triggered at night when your defenses are down and it's sending your nervous system into a vicious cycle of hyperarousal, stress, intestinal pain, exhaustion, and depression. You're sleeping in a battlefield. No wonder you can't function. You're on high alert, like a guy who thinks he'll be gunned down at any second."

"I've only had one near-death experience," I said. "That was the hash overdose in Nepal I told you about. Could that have caused it?"

"It's possible," Greenspan replied. "But we don't need to know right now. First, we've got to get you relaxed. The stress is killing you. We're going to give your brain a new circuit, teach you a new pattern of interacting with the world."

He called in his assistant, who hooked up some of the colored wires to small sensors on my head, chest, and hands. When she left, Greenspan showed me how to slow down my breathing, reduce my heart rate, and even raise my skin temperature by responding to the feedback from the machine.

I got the hang of the relaxation response quickly. I enjoyed the challenge of getting the machine to slow its beeping sounds and flash the good lights. By the end of the session I could feel my tension and anxiety receding.

Before I left his office, Greenspan wrote me a prescription for Dalmane, a sedative, to help me get some restful sleep. The biofeedback would be futile without it, he said. Then he handed me a cassette tape labeled "Active Relaxation" on one side and "Passive Relaxation" on the other.

"Listen to one of these each day," he said. "And get some exercise, running or biking. Getting the energy flowing is the best antidote for depression. I bike every day. In fact, I'm going right now. Sex is really good, too," he added, enthusiastically. "Exercise and sex. Those are nature's antidepressants."

I began seeing Greenspan twice a week for biofeedback, and I welcomed the blissful sleep on Dalmane. Every morning, I made myself run around Stuyvesant Oval or bike through the East Village. When an old flame was visiting in town, I followed doctor's orders and had sex every day for a week. She wanted to do her bit to help me heal.

Greenspan was pleased with my progress. I was still physically weak and prone to anxiety attacks but I did feel able, at last, to face the world. Besides, I had no choice: I was broke.

I went to work as a Disaster Specialist for the American Red Cross. Driving one of their white station wagons, I responded to nighttime fires in the bombed-out South Bronx, taking inventory of the damage and evacuating families to temporary housing. In the previous decade, the South Bronx had become a national symbol of urban decay and destruction, with entire blocks burned to the ground.

On my first night, the dispatcher took me aside and said: "Listen up, my white friend, whatever you do, don't take off that Red Cross jacket. Without it you'll get shot inside ten minutes." There had to be less stressful ways to make money, I thought. Still, I felt like I'd been a disaster specialist my entire life. At least now I was getting paid for it. I moved out of my parents' place and sublet my sister's apartment nearby in Stuyvesant Town.

I fled the Red Cross after three months, just as my health began taking a nosedive. The sleeping pills had stopped working their magic and the night terrors returned in force. My dreams were vivid and unrelenting: heavily armed police dragging me away to be tortured; marauding vandals invading my childhood home and disemboweling my family; young soldiers screaming in pain from their burns, amputations, and shrapnel wounds. Each night, before going to bed, I'd plead with the universe for an hour of sound sleep. I got none.

The relapse might have made sense if I were still chasing fires in the Bronx, but I was now working as a copywriter for a nonprofit fundraising agency, a position I'd found through my mother. I had no clue what fundraising copy was, nor did I care. I just knew it sounded easier than chasing four-alarm fires in the middle of gunfire.

As soon as I started the job I wondered if I'd made a mistake. With the Red Cross, all I had to do was show up, survey the charred remains of an apartment, and shepherd a traumatized but grateful family to their temporary home. I hadn't worked in an actual office since assisting Margaret Mead four years earlier. Now I was back in the land of professionals, feeling out of practice and out of confidence.

"That's bullshit," Josh said when I shared these fears. "You were born to do this kind of work. You're compulsive and a perfectionist."

He wasn't wrong. I had come home from Asia with a meticulous accounting ledger, a killer slideshow, and a dozen fat journals. And I needed this job to occupy my mind or I'd go crazy for sure.

But after a few weeks, I was too exhausted to eat when I walked into my apartment after a long day of work. I'd collapse on the bed in my clothes and surrender to the unremitting brutality of my dreams. One morning, I woke up and my body was rigid with fear. An hour passed and the paranoia wouldn't quit, so I called in sick.

I kept my appointment with Greenspan, though. His assistant hooked me up to the usual array of wires. I braced myself against the leather chair, heart racing, skin crawling, fighting a powerful urge to bolt. It was a full-on panic attack. Greenspan studied me impassively.

"I like to avoid talking therapy if possible," he said. "It tends to evoke more thinking, which, frankly, you don't need." He was starting to sound like Huyen Viet, the Vietnamese monk. "But in your case, we don't have a choice."

Greenspan unplugged me and we talked for forty minutes— about my dreams, my work life, my history. Mostly, though, we talked about my fear: fear of people, fear of death, and, above all, the incessant fear of my own body. When we were done, he prescribed Tofranil, a tricyclic antidepressant, and a different sleeping medication. "The Tofranil will give you some leverage in working with the depression," he said.

I was on the drug for just a few days when the perpetual fear dissipated. I felt oddly detached and apathetic, but it beat the hell out of despair. The bad dreams still played at night but they were dialed back and didn't leave my body racked in the morning. I was able to do biofeedback again. When I couldn't, Greenspan would unhook me and we would discuss my dreams.

"All this violence is bottled-up anger," he said. "You've got a lot of rage, Stephen. You channeled it for years into academic achievement, or else you suppressed it and turned it on yourself. That's what you're doing now."

"I never get angry," I objected.

"Exactly," he said.

The antidepressants made work possible. It turned out I was a natural-born fundraising copywriter. I had an affinity for under-dogs and telling their stories. Within a few months, I was promoted to account rep for the New York Civil Liberties Union and the Native American Rights Fund. I immersed myself in their advocacy, becoming fluent in their issues and programs.

I began seeing friends again and started an affair with a woman at work. She was sexually voracious and lived in a psychotherapy cult, the kind of person you only find on the Upper West Side of Manhattan. Things were going so well I stopped seeing Greenspan that summer. Why incur all the expense?

My REPRIEVE WAS short-lived. I soon fell apart, suddenly agorapho-bic, panicking in the subway and in movie theaters. My dreams were running riot, and I was crying all the time. Sex was a no-go zone. My attraction to the woman at work had vanished, replaced by aversion to this naked stranger. I was losing my grip on the life I'd painstakingly built over the previous half year.

A dream finally pushed me to the breaking point. I was in battle, pursuing my enemy through underground tunnels. When I cornered them, they set themselves on fire. I watched in horror as their faces melted. Then I was captured. Their soldiers wore me down with psy-chological warfare. I tried clinging to my identity, but it was no use. They were preparing to castrate me and turn me into one of their smiling drones. It was only a matter of seconds before I'd become a mindless idiot and have no memory of the person I'd once been.

I woke up in excruciating pain, as if every bone in my body were broken. I was too dizzy to sit and convinced I might have already been emasculated. Or was I finally going insane?

As the dream loosened its grip, I became despondent. I'd been back from Asia for eighteen months and had suckered myself into believing I was better. I wasn't, and I still had no clue what was stalking me. I knew what the next day would be like, and the one after that. Why prolong the misery?

I grabbed the bottle of sleeping pills, unscrewed the cap, and poured a couple dozen into my palm. I searched the label for a warning, wanting to be sure they were deadly enough to do the trick.

"Fucking Greenspan," I said out loud, when I saw his name on the bottle. He had never divulged what was wrong with me, just some bullshit about being angry. If I was going suicidal, he owed me a diagnosis. I put the pills back in the bottle and dialed Greenspan's number. His assistant answered. I told her it was urgent, and she slotted me in that afternoon.

Greenspan welcomed me with a smile, like he'd been awaiting a cry for help. I resented his smugness. He waved me toward his office but I didn't budge.

"I'm not here for a session," I said, my voice quavering. "I won't be coming back. I'm in a bad way. I just want to know what you really think. I know shrinks don't do that. But that's all I want."

"What happened this morning?" he asked. "Why did you call?"

I told him the dream and said, "I'm pretty sure I'm losing it. I haven't been this terrified of my body since Nepal. It all goes back to that, doesn't it?"

"No. It doesn't," Greenspan said, shaking his head. "Your problems have nothing to do with what happened in Nepal."

"Then what do they have to do with?" I asked. "Just tell me. Please."

"Look, Stephen, I don't know what's buried in your childhood, but there's some deep humiliation there. You have a terrible fear of being exposed, of getting caught, as if you've done some god-awful thing and have to spend the rest of your life hiding from the world. All these dreams about watching other people get set on fire, they're about you, the annihilation of *your* body. You're witnessing your own death. That's why the dreams are so terrifying."

"But why now?" I implored him. "Why's it all getting worse now?"

"Because of your job. You could feel safe in a refugee camp or the South Bronx because you had some emotional distance from those worlds. But you're back in *your* world now, with your peers, your people, and when they get too close, you're terrified of connecting. You retreat into shame. You have no authentic emotional contact. So you wind up back in emptiness and despair."

He sounded so cold and clinical. But I had asked for it.

"I don't know," I said. "I was doing so much better for a couple of months."

"The biofeedback and the meds bought you time, but there aren't enough pills in the world to slay the demons you're carrying around."

I wobbled, suddenly unsteady, and found myself sitting on his sofa.

"I give up," I said softly. "Just tell me what to do."

"I've done what I can for you," he said. "You need to get yourself into some intensive psychotherapy. It's going to be painful. Your dreams will get worse for a while. But if you stick with it, you can overcome this. I know you can. But you've got to make the choice to get help. If you don't, you're going to self-destruct."

He didn't sound cold anymore, just concerned. This doctor was telling me I was emotionally damaged but I had the power to help myself. This had never occurred to me before. I experienced a strange new feeling: hope. I promised Greenspan I'd start calling therapists the next day.

That night, I lay in bed, racking my brain over the "deep humiliation" the doctor had spoken of. How could I suffer so much without some obvious cause?

A year later, when I read my journals from this period, I was dumbfounded. They did everything but flash Dan Farinella's name in neon lights. I dreamed of being castrated. I dreamed of a mobster toying with me, like a cat with a mouse, as he bludgeoned me to death. I dreamed I was saluting a ruthless fascist dictator while I jerked off, trying to hide myself in a crowd of sycophants.

I hadn't shared all these dreams with Greenspan, but like Sherlock Holmes, he had deduced from the evidence at hand that trauma and shame lay behind my terror. The crime itself remained unsolved, however. It was as if I were studying a lineup of suspects and couldn't pick out the killer standing right in front of me.

# 23

ONCE I BEGAN THERAPY, MY dreams got worse, just as Greenspan had predicted. They were every bit as murderous, but now they were all set in the same haunted house: my childhood home in East Meadow. These nightmares starred my mother and Ken. Night after night, they ranted at me, assaulted me, and banished me from their home. In one gruesome episode, my mother ate me alive. In these dreams, I was forever digging graves in the backyard, trying to bury a corpse, which only enraged my mother even more.

"You haven't finished burying your father," my new therapist observed dryly when I told him about the nocturnal grave digging. *Finished?* When had I even started?

After interviewing a few shrinks, I'd chosen this one by default. The others seemed too clinical, too preppy, or too old. I had no idea what I was looking for, but at least I could relate to this guy. He'd grown up near me on Long Island and was a familiar character, like one of those brainy Jewish kids in high school chess club. He was in his early thirties and resembled the young Albert Einstein: dark bushy hair, fat caterpillar mustache, deep eyes, and tortoise-shell glasses. He seemed a viable guide for this twice-weekly expedition in search of whatever had caused my crippling humiliation.

The recent evidence pointed toward my mother. After she'd remarried, I grew scared of her unpredictable and sometimes physically abusive outbursts. The closeness I'd once felt with her had vanished, replaced by fear of her anger and rejection. At age seven, while I waited for my father to return, she acted as though he'd never existed, denying our shared past.

Now it struck me that my mother may have been too numb after years of nursing my father to feel anything, much less grieve. She had coped with her ordeal by wiping it from consciousness. No wonder she was enraged in my dreams when I dragged her ex-husband's corpse around. She knew I'd been reading his letters and talking to my uncles, learning more about his life. I was violating her taboo on revisiting the past and dredging up the unspeakable. I knew the dredging was painful, but keeping it submerged would only prolong the pain.

"I'd like to ask you some questions about my father," I ventured one day, having stopped by her apartment while Ken was at work.

Her face soured.

"Stephen, I don't understand this obsession of yours. I mean, are you going to talk to Ken, too, and find out about *his* family history?"

"No, I'm not." I was trying to stay calm. "Ken has a son and daughter. Who are you expecting to remember my father if I don't?"

"I never understood why you rejected Dad," she said, meaning Ken.

"I never rejected him, Mom. I always liked him, but I needed a connection to my real father. I still do. Why can't you see that? Think about your own father."

"What are you saying?" she asked, a look of hurt surprise on her face.

"He died when you were twelve!" I said, my voice rising. "What was that like? How easy was it for you to let go of him?"

She winced, her chin trembling. I'd gone too far, I thought, as my mother retreated into herself. After a few seconds, she looked up, stricken.

"I was nine when he had his first stroke," she said. "My mother took care of him at home for a year. But she was weak from the TB. She had a hard time getting him dressed each morning. He was bedridden. When he became incontinent, she moved him into a Jewish nursing home."

"Did you visit him?" I asked.

"Yes. It was awful. He was a good man, so agreeable. All he wanted was to sit in his rocking chair by the window and read his Hebrew books. But the people there humiliated him because he was religious. I couldn't bear the way they treated him, so I stopped going. My mother went every Sunday. She always cried when she came home."

"How long was he there?" I asked.

"Two years. When he died, it was a big deal. My father was a respected man, a learned man. The rabbis came to sit shiva. They asked me to say Kaddish at the shul." She shook her head in amazement. "You have no idea how unusual this was. It was unheard of for a girl to say Kaddish, and I was only twelve! But I'd been studying Torah. They knew I was the son he never had."

"Did you say Kaddish?"

"Yes. Every day at the shul for a month." She sank into herself and sighed.

"What?" I asked.

"I said Kaddish but I don't think I ever grieved. We were so poor, my mother was sick. We were just trying to stay alive."

"That sounds incredibly hard."

"You know, Stephen, I've often wondered how much my first marriage had to do with my father's illness."

"What do you mean?" I asked. I knew exactly what she meant but was surprised she'd acknowledge the connection.

"My father was an invalid. My husband was an invalid. That was all I knew."

Having shared this, my mother then told me how, after she'd corresponded with my father during the war, they met at a friend's party, carried on a whirlwind romance, and got married two months later. "I'd lived a sheltered life till then. He opened a whole world to me: his brothers, his friends, that big social circle. They did everything together. I suddenly had a tribe."

I asked when she learned of his illness.

"He told me early on," she recounted. "I went to the library and read up on it, but I really had no clue. When we announced our engagement, your uncle Milt came to my office. He's a good man, and he wanted me to know what I was getting into. The doctors at the VA had told him that Si had two to fourteen years to live. I said to Milt, 'If we get two years together, that'll be enough for me.'" She smiled knowingly. "I was so young, so romantic."

After they married, my father could no longer drive so my mother quit her job as a legal secretary. The VA paid her a stipend to get him to NYU and to physical therapy. A year later, he couldn't walk and she began pushing him to school in a wheelchair. When his hands could no longer type, she began taking his dictation.

"He was writing stories and radio plays," she told me. "The NYU radio station produced some of them. He had two professors who were very supportive. One of them had us over for dinner all the time in the West Village. He thought Si's stories about the war were terrific: the deprivation, the prejudice, all those psychiatrists. His writing was dark but funny, too."

"Do you have any of those pieces?" I asked. "I'd love to read them."

"No. I don't know what happened to them. We must have tossed them somewhere along the way."

My patrimony—gone. I felt a lump in my throat.

A good friend of theirs had been writing for *The Fred Allen Show*, the most popular comedy show of the era. He'd promised to get my father in the door. But by the time he graduated, he was in no shape to hold a job. My parents hoped for a silver bullet, but none of the new drugs relieved his symptoms.

"I know you resented my not telling you these things when you were younger," my mother said, "but they were hard to talk about. It's hard even now. I did things that were humiliating, but our dignity was intact because we never moaned and groaned. I'd get upset and go off by myself. That was my pride, nothing to do with your father. I loved him, but I had a lot of anger, so much frustration. I wasn't dealing with it very well. We never talked about his condition. Never. That's what let us get through."

MY THERAPIST ASSURED me I was making real progress, tracing my anger and shame back to the fraught relationship with my mother and the loss of my father. But the nightmares were still jolting me awake, and in them I was now stalked by a faceless, implacable enemy. When he caught me, he would club me or dismember me or burn me alive.

Waking from one of these nightmares, I'd vault out of bed and scour the room for a sign of my tormentor: in the closet, under the bed, behind the door. I'd check over and over until I was sure the coast was clear. Then I'd fall back into the same cycle of terrors.

As Greenspan had observed, the nightly meltdown of my nervous system wreaked physical havoc. By daybreak, I felt as if I'd been crouching in a cage for days: arms and legs bound in place, head battered, neck taut. Numbness spread throughout my body, and moving at all was painful. I would begin the frenzied process of trying to stuff the ghastly images and thoughts back down into their hiding place. It took me two or three hours to exit the dream world, enter daytime consciousness, and stagger off to the subway.

On a bad morning, nothing—no words, no drugs, no prayer—would help. I'd bolt the door and hide under the covers until I could gather the courage to call in sick. It seemed laughable that I had ever imagined there was some physical cause for my condition. I'd watch as terror turned into crushing headache, then intestinal distress, then crippling fatigue, and, finally, all-consuming despair.

It was taking me longer and longer each morning to drive away the demons and recover. It was getting harder and harder to pretend I was okay.

I WAS IN my mother's narrow kitchen one Sunday as she baked *mandel* bread and filled me in on the plans for my sister's wedding. She ticked off the names of good friends and family who'd be attending.

"Did I mention Dan and Betty?" she asked, glancing up from her mixing bowl. "We invited them, of course."

My face flashed hot at this alarming bit of news. I'd managed to avoid Dan for five years, since that summer at Camp Henry Horner, and I'd become so adept at pushing away thoughts of him that I'd airbrushed him out of my parents' lives as well.

"No, you didn't mention them," I said, trying to sound unfazed. "Do you think they'll come all the way from Illinois?"

"Oh, they're not in Illinois anymore. Didn't I tell you? They moved to Pittsburgh last year."

Pittsburgh. That seemed close. My stomach began churning.

"Why did he leave Henry Horner?" I asked, clinging to some shred of hope that he'd left camping after all.

"Oh, he got a great offer running youth programs for the Jewish Community Center in Pittsburgh. And he's the director of their summer camp."

I was appalled. All those people at Henry Horner who knew what Dan was doing, and he'd simply moved on to the next job and the next set of boys. But I had a more immediate problem.

"Have you heard back from Betty?" I asked. "Are they coming?"

"The invitations just went out this week. But I think they'll want to come. Dan was always fond of Donna and he'll want to see you."

I left my mother's apartment frantic, imagining Dan at the wedding, shaking hands, smiling, pretending we were friends. I felt a spray of acid rise in my throat. I stopped and hocked a gob of green bile onto the sidewalk. My body wasn't going to let me be in the same room with Dan Farinella. It was him or me, and I wasn't going to miss my sister's wedding.

The next day, I called directory information in Pittsburgh and got the number for the Jewish Community Center. Then I sat at the small desk in my bedroom for several minutes, my right hand clutching the phone as I stared vacantly at the bare trees outside.

This was the call I'd been dreading for years. Back in Madison, there had been mornings when just the thought of this call would send me straight to Tommy's house for a needle in my arm and a wave of blessed forgetfulness. But there could be no turning away now. Calling Dan was scary, but seeing him in person was unthinkable.

I steeled myself and dialed the number. The woman who answered told me Dan would be back in an hour. I thanked her, hung up, and collapsed on the bed, my face buried in the pillow. When I called again, the same woman asked for my name and patched me through to Dan's office.

There was a click on the other end, then the familiar, tough-guy Bronx accent.

"Hey. How ya doing?"

Chills down my spine. I was thirteen again.

"I'm okay."

"I heard you were sick," he said. "Your mom told me."

"Yeah, I was. But I'm feeling better. Listen, Dan, my mother told me she invited you and Betty to Donna's wedding."

"Yeah, we just got the invite. That's great news, huh?"

"Look, it's not a good idea for you to be there. It's just not."

He didn't say anything for a few seconds.

"Don't worry," he finally said. "I'll come up with an excuse why we can't make it."

"Good. Thanks."

I wanted to remind him of his promise to get out of camping. I wanted to say I was horrified that he'd taken another job working with kids. But I couldn't see the point. He wouldn't stop anyway. Besides, just making this call had taken all I had.

"I don't want to make things hard for you," he said.

"All right," I said, trying to get off. "Take care."

"Yeah, you too."

I BEGAN MY next therapy session by sharing my latest romantic disaster: a date in which I'd gotten so stoned I wound up hiding in the bathroom, having full-on hallucinations. When she and I finally got around to sex, I couldn't. The night was capped off with a castration dream: my dick withered away and broke off in my hand.

I was in the middle of recounting this story when I casually let drop that I'd spoken to "this guy," someone I'd had a confusing sexual relationship with when I was a teenager. Then, as abruptly as I'd raised it, I moved on to the next topic.

"Hold it right there," my therapist interrupted, his eyebrows leaping upward. "Could you repeat what you just said? Because I'm pretty sure it's important."

I went back, offering slightly more information: Dan's name, age, and profession. I studied my therapist's face for any hint of judgment.

"How old were you when this started?" he asked, his pen poised over the ever-present yellow memo pad.

"Thirteen."

"That doesn't sound like a sexual relationship. That sounds like something else."

He asked me to start at the beginning. I offered up fragments and talked haltingly, staring at my balled-up fists, glancing up occasionally to gauge his reaction. After ten minutes or so, I went silent. My whole body was taut, braced for fight or flight, half expecting my therapist to vault out of his chair and attack me. But he only nodded and took notes.

At our next session, when I struggled to say more, he suggested I try lying on his couch. *No fucking way*, I thought. That thing looked like an overstuffed relic from the Freud museum. If I got on it I'd be defenseless. I double-checked my escape route to his door. Then I said okay, anything to dodge forty-five agonizing minutes in the chair.

The couch worked like magic. From the second I lay back, my therapist receded. He was there, yet not there. With my eyes closed or fixed on the ceiling, I gave myself permission to talk.

I related the events of the first year I knew Dan. Recalling them felt like uncovering a story written in invisible ink. It had never been read, never been told, but now it took on the shape and weight of reality. These things hadn't happened to someone else, they had happened to me.

I'd spent so much energy for so many years denying these memories that I'd lost track of who I'd once been. But there he was, waiting: a thirteen-year-old fatherless boy, at odds with his mother, who craved love and attention.

"He trapped me," I whispered. "Then he tore my heart out."

In a flash, I was consumed by rage toward Dan Farinella. He had stepped into the role of father, then exploited me like some disposable object to gratify his twisted sexual needs.

"I want to kill him," I said. "I *have* to kill him!" The violence of my words hung there for a moment, before I added: "You know what the sick part is? There's this voice inside me saying, 'How could you even think that, Stephen? He cared about you. You know he did. He's a good person. Everybody knows Dan's a good person.'"

IN 1983 THERE were no road maps to healing from childhood sexual assault. The language of trauma and PTSD had not begun filtering into the tradition-bound practice of psychotherapy. Another twenty years would pass before the national media began covering the sexual abuse of boys in the Catholic Church.

I had washed ashore on terra incognita and would have to find my own way, guided by a therapist who was discovering the terrain along with me. I'd made a start by mustering the courage to describe what Dan had done. I'd let myself feel the stabbing pain of his betrayal and the white-hot fury of hatred.

Over the following months, I'd come to see that my terror of Dan was not a thing of the past. It seized me each time I lay down on the therapist's couch, petrified that this small affable man, like my abuser, was only pretending to help me. Sooner or later, when I least expected it, he'd overpower me, too.

Instead, I came to trust him, which in turn prompted other changes. I had often told him that I seemed to be watching a movie of my life instead of living it. I'd been outside looking in for so long—detached and powerless—that I felt no sense of control at all. Now I began trying to steer my fate.

I loved my work, but the workplace itself had become dysfunctional. It hadn't occurred to me before this to find a different job. Then, in the fall of 1983, I put the word out to nonprofit groups that I was available. The Natural Resources Defense Council, a national environmental organization, called. They wanted to hire me to build their Membership and Public Education program, and I said yes.

I was making new friends and playing poker in a home game. My nightmares were less frequent and my physical symptoms receded, present but not disabling. I got involved with a woman in her late twenties who ran an environmental foundation.

Still, after a year with my new girlfriend I began looking for an escape hatch and broke off the relationship abruptly. In all that time I'd never mentioned Dan Farinella. It wasn't a conscious choice. Thought never entered into it. My body had decided that telling her wasn't a safe thing to do.

# 24

I was thirty years old and had never been romantically involved for more than a year. If you had asked me why, I would have said that I hadn't met the right woman yet.

The truth was a lot simpler: it was the double life I'd been leading since I was thirteen. The guy who went on dates, the one wearing a mask of normalcy and pretending to be available, was a front man for the kid trapped in a psychic bunker. But I didn't understand that yet. I just thought I was bad at picking women.

One night I called a good friend. "Look, I'm always with the wrong person," I said to her. "Just tell me who I should go out with." She laughed. "I'm serious," I said.

She told me I needed to meet this woman, Susan. "She's in Renegade Theater. She's gorgeous, artistic, funny. You two would be good." I needed to move fast. Susan was leaving soon for a month in France.

She agreed to meet me two days later for a drink. At the appointed hour, I walked through the door of Around the Clock, a bohemian café in the East Village, and scanned the packed room. A flash of red lipstick near the bar caught my eye. I took in the woman behind the lipstick: a tall, Black Irish beauty with high cheekbones, almond-shaped eyes, and abundant dark brown hair swept back in a pony-tail. She was standing alone, a picture of downtown chic.

My friend had described Susan as gorgeous, but I didn't know she meant *gorgeous*. If this was her, I was in trouble: she was out of my league, one of those women who turns heads on Seventh Avenue. When I introduced myself, she seemed surprised, as if she'd been waiting for some self-confident master of the universe, not whoever the hell I was.

But once we began talking I realized she wasn't surprised, only nervous. Susan came from an Irish German family in Bay Ridge, Brooklyn, one of seven children. Her father was a butcher, her mother a math teacher. She'd gone to all-girls Catholic schools, then to Skidmore College, where she studied dance. Back in New York, she'd worked in the fashion industry before quitting to devote herself to acting and the theater she'd helped found.

Beneath our cultural differences, we had a lot in common: lower-middle-class roots, a love of the Talking Heads and Elvis Costello, alienation from our families, and a serious stint in psychotherapy. But more than any of that, we shared a passion for contemporary theater: August Wilson, John Patrick Shanley, Caryl Churchill, Athol Fugard.

When I talked about a play, I parsed the text as if I were studying Talmud: what the playwright meant and how the words conveyed that intention. Not Susan. She bored into characters: their motives, their behavior, what they said, and especially what they didn't say. She was after emotional truth. She waved her hands, Brooklyn-style, speaking rapidly, almost free-associating, as she pursued the secrets of the human heart. When she uncovered them, her delight was complete, almost childlike.

I got us tickets to see Sam Shepherd's *Curse of the Starving Class*. Afterward, we walked eighty blocks, dissecting the play scene by scene, before moving on to probe our own familial wounds. In a bid to impress her, I called on my cousin, a rock 'n' roll producer, for close-up seats at Tina Turner's next show. Tina was electrifying and, after dancing nonstop through her set, we gyrated for hours at the Limelight on the steamiest night of the summer, before shedding our clothes on Susan's floor and making love.

A couple of days later, as Susan left for France, she handed me a copy of *The Words to Say It*, an autobiographical novel by Marie Cardenal, a French Algerian writer, about a woman's recovery from mental illness. I spent the next two weeks devouring the book. Midway through, I came upon this line: "During the first part of analysis, I had won health and the freedom of my body. Now, slowly I was going to begin to discover my self."

Cardenal's words held up a mirror to my life. I'd been in psychotherapy twice a week for three years. Without a doubt, the process had helped transform me from basket case to functioning human. But I sensed a void where my self should have been, as if it were still pinned down on the invisible battlefield that Greenspan had identified years earlier.

By the time I finished reading *The Words to Say It*, I was ready to venture into that mysterious territory. I had no idea how to get there, much less what I'd find. But I sensed that this woman I'd just fallen for, the one who had given me this remarkable book, might be the one to go with me on that journey.

NOT LONG AFTER Susan returned, we found ourselves lying on my velvety gray sofa, a boxy Scandinavian thing I'd installed the year before to signal I was no longer a vagabond. With our bodies intertwined and faces inches apart, we compared notes on our sexual histories, that ritual exchange between two lovers.

"Did you ever sleep with a man?" she asked.

I tensed, wanting to disappear.

"I'm not sure," I mumbled.

"What do you mean you're not sure?"

Every cell of my being was screaming, *Don't tell her about Dan. You'll ruin everything.* "I don't know," I stalled. "I was young. Stuff happened. I'm not sure what it was." I forced a smile, hoping she'd move on. But Susan was a bloodhound for emotional secrets, and she'd caught the scent of something buried.

"What are you not telling me?" she asked, propping herself up on one elbow.

"I was experimenting. You know, a rite of passage."

"Hmm," she said, as I withdrew. "It feels like you're not here anymore."

There was no hiding from her. She coaxed it out of me, like a detective questioning a shaken victim at the crime scene: *Then what happened? What did he say? How did you feel?*

I'd shared most of this in therapy. But telling a woman, this woman, felt excruciating, like she was drilling directly into my well-spring of shame. I was broken and unlovable, and she was sure to dump me. But there was no judgment in her voice, only insistence and compassion.

When it was over she said, "I can't believe what he did to you, Stephen. He's a predator. Someone needs to stop him."

I'd had that thought many times since Camp Henry Horner, but no one had ever said it out loud. It sounded so . . . definitive. It left no room at all for Dan the good guy. I knew she was right, but I could barely bring myself to *talk* about Dan Farinella. How in God's name would I ever summon the courage to stop him?

Still, the world hadn't ended. Susan hadn't run screaming from the room. She held me close, and I floated in a strange, new reality: she knew my darkest shame.

SUSAN'S PREVIOUS BOYFRIEND was a chemist, a researcher at one of New York's leading cancer institutes. He mentioned that his colleague was making MDMA—Ecstasy—in their lab and asked if we wanted some. "It'll open your hearts," he promised.

I knew that Ecstasy, a psychoactive drug, had been banned that year, 1985, right before Susan and I met. A group of psychothera-pists said that MDMA made their patients more receptive to treat-ment, but Ronald Reagan's FDA decided that the drug had "no accepted medical use" and classified it as Schedule 1, along with heroin and cocaine. Still, who didn't want their heart opened?

We got two hits and brought the green capsules with us on a trip to San Francisco. After crashing with friends for a few days, we sought out a more secluded environment for our foray into Ecstasy. We drove around town and rejected a dozen hotels—too tacky, too corporate, too dark—before finding ourselves in a white, three-story Victorian Baroque in Pacific Heights. We chose a room with a four-poster bed, private balcony, and large tub.

Then we set about creating the most tranquil, romantic cocoon possible. We put on the white terry cloth robes we found in the closet, pulled the shades, lit a roaring fire in the fireplace, and drew a hot bath. Then we swallowed the green capsules with a swig of champagne and lay down on the bed.

Forty-five minutes later, my body was bathed in a warm glow. With each breath, my heart center expanded in sync with the uni-verse. I could tell from Susan's dilated pupils and the grin on her face that she was feeling it, too. She moaned and began massag-ing my shoulders. Her touch felt transcendent. I seemed invisibly melded to her—through her hands, her presence, her energy. Who needed sex when you had this kind of cosmic love bubble? Every-thing around me was crystalline, as if I were seeing the luminous nature of reality for the first time. How had I missed it before?

"Whoa," I said.

Susan got up to pour some champagne, then began rearranging the room to get our nest just so. When she was done, she sat down facing me, cocking her head this way and that, like a bird studying a worm. I had gone mute, as I so often did on psychedelics, unnerved by the powerful sensations in my body and suddenly scared of los-ing control.

"Where'd you go?" she asked.

I felt a flash of paranoia: Had she detected the dead zone inside me? My ex-girlfriends all said I was a stranger to the bitter end. They knew me no better on the last day than they had on the first. Susan had just gotten there at lightning speed.

"I don't want to be seen," I said. Ecstasy felt a lot like truth serum.

The subject of Dan Farinella didn't come up that day. That would have been too much too soon. I was learning to trust for the first time, and we both had to acquaint ourselves with this new realm of vulnerability. In the following months, we would return to MDMA over and over. Inside our cocoon, the drug would surface whatever needed to be known. Some wisdom function took over, aiming my new, truth-telling power at buried pieces of my past.

The second time we did Ecstasy, I began retracing my history with Dan. It was like moving through one haunted room after another, yet feeling utterly serene. I couldn't know what awaited me behind the next door, but as soon as I entered a memory—say, my cousin Dave walking in on me half-naked in Dan's bed—I felt compelled to relive it. I would replay the scene, plumbing the depths of fear and shame before my psyche allowed me to move on.

This was nothing like therapy, at least not like any therapy I'd done. Much of the processing happened in my own head, with Susan sitting opposite me. Sometimes, her presence alone was enough. Other times, I would check in verbally, share an insight, and ask for her response or a hug. In turn, I was present for her, because she had her own realms to explore.

During that second time on the drug, after two hours or so, I entered a room and recognized it as ground zero: the infirmary at Camp Ella Fohs. I was thirteen, lying on my back with my jeans pulled down, the bed's metal coils creaking beneath me. An enormous body obscured my view. Dan was roughly massaging my crotch. *You give up yet? You give up yet?*

I was a small, soft-bellied animal caught in the powerful grip of a half man, half beast with razor-sharp claws—the creature I had dreamed of in Songkhla. The beast was toying with me, preparing to kill me. Utterly helpless, I froze. A rush of endorphins flooded my brain, liberating my spirit from my doomed body. Nature was making sure I would die as painlessly as possible. I hovered above, waiting for death to come.

Ever since that afternoon in the infirmary I had rebuked myself for not telling Dan to stop. Why had I said nothing? On Ecstasy, the answer was stupidly obvious: there was no one there to speak. I had gone into shock. My front brain was off-line, my capacity for speech disabled. My thirteen-year-old body did its job of getting a hard-on, while my disembodied self watched from above, anesthetized, awaiting annihilation.

But, and here we get to the heart of the matter, death never came. At age thirty-one, I was still waiting, still braced for obliteration. Greenspan's words came back to me: "All these dreams you have about watching other people get set on fire—they're about you, the annihilation of *your* body. You're witnessing your own death." On that crisp fall day in the Camp Ella Fohs infirmary, hours before Jim shot the lake turtle, Dan Farinella took possession of my soul.

Yes, I staggered on. My body rose from the narrow metal bed and went about Stephen's life. I ate dinner with Dan in the Italian restaurant, pretending he hadn't destroyed me. I returned home the next night and posed as the same unbroken child my parents had sent off two days before. I went to school and acted the part of student and friend, desperate to get back inside my life but already aware that I could not.

Day after day, year after year, this haunted, undead person went through the motions. His existence was animated by a single purpose: making sure the truth would never be known. There was no need for Dan to swear me to secrecy, much less threaten me. In fact, I'd never been keeping a secret at all. It had been keeping *me*, paralyzing me with terror.

Staving off annihilation, containing the emotional chaos, was an all-day, all-night affair. It was Farinella who ruled both realms.

By night, he was the executioner, the killer who stalked me in my dreams. By day, he was the unseen hand behind my crime spree, my drug habit, my lunge for the train tracks. When my terror became too great, when the chaos and panic could no longer be contained, then my mind and body shut down.

Mrs. Pham, the Vietnamese fortune-teller, had been right: the evil spirit had been gaining on me for years. You can't outrun trauma.

Returning to the scene of the crime on Ecstasy was painful. But on the bedroom floor, in Susan's presence, I felt no impulse to turn away. On the contrary, I felt a primal pull toward the memory, as if it were demanding nothing less than my complete attention. Fear is what drives trauma underground, where it pulls the levers beneath conscious awareness. In the absence of fear, dissolved by MDMA, the potent truth of experience reveals itself.

"This happened to me," I said to Susan. "This actually happened."

And I didn't die. I survived.

If denial is the body's way of damming up what desperately needs to be felt, then the little green capsule opened the floodgates. The effects were cascading. When the drug wore off that night, I began crying. I cried for the boy who'd been enslaved by a sick man. I cried for how utterly alone I'd been throughout the years of my ordeal. I cried for the young man whose self-hate drove him to try to erase his life for a crime that was not his own.

I'D BEEN CERTAIN I would never tell my parents what Dan Farinella had done. But my certainty was starting to crack, and I found myself looking for excuses to avoid that unimaginable conversation.

"Why can't I resolve this on my own?" I asked Susan. "Do they really need to suffer, too?"

"You'll be sharing what's true, what's already there," she said. "Maybe that will change something, because right now you're stuck in hating them for what happened."

We decided to take MDMA again on the anniversary of my

father's death—the twenty-sixth anniversary to be exact. In the days leading up to it, I'd been filled with grief and foreboding.

As soon as the drug kicked in, I replayed the harrowing dream I'd had at Camp Ella Fohs when I was fifteen, the one about head-less soldiers. It was the dream that had prompted Farinella to con-sult with a psychoanalyst, who said it related to my father's loss of speech. On Ecstasy, this interpretation seemed so preposterous that I began laughing in amazement.

Susan was lying on her back, emitting deep, vibrating tones like a whale. We had veered off into our own worlds. I was in Ella Fohs, she was in the ocean.

"What are you laughing at?" she asked, breaking off from her song.

"Do you think when Farinella spoke to the psychoanalyst about my dream he told him he'd been sexually molesting me for two years?"

"I'm guessing that didn't come up," she said.

"Right. So he spoke to this famous shrink about my dead father and forgot to mention that he, my father figure, was raping me."

Had the psychoanalyst known the truth, perhaps he would have seen what Ecstasy now revealed: a boy, poisoned with shame, sum-moning his dead father to save him. From age seven I had believed my father watched over me, so he must have seen every unspeakable thing this man did. The soldier's missing head had never been about my father's power of speech. It was my certainty, and my despair, that my father was powerless to rescue me.

Then I recalled a fantasy, one I'd long forgotten. When I was thirteen I would lie in bed each night, the covers pulled over my head, and imagine my parents finding out about Dan. It would happen magically, without my needing to tell them. That way, he wouldn't kill us. They would just know and the nightmare would be over. Then they'd keep me at home and I'd never have to see Dan Farinella again.

Those few seconds of mental escape were my only reprieve. From the moment I came through the door after that first weekend, my life was in danger. My parents might discover the truth at any time. I spent my middle and high school years in that hypervigilant state, doing my best to disappear. With each day that my bedtime wish wasn't granted, I hated my parents more for not knowing.

Susan was right: I was still living the lie. Farinella had imprisoned our family inside that lie. I'd been blameless for remaining silent as a child, but now I was the only one who could free us.

# 25

I INVITED MYSELF TO MY parents' apartment for brunch. After we ate, I cleared the dishes. Ken washed them, as he always did, and I dried them, as I always did. While I toweled each plate, I repeated a mantra: *Be with the truth.*

We moved into the living room and took up our usual positions. They eyed me nervously, knowing I hadn't invited myself just to chat. I half expected to see Dan's hulking presence next to me. It was the same sofa he'd sat on the night he invited me to the Bahamas.

"You know I've been going to therapy for a few years," I began. "I don't need to tell you the details. But there's one thing that happened when I was a kid that you do need to know about. It's important you know the truth." I paused, a lump in my throat. "When I was thirteen, I was sexually molested by Dan Farinella. It went on for two years."

My mother's body went rigid, her face contorted in agony. She swiveled toward Ken, in search of something. Comfort? Shock? Ken seemed lost in his own world, as if he hadn't heard me. My mother turned back, her head bobbing from side to side.

She said nothing and I kept going. I described how Dan had engineered everything: how he drew me in that first summer, how he set up my mother by calling her, how he held me hostage in the infirmary, how he sat on this very sofa and conned them so he could abuse me in the Bahamas.

I went on for ten or fifteen minutes, leaving out the specifics of what he'd done to me sexually. I was prepared to tell them if they asked, but they never did. When I was done, we sat in silence.

"I had my suspicions about him," my mother finally said. "I thought I was just being crazy. It seemed too extreme." She looked to Ken, waiting this time for a response.

"It never occurred to me," he said.

"Mom, if you had suspicions, how come you never asked me anything?"

"Because you never said a word. My God, all those years. Why didn't you tell us, Stephen?"

*Why didn't you tell us?* Those five words would become her refrain, a kind of lament. I understood the logic—*We could have saved you!*—but I bristled at the question. My mother presumed that at thirteen, I would have confided in her, which I hadn't done since I was six. She had been my adversary, not my confidante. She also overlooked that her lionizing of Farinella had fostered my own trust in him. But I couldn't get into that just yet.

"I was in shock," I said. "I had no idea who Dan was or what he wanted. I was sure he'd kill me. There was no chance I would turn on him."

My mother looked confused, puzzling over something.

"He came to our home on the holidays," she said in disbelief. "He pretended to be our friend."

"That piece of shit," Ken spat out. His face finally registered the betrayal, like a man realizing he'd been shot.

"I don't know why I didn't do anything about my suspicions," my mother said. "We failed you. I'm so sorry, we failed you."

My mother took two steps toward me. I got up and wrapped my arms around her. She rested her head on my chest and wept, then kissed me over and over like I was a child.

"I feel like I have my son back," she said through her tears.

I held her tight, wanting to console her. It was awful, passing on this burden, transmitting such pain. But I felt lighter, almost weightless.

"You suffered alone for so long," my mother said. "I hope you can forgive us." But I wasn't ready to forgive, not yet. I waited for her to stop crying and return to her chair before saying more.

"I'd like you to think about your role in what happened," I said. "That's important to me. Then we can talk about it. Until then, I'm not sure what kind of relationship we have. It's all wrapped up in him and the lies. I can't do that anymore. I need to take care of myself first."

"Of course," Ken said.


THAT MY MOTHER had suspected Farinella in any way came as a total surprise. I discovered the source of her suspicion when I went to Connecticut to visit my cousin Dave. I'd scarcely seen him in the years since high school, and I wanted to begin repairing the relationship that Farinella had destroyed.

After I told Dave all that had happened at camp that last summer, he revealed that he had talked to his parents within days about finding me in Farinella's bed on the night of the car crash and my disappearance in its aftermath. He remembered: "The first thing my mother said was, 'Do you think Dan is molesting Stephen?' I wasn't entirely sure what that meant. I didn't know what to say."

It turned out that my aunt and uncle had tried to talk to my mother when the summer ended. So had Dave: "I said to her, 'Don't you want to know what happened at camp?' She said, 'Oh, you're just jealous that Dan spent more time with Stephen than with you. You're a troublemaker.'"

"That sounds like Farinella talking," I observed.

"He poisoned her against me," Dave said. "I was pegged as the kid in therapy, the one with problems. Farinella told her I was a liar, so she told my parents I lied about everything."

I recalled how my mother had made her loyalties clear when she invited the Farinellas for Rosh Hashanah that fall. Her ties to my aunt and uncle frayed badly after that. I had never understood their rift and it pained me. Delle and Harold had been my mother's mainstays since she married my father, and they'd always been like parents to me. Sixteen years later, my cousin was still stunned that my mother had refused to hear him out.

Dan Farinella was a bomb that went off in the extended family, leaving no relationship unscathed.

I CALLED MY mother to say I wouldn't be coming for Passover. I needed time to think about things. The conversation with Dave was fresh in my mind, and I asked her to reflect on why she had trusted Dan so completely, so blindly.

"I tried, Stephen, but I just can't dredge up the past anymore. The day you told us about it, I thought I was losing my mind." She wanted only to survive, to escape the pain, she said.

"You may keep your sanity, Mom, but you're going to lose me if you don't tell me what you were thinking and feeling while this was happening. You were there."

"I know and we feel so guilty. But most of this was Dan. He did this."

"That's too easy," I responded. "I took on a stranger as a father figure. I became part of his family. I went on their vacations. Are you telling me you had nothing to do with that?"

"I probably did. I had my own problems from childhood. All of that gets involved. I see that now. So much of it is unconscious."

But she would say no more. She sounded broken.


WEEKS LATER, MY mother asked me to come see them. She seemed tense, and when I arrived they were somber.

"We wanted to tell you that we went to see a therapist," she said.

"I'm glad to hear that. And?"

"He thinks there's nothing we could have done since you never told us anything."

"Oh, so you're off the hook then?" I asked. "That's convenient."

"What could we have done, Stephen? We didn't know."

"So it was my fault for not telling you. You had no responsibility for sending me off with someone you had just met for the first time. This is just a wild guess, but it sounds like your therapist has never dealt with sexual abuse before. Are you going back to this person?"

"No. We didn't think there was anything else to discuss."

I covered my face with both hands.

"Wow, I'm speechless," I said.

"Something else came up that we wanted to ask you about," my mother went on. "Didn't you go to work for Dan at Camp Henry Horner before graduate school?"

"Yeah, I did."

"We're struggling to understand that. You weren't a kid anymore. Why did you do that?"

I feared this question. A decade later, I'd know how to answer it. Like so many victims of childhood sexual abuse, I had been held physically and emotionally hostage. Farinella had forged a bond of dependence, steeped in terror, that felt indispensable to my survival well into adulthood. But in that moment, as my mother waited for an answer, I felt only shame.

"I thought Dan was my friend," I said. "He was some kind of

saint because everyone said he was, including you. Facing the truth would have been much too scary. Can you understand that?"

"I think so."

"I can tell you one thing," I said. "Some part of me wanted to uncover the truth. I went to Henry Horner and saw he was still molesting boys. I'm not saying I planned that. I didn't. But he and I had unfinished business. I had to catch him in the act to wake up. So I'm glad I went. At least I confronted him. It's taken me another eight years, but I'm finally ready to try to stop him. I don't know how, but I'll figure it out, because I sure as hell don't see anyone else doing it."

"You know we support you in that. But the most important thing is that we get to see you and be a family," she said. "You could have called on the holiday. That's not how a son behaves."

"What does being a son entail exactly?"

"You're being disingenuous," she said, sharply.

"No, I'm not. I don't know what you expect of me."

"A son is someone who cares whether you're dead or alive, calls on your birthday, spends time on holidays."

"I guess that's not me. I'm not going to pretend to be that son anymore. That was bullshit. This family has been nothing but lies for twenty years—pretending I had no birth father, pretending we had no past, pretending I wasn't getting abused. I've built a small life where I can be honest, be myself. I want people in that life who will face what actually happened. You've made it clear with your one therapy session that you're not willing to do that. You want to act like it's all behind us. It's not behind us."

"Well, what do you expect us to do now that you've laid this on us, Stephen?"

"Laid this on you?" I felt the blood rush to my face and, for the first time in my life, I began screaming at my mother. "That slime bag was sucking my dick for two years! I was his slave. You have no fucking clue what that is. No one does except someone who's been through it. I stopped being your son the first weekend you sent me away with that psychopath. Don't you see that? I'm not saying it was your fault. But you stopped being my parents that weekend. I hated you for not knowing, and I was terrified of what you'd do to me if you ever found out. What kind of family is that? Tell me!"

My mother collapsed in her chair, devastated. I was shaking uncontrollably.

"You never told us," she said softly. "How could we be your parents if you never told us?"

"I don't know. I really don't. It feels like you just want to move on and have it all go away. But it doesn't go away."

"So we're not your parents anymore? We've been trying to help you but you don't want help. What are we supposed to do? Your life may be hellish but you're making it hellish for other people, too."

I wanted to scream. Instead, I covered my face with my hands again.

"We're sick," she went on. "We have heart problems. Do I have to spell it out for you? Our life is finite. Have you ever once asked how we feel? You don't care. After we're gone, you're going to have to live with it."

"You're not scaring me, Mom. You've been threatening to die since I told you I was moving to the yeshiva. But I see you're still going strong."

"I'm not trying to scare you," she said. "I'm just telling you the reality. I know that's how I'd feel about it if the roles were reversed."

"I'm not you."

"So you'd rather we didn't bother you?"

"Yes. I'd rather you not bother me." She winced. "I know you're good people," I said. "I know you think you're trying to help. But the only way you can help is by looking at your role in letting that monster into our lives. Until then, we have nothing to talk about."

# 26

I HAD NO IDEA HOW to go about stopping Dan Farinella. I decided to start by learning more about his employer, so I called the Jewish Community Center in Pittsburgh and asked them to send me their program guide.

As I read through the material I felt queasy. It seemed so familiar. The center's Emma Kaufmann Camp, like Ella Fohs and Henry Horner, had been created nearly a century before as a "fresh air retreat" for Jewish children, in this case to escape Pittsburgh's summer heat and pollution. The rustic, outdoor experience had been a fixture of life for generations of kids from the tight-knit Jewish neighborhood of Squirrel Hill.

Farinella had been directing the camp, which was just across the state line in West Virginia, since 1982. The upcoming summer, 1986, would be his fifth. I wanted to make it his last.

My therapist suggested that I file a complaint with the New York State Office of Professional Discipline. They had issued Farinella's license to practice social work and they had the power to revoke it, which, presumably, would make it impossible for him to keep his job as the supervisor of youth programs in Pittsburgh.

An official at the New York agency explained that I'd need to fill out a form and provide the names of other victims in the state if possible. He warned me against notifying the Jewish Community Center. "This guy can sue you for slander if he wants to defend himself," he said.

The most promising way to find victims would be contacting kids I'd known at camp, but that abuse would have happened in Connecticut. I was eligible to file a complaint in New York only because Farinella had molested me that one time in the Catskills.

I decided to call Vinny, the former maintenance man at Camp Henry Horner. Vinny lived in Chicago, but he'd seen campers and staff revolve around Farinella for more than a decade. He might have a lead in New York.

Vinny was happy to talk with me. The whole thing weighed on his soul, he said. He recalled the four other employees at Henry Horner who had suspicions back in 1978—the ones he'd told me about. But now he added a fifth: Adam, who had been a counselor that summer and worried to Vinny about a boy in his bunk.

"Find Adam," Vinny said. "He's from New York. He told me Danny abused a friend of his when they were kids."

After a chain of calls, I located Adam, now in graduate school for clinical psychology. He recalled that Farinella had been spending a lot of one-on-one time with a boy in his cabin in 1978. Adam confronted him, accusing him of having sexual contact with the boy, and Farinella didn't deny it. Instead, he assured Adam he'd be moving to a desk job after camp ended, the same line he'd used with me that summer. Adam said he was still wrestling with his guilt about the boy, whether he'd done enough.

He also confirmed that Farinella had molested his friend years earlier in New York when they were in middle school. When he told me the name, my heart sank—I knew Eric from Camp Ella Fohs. I'd been to his home and met his mother. Now I learned that after the boy's father died, Farinella had befriended the mother and begun abusing him. I felt sick.

Adam was reluctant to pass on Eric's phone number until I said I was determined to stop Farinella. "Maybe you'll inspire Eric to act," he said. "But don't be surprised if he doesn't want to replay his past right now."

Before we hung up, Adam told me something else: he'd spoken with former students from Oyster Bay High who believed that Farinella had been forced to resign his job there in 1971. He gave me the names of three administrators who would know the real story.

That night, I lay in bed imagining how relieved I'd be to join forces with another victim. But when I fell asleep, I dreamed I was a child on trial, facing an accuser who held the power of life and death.

I couldn't get out of bed the next morning and called in sick to work. Susan urged me to follow through with my plan, and I made myself dial Eric's number. When I got his answering machine, I left an innocuous message about wanting to catch up.

Eric got back to me that same evening. Of course he remembered me from Ella Fohs, he said. I told him why I'd gotten in touch, leaving out what I'd learned from Adam. Dan Farinella had sexually abused me, I said, and I was going to file a formal complaint. I wanted to know whether he'd ever heard similar stories.

"Everyone knew Dan grabbed boys in the crotch," Eric said. "But he never went further than that with me." He was going right to denial, as Adam had warned.

"Would you be willing to say you saw him grab boys?" I asked.

"I'm sorry, I can't," he said. "This brings up a really painful part of my life. I respect what you're doing. It's just too painful."

"Can you tell me why?" I asked.

"Dan was there the day after my father died."

"Why was Dan there?"

"I don't want to talk about that."

"Of course. I understand. But you knew what Dan was up to with boys?"

"Yeah, I know what Dan did to other kids. He picked the weakest ones and used them. I was just fortunate he never did that to me."

I changed tack, sharing some of the details of my own molestation. I thought it might help him open up.

"I never realized that Dan was actually sexual with kids," he said when I finished. "I didn't know it went that far," contradicting what he had just told me.

Since he had witnessed Farinella groping children, he might be called to testify at some point, I said.

"I'd testify if I were forced to, but please don't call me anymore."

I hung up the phone, despondent. Adam had been right. Who wanted to replay their history with Farinella? Talking to Eric was like talking to the old Stephen, the one who'd lied and denied so expertly. And what was wrong with a little denial?

Within hours, though, I hated Farinella with a new intensity. The more I thought about the call, the more I saw a predator who specialized in crushing fatherless children. I hated the web of fear, shame, and silence he'd spun around each of us. I hated the system that propped him up, letting him move stealthily from camp to camp, preying on fresh groups of unsuspecting boys.

The thirteen-year-old in me wanted to give up, to lie down and die. But Eric reminded me how it felt to be buried alive: mute and frozen in terror. I was done with that. I was innocent. As long as Farinella worked with kids, I was going to hound him. If no one else would join me, then so be it.

I FILLED OUT the New York State Complaint Form, including a statement about my own abuse. I left Eric's name out of it, but I did give Adam's, with his permission. I listed Farinella's employers since 1966: the administrators at Oyster Bay High School and at three Jewish agencies. They could provide information about any complaints, as well as explain why Farinella had left his previous jobs.

I concluded by invoking the children in imminent danger. "It is incumbent upon the State of New York to protect those children by revoking Mr. Farinella's license and taking all possible measures to end his social work career in other states as well."

The night after mailing the material, I dreamed I was back at Ella Fohs as an adult. A horror-movie version of Farinella—gigantic, grizzled, and bloodthirsty—had trapped me in a small cabin. He was out of his mind with rage. He was going to make me suck him off, then kill me. He knew I'd betrayed him. I didn't want to die. *But at least I filed the complaint*, I thought in the dream.

I spent an awful month waiting for a response until an investigator named Bill Klaus called me. "Your case is very credible and well documented," he said, before asking me to confirm that there had been an incident in New York State. We discussed the episode at the Homowack Lodge in 1969. Klaus thanked me and said he'd be contacting Farinella. He was confident he could "break" him. He was willing to go to Pennsylvania to do it.

Klaus's next call came a few weeks later, and now he sounded sheepish, apologetic. His superiors had decided to "green stripe" the case, meaning they wouldn't pursue it. Farinella hadn't been licensed to practice in New York for ten years, so he was beyond their reach. "If he tries to register here again we'll nail him," he said, in a pathetic attempt at bravado.

"That makes no sense," I insisted. "All you need to do is start an investigation and contact the Jewish Community Center in Pittsburgh. That should be enough to stop him. I can't do that. You can."

Klaus didn't budge. "The bottom line is, the citizens of New York are safe from this guy," he said. I gasped at this cynical logic. Klaus conceded that he didn't agree with his superiors and, to prove his goodwill, he would contact Farinella himself and "try to extract an admission."

If only. Klaus did speak to Farinella, he reported back, telling him there were problems with his license in New York, that there were allegations of child abuse. Did Farinella want to talk about them? No, he did not. Case closed. Klaus, embarrassed, apologized to me yet again. His parting advice: contact the licensing agency in Pennsylvania, which is what I did next.

The official I reached at the Pennsylvania Bureau of Professional and Occupational Affairs listened to my story, then explained they couldn't do anything about it. Social workers didn't need to be licensed or registered in Pennsylvania. Why not try the state attorney general's office? I did, and they told me to call the Office of Chief Counsel in the Department of Public Welfare, the agency in charge of enforcing the state's child abuse law. It sounded promising.

After getting through to the right person, I explained the situation for the third time that day: a social worker who had sexually abused me and other boys was now working with children in Pennsylvania. The official thanked me and said that Act 33, passed just the year before, was meant to handle exactly this situation. The law screened professionals working with children.

"That's great," I said. "How does it work?"

I'd need to speak to an attorney in the Office of Children, Youth and Family, he said. So I dialed their number and left a message. Eleven days later, the assistant counsel called me back and yet again I explained the imminent danger posed by one Daniel Farinella. By this point, my twenty-year tale was a compelling sixty-second elevator pitch.

"I'm sorry," she said when I finished, "but in Pennsylvania, social workers are not responsible for a child's welfare."

"No, no, maybe you misunderstood," I persisted. "He is definitely responsible for the welfare of hundreds of children."

"That may be," she countered, "but social workers are not subject to employment screening under Act 33 unless their job is in child care services, like day care. And even if they were, the law is only triggered by an act of abuse in this state, not by the threat of abuse or by abuse that happened in another state."

"So if New York State confirmed he had abused children and they revoked his license, that wouldn't matter to the state of Pennsylvania?"

"That's correct."

I was getting the picture now. New York wouldn't alert Pennsylvania to a child predator in its midst and, even if it did, Pennsylvania didn't want to know.

I took one last swing.

"Are there any laws at all, at the state or county level, to protect children against an imminent threat like this one?"

"No," she said. "But I'll be happy to send you a copy of Act 33." We hung up.

I suppressed an urge to throw the phone at the wall. "Fucking Farinella!" I screamed. The guy was untouchable, protected by some invisible shield. For the first time, it dawned on me that there might not be any legal means for stopping him. I'd have to go directly to the Jewish Community Center, as I'd been warned not to do. I'd send a letter to every member of their board and demand they protect the children in their care.

But alerting them might not solve the problem. Farinella would just move on to the next Jewish camp. For all I knew, someone like me had blown the whistle before, which is why he'd left the other camps.

I'd have to stop him myself, physically. I'd strangle him. Or I'd show up with a concealed weapon, extract his confession, then blow his head off. Better yet: torture him first.

These fantasies seemed self-explanatory to me: revenge was sweet. But my therapist wasn't buying it. He said my homicidal urge reflected a deep and abiding fear: I had to get him before he got me.

I noticed I was latching the chain lock on my front door, a precaution I'd never taken before. I was scanning the subway platform, checking behind the shrubbery at the entrance to my building, peeking into the stairwell by the elevator. Manhattan had turned into Camp Ella Fohs and Farinella could be anywhere.

As for the pain, it seemed indelible, like a tattoo, but going all the way in, a thousand layers deep. It had polluted the wellspring of my sexuality and selfhood, that pool of childhood innocence that many people never even notice, because why would they? One drop of poison can contaminate those waters forever. That's where he had injected shame and self-loathing. I wouldn't be rid of them if I lived a million years.

One day in therapy, I paused for effect and said, "Killing him is the rational thing to do. It may be the only way to stop him. And it's the only way I can respect myself."

My therapist saw that I was serious, or serious enough.

"You hold all the cards, Stephen. He's the one who should be scared. Don't play into his hands."

FIVE MONTHS INTO my quest, I was flailing. Then I had an idea to try the National Center for Missing and Exploited Children. It had been founded two years earlier by an act of Congress in the wake of several, high-profile child abductions. Like most people, I knew them as the group that put photos of missing kids on the side of milk cartons, but the center was also the national clearinghouse for information about victims of sexual abuse.

One of the center's founders, Jim Scutt, called me back the same day and I knew right away I'd found my guy. Jim had the no-bullshit demeanor of a detective, which had been his previous job, investigating homicides and crimes against children.

"First things first," Scutt said. "You need to get the FBI involved."

"The FBI?" I thought he was joking.

"Absolutely. From what you've told me, this guy was transporting minors like you across state lines. That's a violation of the Mann Act. I want you to call Ken Ruffo at the bureau. He's with their Sexual Exploitation of Children Task Force in New York. I'll give you his number. Tell him I sent you."

"Two more things. Do not contact this guy's employer. You could face a countersuit. Leave it to law enforcement. Also, you're going to need cooperation from other victims. Without that, it will be tough for the police and FBI to move forward."

"Got it. Victims."

At the FBI, Ken Ruffo asked me for the basic facts, then said I'd be hearing from someone on his task force. By the end of that day I had a meeting scheduled at the FBI office in Queens. Now, I was energized. If the FBI needed victims, then I was going to find them. Even better, I was no longer restricted to abuse that had occurred in New York—the more states, the better.

There had to be a far-flung network of men who'd been abused by Farinella. Who was in that silent brotherhood? I began conjuring the names of the boys who'd been at camp with me, calling up their faces, one by one.

## 27

AT THE TOP OF MY contact list was Leonard, a family friend who'd gone to Ella Fohs for several summers. Leonard and I had spent a good deal of time together as kids. He was now a pediatrician at Long Island Jewish Medical Center but I hadn't talked to him in more than a decade. I steeled myself before dialing his number.

After we chitchatted for a minute, he said, "So the suspense is killing me. What are you calling about?"

I gave him a slightly longer version of my usual account. When I finished he said, "Steve, two years ago, a friend from camp told me the same story about Farinella." Here I was, five minutes into my first call and I'd found another victim. It had never occurred to me it might be this easy.

Leonard hadn't been sure if he could believe his friend's story, he said. It just seemed too outrageous.

"But the warning signs were there," I said. "Don't you remember Dan's behavior at the waterfront: fighting with boys, grabbing them by the balls, yanking their bathing suits down?"

"Yeah, of course. But that was just horseplay. It was so common then. My junior high gym teacher did the same thing."

"That wasn't horseplay, Leonard. That was sexual. Dan wanted us to *think* it was horseplay." In the quiet that followed I could practically hear him, a respected pediatrician, recalibrating his memories.

"You're right," he finally said. "I'm sorry. I want to help. Let me call my friend and see if he'll talk to you."

My phone rang fifteen minutes later and when I answered I heard a voice from long ago.

"Hey, Steve. It's Bruce. From Camp Ella Fohs."

For a moment I was too bewildered to speak. I'd known Bruce as a camper and then we'd worked together in the kitchen. He was a popular guy, someone I'd looked up to. Some part of my brain couldn't compute that Dan had done to him what he did to me.

"Holy shit, Bruce. I had no idea."

"Yeah, I know. Same here," he said. "It's weird, huh?"

Our stories were remarkably similar. Farinella had infiltrated his family, taken him to camp in the off-season, and bought him gifts he craved. "I was so needy," Bruce said.

I began wondering how Farinella had coordinated all this.

"Dan always got me in the mansion," I said. "On the first floor in that secret room he had. What about you?"

"Never in the mansion, for sure in the infirmary. He took me there during the winter. And he'd bring me there every summer before camp started."

"But you don't remember where it happened during the summer?"

"No. Honestly, Steve, for something that went on for so long, it's amazing how little I can recall. I've blocked a lot."

"That's understandable," I said.

"But I do remember who else was in the room."

"What do you mean?" I asked.

"Sometimes Dan would abuse two of us at the same time."

I hadn't seen this coming. It was so at odds with the isolation of my experience.

"Can you tell me who?" I asked.

"Remember Andy?"

"Of course." Andy was a great softball player, one of my regular rivals on the field.

"Kevin, too. Dan abused us together before camp started." Kevin was a local boy who worked in the kitchen.

"He had a friend named Eddie, right?"

"Yeah, Dan was abusing Eddie, too," Bruce said. "Not with me. But definitely."

"Jesus Christ. Anyone else?"

"Charlie."

"Charlie?" He was a quiet kid who washed dishes. Then I remembered something: "Charlie followed Dan to Camp Henry Horner in 1972. I was surprised. Like, why would he go all the way to Illinois to wash dishes?"

"Now you know why," Bruce said. "I heard he killed himself."

"That bastard," I said. I recalled a bit of news that had seemed innocuous at the time. Dan wrote to me saying he'd sent Charlie home from Henry Horner because he had some kind of breakdown. He also reported that most of the kitchen boys from New York fell apart and left. In light of what I now knew, it was a chilling statement, suggesting that Charlie had not been the only victim who'd followed Dan to Illinois. How many breakdowns had there been, how many suicides? God knows, I'd almost wound up in the deceased column of Farinella's ledger.

"There were others," Bruce went on. "I could just tell from who was on the scene with Dan. Do you remember Walter, the maintenance guy? He was kind of like Indiana Jones?"

"How could I forget?" I said. "He had no teeth and tied mice to his car antenna."

"Right. He walked in on Dan while he was abusing one of the kitchen boys. We all knew. It wasn't a secret."

"I must have been on fucking Mars," I said. "How did I miss all this?" That day at camp when one of the kitchen boys said "Dan's a homo," I had frozen, like a possum. I was so scared of being found out, I'd barely noticed everyone else shrugging.

"Do you remember how the abuse ended?" I asked Bruce.

"Yeah. After three years, I couldn't get a hard-on anymore. I wanted out. I remember thinking, how the hell do I get out?"

Bruce had told his wife and said it had affected his ability to trust. He felt much safer with women than with men. But he struggled to articulate the emotional fallout and was adamant that Farinella should get treatment, not jail time. That sounded familiar—it was what I had once told myself. As for signing a statement, he wanted to help, but only if he could remain anonymous, scared that people at his job would find out.

Still, I had the names of five guys now. Bruce promised to get in touch with Andy, Kevin, and Eddie; I'd contact the others he'd mentioned. I wasn't working alone anymore.

Special Agent Steve Braus of the FBI sat in a cramped, fluorescent-lit office at 9525 Queens Boulevard. As a kid, I had watched *The FBI* on TV in black and white every Sunday night. In that show, Inspector Lewis Erskine and his G-men always solved the crime in twenty-nine minutes, with justice meted out in the final sixty seconds. Hoping this would be like one of those TV episodes, I came prepared as the best informant in history.

I walked Braus through Farinella's employment record: two decades working with thousands of children in six different states. And that didn't include the years he had worked in the Bronx and at Camp Willoway before Camp Ella Fohs. My calls had turned up ten likely victims in short order—there must have been many more. Braus made copies of my documents, asked questions, and took notes.

He explained the Mann Act: the statute of limitations was seven years, so Farinella couldn't be prosecuted for crimes committed at Camp Ella Fohs. But that law *would* come into play if he were transporting kids from Pittsburgh to the camp in West Virginia during the off-season, which was likely, given his pattern. Braus would use my information, he said, but there was no need for testimony from past witnesses. The FBI would need current cases with boys in Pittsburgh. He'd start by running a state-by-state check to see if Farinella had a criminal record.

Before leaving, I mentioned that some of us thought that Farinella should receive treatment rather than jail time. Braus shot me a no-nonsense, G-man look.

"This would be a straight criminal case, Stephen. Treatment is ineffective anyway. You were victims. Feeling guilty about it or wanting to help this guy is just an extension of thinking you did something wrong. You did nothing wrong. He's a criminal. End of story."

God, I loved the FBI.


BRUCE AND I worked the phones. Even if past victims couldn't help the case, we wanted to find more of them, if only to increase pressure on law enforcement. There was something else, too: I was becoming obsessed. As the scale of Farinella's crime began to sink in, I couldn't stop compiling lists of camper names, mapping their connections, and puzzling over how to get to them. I needed to know who had suffered as I had. It made me feel less alone. And I wanted to hear, twenty years on, how they were coping, or weren't, with the deep shame and enduring fear.

Andy told Bruce that he'd never talked about the abuse to anyone, not even his wife, and didn't want to discuss it. Kevin warned him to never call again. Eddie refused to speak to him at all.

I got hold of a guy I knew from camp who had lived in Oyster Bay and lost his father when he was a boy. Yes, he said, Dan had taken him to camp in the off-season a few times.

"He tried something once and then I avoided him for a while until he got the idea."

It seemed improbable that Farinella would have brought a boy to camp multiple times and *not* abused him. I asked if he knew of others in Oyster Bay who might have been molested, but he balked at giving me names.

"Look, Steve," he said, "everyone at Oyster Bay High knew Dan had a problem."

JESSE WAS FROM the Bronx and had gone to Ella Fohs forever. He'd known everyone, or it always seemed that way to me. If there had been a most popular camper award, Jesse would have won it.

When I tracked him down, he wasn't surprised to hear my story. A friend had confided in him years earlier. "I keep telling my buddy: 'We know where Farinella lives. Let's go get that son of a bitch.'"

Farinella had tried trapping Jesse, too, when he was fourteen, inviting him to the director's cabin, then lying down on the bed, propped up on one elbow. He asked Jesse to come sit with him. But Jesse's mother had been so concerned about predators, she'd warned him to be on guard against older men. Feeling uneasy, he blurted out that he had to go to dinner and quickly left.

"Later on," he said, "I noticed that Danny was taking certain boys to Candlewood Lake to go out on a motorboat. It seemed weird, like why are they getting the VIP treatment? I'd seen him groping boys in the pool, but when he spent so much time alone with certain guys, I knew something was up. That's when I started referring to all of you as the Penii Brothers Club."

"Penii—as in plural of penis?"

"Yeah. That's what I called you guys."

*You guys.* I was in the club. Jesse wasn't.

I'd completely forgotten about Farinella taking me to Candlewood Lake. Clearly, he had upgraded me to motorboat status at some point. During my ten long weeks cloistered in the mansion, moving from attic to dungeon to Ella's parlor like a restless ghost, I thought I was special, the chosen one. Instead I was just ordinary, one more member of the Penii Brothers Club.

Farinella must have spent a hundred hours with me that summer. Yet he was also abusing half the kitchen staff and any number of campers. My mind balked at the logistics of all that molestation: the stalking, the trapping, the lying, the damage control when he got caught. How in God's name did he have time for anything else? The director's job was just a pretext for a staggering amount of sexual assault. He had turned Camp Ella Fohs into a top-down criminal enterprise.

MICHAEL HAD BEEN at camp with me for several years, and Bruce and I added him to our "likely" list. When I reached him at work in New York, he remembered me right away.

"Why are you calling?" he asked, warily. By this point, I understood that the question was really about the person on the other end, and I replied more like a private investigator than an abashed victim. Had he ever heard anything or did he know someone?

The line was silent for what seemed a long time.

"Yeah . . . I know something," he said. "But please don't call me here again. And not at home, either."

Pressed, he agreed to meet, and suggested St. John the Divine on Amsterdam Avenue. It seemed a strange place for a reunion.

"You sure you don't want to meet for lunch?" I asked.

"I won't be hungry," he replied.

The next day, I waited on the stone steps in front of the imposing Gothic Revival cathedral, surveying the stream of worshippers and tourists. I recognized Michael at once in his jeans and button-down shirt. It was the same twelve-year-old boy, hiding inside the body of a man. He headed right for me. When we shook hands, I felt a fraternal bond, like I were bringing in a spy from the cold.

"This is hard," he began. "I didn't sleep at all last night. I've never discussed this with anyone. I thought it was all behind me." He was fidgety, his shoes *tap-tapping* on the step below.

"Dan was like a second father to me," Michael went on. "He was always kind, always free with the gifts and the money. And he had those magazines and stuff. He told me it was harmless, what he did to me. He said my sexuality was already formed."

"Yeah, I got that speech," I said. "Freud said it was all okay." Michael forced a smile.

Sure enough, his father had died when he was little. Dan took him for a walk at camp early on, asking about his family, his friends, his problems. Picking the right kid, one who couldn't bear losing another father, meant the secret would keep itself.

"I feel like it was my fault," he went on. "I mean, maybe one time I could understand. But how could I have let him do that to me for years? I could have said no . . ." His voice trailed off and he stared blankly at the step below.

I asked if he'd ever told his wife.

"No," he said, his eyes growing wide. "That's out of the question. Whenever it comes into my mind, I just shove it back down. So far it's worked. I mean, I'm normal. Maybe in ten or twenty years, I'll be fucked up. But when you called, I felt relieved. I always thought I was the only one. It never occurred to me there were others. I want to help. I just don't want my name to get out."

We were all scared of Dan, I said. I told him about the nightmares Bruce and I had about Farinella threatening us.

"I don't remember physical fear," Michael said. "I do remember being really scared that Dan would tell my parents what I did."

"What *you* did? It's funny, isn't it? We were all terrified of getting caught. We never thought he was the one who should have been scared. He's the criminal. Let him answer for his crimes. I'm tired of carrying his shame."

Michael looked stunned, as if what I'd just said were both true and completely insane.

"I need time to think about it," he said, when I asked him to sign a statement. "I want to help you, I do. But I need a couple of months."

"This could be over by then," I pleaded. "Try to think about it this week. Please."

We stood up to leave but I could tell he had something else to say.

"What?" I asked.

"If you do go forward, watch out for Dan. He'll come after you."


BRUCE WAS STILL reluctant to sign a statement, but one night he called me and read two different versions. The first said he had seen Farinella "grab kids in their crotch." The second one began, "I was sexually abused by Daniel Farinella." If I wanted to go with the second, it would have to be anonymous.

"I guess you think I'm holding back," he said.

He *was* holding back, I insisted. "I understand the fear, but if we keep living in fear we're just perpetuating the silence. That's what Dan's counting on." Bruce was especially worried about the myth that boys who are abused go on to abuse other children. But if we weren't willing to speak up and dispel those fallacies, I said, we couldn't expect anyone's views to change.

Bruce said he'd talk about it with his wife and decide over the weekend. Well before that, he called again.

"I had a nightmare last night," he blurted out. "You and I were in a room with Dan and his secretary. She said she'd received requests for information about Dan. He pulled out a knife and threatened you. He made you suck him off. I ran out of the room and tried to call the police. I couldn't get through. I couldn't help you."

"What do you make of it?" I asked.

"It doesn't need psychoanalyzing," Bruce replied. "It's a sign I have to join forces with you. I'll sign the statement saying Dan abused me. I'll do whatever you need me to do."

In a note handwritten on lined memo paper, Bruce confirmed

that Farinella had abused him at least ten times at Camp Ella Fohs. He requested confidentiality but was willing to testify in court, he wrote, adding that we were "determined to prevent this disturbed man" from working with children. "We have made you aware of this tragic situation. Please start the investigation now."

Leonard, Jesse, and Adam provided witness statements that vouched for the victims and corroborated Farinella's predatory behavior at Ella Fohs and Henry Horner. Leonard, the pediatrician, provided his on the letterhead of the children's hospital at Long Island Jewish Medical Center. Jesse wrote as the experienced director of a nursing service.

Then a letter came from Michael. It had no return address on the envelope. About Dan Farinella he wrote, "I must also admit to being sexually abused by him when I knew him as a camp director approximately fifteen years ago." He called for action by the criminal justice system. "Nothing else has stopped him from these abuses in the past."

## 28

Agent Braus at the FBI would be interested in my progress, I figured, and I wanted to check on his investigation. But his tone had changed. He had run a check on Farinella in New York and couldn't share the results. My victim statements would serve no purpose, he reiterated. The file was now with the Pittsburgh field office and out of his hands.

They wouldn't want to talk to me, he added. "No prosecutor or agent is going to include you in any discussions or strategies. You're a potential witness, that's all. Unless you can turn up a current case, you won't be very welcome."

My fantasy of the FBI saving the day was fading fast. Maybe the Pittsburgh bureau would jump on investigating Farinella and come to me for more information, but I wasn't going to sit around waiting for the phone to ring.

Josh's sister, Erica, who was a criminal defense attorney, advised me to find someone in the Allegheny County District Attorney's Office in Pittsburgh. She knew a well-connected private investigator in Pennsylvania, who in turn gave me the number for someone who could open doors: an ex-DA for Allegheny County. I left a message but got no reply. A week later and still nothing. Even worse, I was out of names to call.


I HAD BEGUN seeing my mother again every couple of weeks. We never talked about the abuse itself—it was clear she couldn't confront our past—but she encouraged my quest to bring Farinella to justice, and I welcomed her involvement. We connected in the realm of the practical: strategizing, networking, following up. She made suggestions and had good instincts. Now I told her I seemed to have hit a dead end.

"Sara-Alyce Wright," my mother said emphatically. "Call her."

She'd been telling me this for weeks, and I'd stubbornly resisted. Sara-Alyce Wright had created and overseen the program for youth and families in the Black housing project in Freeport where my mother had worked and I volunteered as a kid. We only ever referred to her, respectfully, by her full name.

She was now the executive director of the National YWCA and was, as my mother liked to remind me, at the top of the social work field. I couldn't imagine how Sara-Alyce Wright could get me to the Pittsburgh DA, and it would be a painful conversation—she believed social workers were doing God's work. But I had nowhere else to go.

"A social worker? Jesus wept!" Sara-Alyce Wright cried out when I dropped the news on her. "This breaks my heart, Stephen. But we're going to make it right. Yes we are. We're going to make this right."

It turned out that she was from Pennsylvania and had gotten her master's degree at the University of Pittsburgh. "I'm going to give you the number for Dr. Barbara Shore. She helped start the Center for Victims of Violent Crimes in Pittsburgh. She'll get you to the DA. I can promise you that."

I reached Dr. Shore a few days later. "The Jewish Community

Center is a good organization," she said. "But they'll probably try to hide this." Her bluntness surprised me, but no one knew this terrain better than Shore. An esteemed professor of social work, she had just chaired a commission that issued a blistering report on the failure of the Allegheny County welfare office to investigate the sexual abuse of children, prompting a shakeup of the agency.

Dr. Shore introduced me to her colleague at the Center for Victims, Izzie Rideout, to whom I recited the Farinella saga yet again: six states, countless victims, still working with children. She listened, then waved what seemed like a magic wand, connecting me to Anthony Krastek, the head of the Crimes Persons Unit in the Allegheny County DA's Office—the victims' attorney, as she called him.

Just before we hung up, Rideout offered a piece of advice: "Leave this to the DA's office. Do not approach the Jewish Community Center. You could be open to a civil suit if he's somehow found not guilty." She wasn't quite done with me, though. "What you're doing is very admirable," she said. "When you were abused there were no agencies around that were concerned with the victim. Now there are. We need to do better. A lot of people would throw up their hands and say your case is ancient history, but this is about the kids who are getting hurt right now. We need to act."

THE VICTIMS' ATTORNEY, Tony Krastek, was ready for my call and wanted to see the materials as soon as possible, urging me to send them to the DA's office in West Virginia as well. He would review the background and then share it with detectives in the Pittsburgh police department. They had the ability to investigate the Jewish Community Center quietly and talk to children if necessary.

It sure seemed necessary to me. Otherwise, how would they find current victims? But I had no idea how the DA went about building cases and, besides, I was just grateful they were taking action.

In the cover letter that I sent with statements from past victims and witnesses, I provided a promising lead at Emma Kaufmann Camp: the man who'd been Farinella's assistant director for several summers. The tip had come from Vinny, the maintenance guy at Henry Horner, who had gone on to work for Farinella at Emma Kaufmann.

"He's a good person," Vinny said of Farinella's assistant, "and he didn't seem that loyal to Danny. He'd have noticed which boys Danny was spending time with."

The night I mailed the evidence to Krastek, I was jolted out of a dream, awake but disoriented. *Where was I? Who was I?* There was a human form next to me beneath the covers: a man preparing to rape and kill me. I leapt out of bed and fled to the bathroom, slamming the door behind me. I gasped for breath as I leaned against the door with my full weight.

A minute passed. The puzzle of my identity was reassembling itself, one piece at a time. I could remember my name. I could remember where I lived. Then I remembered who was under the covers: Susan.

I sank to the cold tile floor, shivering and crying.

KRASTEK MOVED QUICKLY. Within a week he had discussed Farinella with the Pittsburgh police department and the FBI. They were jointly considering three options, he reported.

The first one, favored by the DA, was confronting Farinella. It had the advantage of immediacy. The downside, Krastek said, was that it might run him out of town. The second option was going to the Jewish Community Center. The drawback here was the potential liability, he explained. The third approach was to get boys to come forward, maybe by setting up a talk on sexual abuse at the Jewish center. Sergeant Ray McNowsky of the police Sex Assault Squad apparently favored this idea. He wanted to engage with the kids directly, find victims, then prosecute Farinella.

"I'm with McNowsky," I said.

"I understand," Krastek replied. "But teenage boys are the toughest to get to talk. It'll take too long. We can't wait. If someone's abusing boys in my county, I can't put it off. We'll do something in the next two weeks."

"If you wind up running him out of town, you'll look bad later if more boys are abused," I said, alarmed at the prospect of Farinella getting away. He acknowledged this was a possibility but said speed was paramount.

Krastek's preferred plan was the worst option, it seemed to me. My fellow victims and I wanted swift action, but not if it put other kids in danger somewhere else. Yes, teenage boys were reluctant to talk, but wasn't that what detectives were paid to do—get victims and witnesses to open up? The Pittsburgh police were willing to go to the kids. Plus, they had the name of a potential informant. If they spent thirty minutes with Farinella's ex-assistant, he could probably provide a list of families to approach.

Besides, didn't *all* the families at the Jewish Community Center deserve to know they'd had a sexual predator in their midst for five years? How would the victims ever get the help they needed if this all got swept under the rug?

I knew for a fact that investigations were able to turn up new victims. Just days earlier, my mother had given me an article by Calvin Trillin in the *New Yorker*. Something about it had spooked her. "It's tough stuff," she said, handing me the magazine. I assumed I was in for a graphic account of sexual abuse, but that wasn't it at all.

In central Oregon an informant had alerted the local authorities to a scoutmaster who was abusing boys in a Mormon congregation. When they failed to act on his report, the informant went to the state police. According to Trillin, the state police "weren't troubled by the fact that so many of the allegations were beyond the statute of limitations." They were confident of developing current cases because "the behavior pattern of a pedophile tends to be so unvarying." They quickly located a fifteen-year-old victim and then extracted a confession from the perpetrator.

The piece ended with justice meted out, and it was chilling. In return for a guilty plea on two charges of sexual abuse, the county DA agreed to drop further investigation of similar charges involving other boys. The abuser, who had been preying on Boy Scouts for more than two decades, was sentenced to a mere twenty days in jail. Five days after the sentencing, the fifteen-year-old boy killed his abuser with a sawed-off shotgun.

*There but for the grace of God*, I thought. I knew how unbearable shame could turn to blinding rage. I lived with that oscillating current in my bones every day. I couldn't count the number of times I'd fantasized about blowing Farinella's head off. It was only by channeling my anger into the task at hand—finding others like myself, securing statements, bird-dogging law enforcement—that I stayed grounded. When I stopped working on the case, I grew depressed, or homicidal.

After reading Trillin's article I was glad the Farinella case was not unfolding in some small town in central Oregon where pedophiles got twenty-day sentences. Then came Krastek's three options. I didn't know which agency would have the final say, but his comment that "we can't wait" made it clear the DA would not be building a case against Farinella.

A MONTH OR so later, I was at my desk at work when Krastek called.

"Steve, we just met with the Jewish Community Center," he began.

"Okay," I said. "Who was there?"

"On our side, it was me and an agent from the FBI. We met with officials from the Jewish center and their attorney."

"And?"

"We shared the information from you and we got a good reaction. They're ready to act. There's no need to apply pressure. We're going to work with them."

"You mean they'll just show him the door?"

"Right. They haven't notified Farinella yet. They said they hadn't had any complaints about him. They said he turned their camp around."

"Yeah, I don't doubt he turned their camp around," I said, "but you can be sure he was abusing boys while he did it. You can't let him walk. He'll just go somewhere else and start over. If you're not going to prosecute, you have to at least stop him from getting another job with kids. You need to contact his previous employers and the camping networks. Please do something. Otherwise we'll be right back where we started."

"The FBI is going to talk to witnesses and past employers," he said. "Then they'll go back to the Jewish Community Center and make sure that Farinella is out. If there's any current evidence in Pennsylvania, then we'll try to get the state to prosecute."

*If* there's evidence? Why not *find* the evidence? Why weren't they going after a serial predator?

"Is there any way for me to track what the FBI is up to?" I asked, desperate for some way to stay plugged in.

"Bill Lintz is the agent they've assigned. I'm sure you'll be hearing from him."

I was numb. Of course the Jewish Community Center wanted to hustle Farinella out the door in the dead of night. Dr. Shore had predicted as much. But why in the world would the DA let them do it? Since when did law enforcement "work with" organizations, as Krastek had put it, to cover the tracks of criminals? Who was left to speak for the children?

# 29

I WAS EATING LUNCH AT home when the phone rang. I picked up and said hello but there was just dead air. Whoever it was hung up. The same thing happened the next day.

I was sure it was Farinella. The Jewish Community Center had probably broken the news to him. He would have seen my letter to the DA. He'd know I was the one behind his ouster, and that was fine by me. In fact, I wanted Farinella to know that I wasn't going to quit hounding him. That didn't mean I wasn't scared. I was pretty sure he'd be coming for me, and these phone calls were creepy.

If we wound up speaking, I planned to record the call and somehow get him to confess, which would help in the event of a criminal or civil case. But I had another reason for taping: if he killed me, there'd be evidence.

I picked up the phone the next day and heard the same dead air.

"Hey, it's me," Farinella finally said.

"Yeah," I said coldly. "Why are you calling me?"

"I just want you to know that . . . I'm sorry. I've changed. I'm not hurting anybody now."

"I don't care about your apology," I said. "You need to live with the consequences."

Susan appeared in the doorway. She was stabbing the air, pointing at the answering machine. I'd forgotten to turn it on. I hit the RECORD button and the cassette began whirring.

"It's torment for me to know I've hurt somebody and I live with that every day." He sounded anguished, as if he were suffering more than anyone. "I mean, you don't understand, when I get up in the morning and I think of what I've done or when I'm in the car and driving and you come into my head, there's the torment that I hurt you. And I have to live with that, you're right. But I just don't want you to have to hate. Because I never was intentionally wanting to hurt anybody."

"I can't help you," I said. "If you understood what you put me through, not to mention everyone else. I won't run down the names because you know who they are. You'd kill yourself."

"Well, it's pretty close to that."

"You make the decision. You changed? Maybe you did, maybe you didn't. You were always a compulsive liar. Why should I believe you?"

"I was never a compulsive liar," he said.

"You were always a compulsive liar!" I yelled. "You played friends with my parents for how many years?"

"I know," he said softly.

"Who are you trying to kid? You were never straight in your life with anyone." My body was shaking with rage.

"Well, I never have any friends," he went on. "I don't get close to anybody. Don't you think I know I'm a lie? It's a cheat, it's a fraud when I look at somebody? The only people I ever got close to were your parents. And I probably hurt them to no end. I can't do anything, but there was never the intent."

"What does intention have to do with it?"

"Well, the road to hell . . ." He broke off. That had always been one of his favorite sayings. "I know I always tried to do what was right. But there was always that deceit, that thing in the back all the time. I lived a lie all my life."

"I can't imagine what you want from me," I said. "What do you want me to do, forgive you and say it's all right?"

"It's not all right," he said. "I just don't want you to feel the hate."

"Why the hell shouldn't I feel hate? You did a horrible thing to me. You used me."

"But I never saw it that way," he said. I laughed at this. "It was like being accepted as what I was," he went on. "And the more you accepted, the more I came back, and it was like a trick I played on myself. It wasn't like a dishonest kind of thing."

"I wasn't the only one, Dan. I was nothing special. There were plenty of others the same summer. Don't give me this shit about making you feel okay. It's got nothing to do with me. I was an innocent, vulnerable kid, and you used me, period."

"And I was sick."

"Yeah. And you're kidding yourself to think anything else. Because I wasn't the only one. You checked every kid out. And anyone who was fair game, you hit on them."

"That's not true."

I laughed again. "I can name a dozen," I said.

"A dozen," he repeated. "All right."

"Am I wrong?"

"I don't want to get into numbers," he said.

"Am I wrong?" I asked again.

"A dozen. I don't think so. Anyway, it's a sickness. It's gone. No more. I don't want to hurt anybody else."

His self-pity was nauseating. I wanted badly to hang up, but I wanted a confession even more.

"Look, I've done terrible things," he said. "I just want to reassure you, there is no more of that. I can't do anything but hope that there could be just a little bit of understanding on your part."

"Why should I when you never had any?" I asked.

"I've always had for you. It was not using you as you think it was. It was that you were a friend. In my own sick way, I thought you were something super special, that you accepted me and that you liked me."

"Do you know how terrified I was of you? Do you know how terrified every kid was of you?"

"No, I had no idea. I had no idea you were terrified. I always thought you liked me."

"We all had the same nightmares, Dan. The same fucking nightmares. Some of us are still having them. You believe that?"

"Yes. Sorry. I have mine. I know I hurt people, but I never want to hurt anybody again. And I only want to try to have you understand that that's the way it is now, so you don't have this hate. Someday maybe there can be a bit of understanding that would remove that from you."

"It's pretty convenient to ask for it now," I said.

"Why?"

"Beause it's got nothing to do with me anymore." He knew what I meant. He had to answer to law enforcement.

"Well, it's you, I guess, that . . ." He broke off, unable to say that I was the one who'd reported him.

"You told me you were going to get out of camping," I said. "Why didn't you?"

"I tried," he said. "I'm trying now."

"What do you mean you're trying? That was eight years ago."

"I'm trying to get the house up for sale so we can get some money and I can open a little restaurant or something."

"You're the one who was always saying you have to be responsible for your actions. You got to deal with that."

"All right. I don't want you to think it's a free ride for me. I'm paying."

His suffering act made me seethe.

"You murdered me. You killed something in me I'm never going to have back. If you think I'm going to feel compassion for what you're going through, forget it. I don't have it in me. I can see you're so totally unconscious, you have no idea what I went through."

"I never saw it at the time. I never thought I was hurting anybody. I played the game with myself. I know now, and that's the pain. If I understood a little bit more then, I wouldn't have done anything."

"That's make-believe land. That stuff doesn't mean anything."

"I know. Look, I'm afraid to come to New York because I run in to see my aunt. I run out the same day. She's sick. I want to go see her, but I'm afraid."

"What are you afraid of?"

"I'm afraid that you'll see me or you'll want to . . . So I just try to stay away."

"How about my parents? You think you can ever make it better for them? All those horrible years."

"What do you mean horrible years?" he asked.

"They lost their son. Don't you understand that?" He was silent. "You never saw that part, did you?"

"No. Why didn't you talk to me?" he asked. "Tell me to fuck off, get lost."

"You controlled every fucking thing we did. And physically controlled us. You think anyone had the power to say no to you?"

"I want to believe it."

"Come on. You knew exactly what you were doing."

"You give me too much credit."

"You knew."

"I can only know what I can do in the future. Try not to hurt anybody."

"You said that to me in '78, Dan."

"I know."

"And you lied. Because I know you were abusing kids after that. I know the kids."

"In '78?"

"Yeah."

"I don't know," he said.

"You know," I said. "You just don't want to face it."

He said nothing for a full minute. Then he sighed heavily. I saw my opening.

"Do you understand that what you were doing was sexually abusing kids?"

"I understand now," he replied. "I went for help. I spent a lot of money and a lot of time with some of the biggest psychiatrists. All they came up with was that you're only hurting yourself and that it's your mother and your father and all that bullshit that was prevailing in those days. I was the victim was what they were saying. That was the whole therapy business that went on for years and years. And I began to believe the bullshit that they were giving me. Now, times are different and people see things differently, and I do."

"Dan, I know how strong your sexual thing is for boys. I don't believe, no way, if you're working around kids that you're on top of that."

"I am. I haven't had a sexual experience with any other human being in the last five years. That I know. I don't have to bullshit anymore. That's true. And there's lots of reasons why. First, I take pills that desexualize."

"What kind of pills?"

"Inderal or Isordil." Those were heart medications. "Two, I control it. I have no desire. Whatever I do, I do it in my own head. Look, I don't want to keep beating a dead horse. I don't want to upset you or hurt you."

"You already did that. There's nothing you can do to me now. I know who you are. I know what you are and what you did. Nothing you say means anything to me."

"All right. Thanks for talking to me," he said.

"Okay," I said.

"So long."

My body was vibrating from the rush of fight or flight coursing through me. For the first time I hadn't frozen or fled from Farinella. I'd stood my ground and fought.

I hit the EJECT button and popped the cassette out of the answering machine. Our exchange had been so intense I could barely remember what we said. I was pretty sure I'd gotten him to confess, but there was no way I'd be listening to the tape any time soon.

## 30

IT TOOK ME A WHILE to catch on that the FBI wasn't going to investigate Farinella.

Agent Lintz promised he'd be coming up to New York to interview me. He was impressed to hear I'd recorded the call with Farinella, and laughed at Farinella's claim that he'd stopped abusing kids. "I've been at this for a lot of years," Lintz said, "and I know this type of guy. He just can't keep away from the candy store."

Lintz definitely wanted the new lead I had: the name and number of a kitchen boy at Emma Kaufmann Camp who had likely been abused. It turned out that Farinella had submitted his resignation, Lintz reported, but that would not stop the FBI from pursuing a case with the US Attorney's Office in Pittsburgh.

I believed all of the FBI's promises—until I couldn't believe any of them. I soon learned from Lintz that, despite his resignation, Farinella was still working at the Jewish Community Center, nearly three months after they had been told that their youth supervisor was a known pedophile. I was horrified by this news.

My faith in the FBI shattered, I did the only thing I knew to do:

unearth more evidence. The FBI had never contacted Farinella's former assistant director at Emma Kaufmann, so I took it on myself. Yes, he said, Farinella's pattern with boys had been obvious. In fact, he'd even confronted Farinella over his favored treatment of certain kids.

I couldn't seem to stop working the case. I produced leads that no one wanted and witnesses who would never be called. I built an airtight argument that would never get tried.

Farinella did finally leave his job and bought a diner called R.J. Scott's, I learned from a source inside the Pittsburgh police department. Given his history with kitchen boys, his new haunt was both predictable and disturbing. It wasn't a stretch to imagine him hiring teens from the Jewish Community Center to work in the diner. He had found the commercial equivalent of a camp: easy access to boys and a great cover for sexual abuse. The problem was, no one else seemed to care, at least not enough to do anything.

"I wish you luck, Steve," said one man who had worked at Henry Horner. "But let's face it, we'll never get Dan."

The most disheartening calls were with the social workers—Farinella's colleagues. One flatly denied that he could have abused children. Others were shaken but still held him in high esteem. "He did so much good," they said, as if that compensated for the lives he'd destroyed. They had been conned by a master, and it was easier for them to believe a comforting lie than face the devastating truth. God forbid they might have to ask tough questions of themselves and of the agencies that had enabled his decades of predation.

With a criminal case slipping out of reach, I considered every possible way of getting at Farinella. Given the statute of limitations, I couldn't file a civil suit. I could hire a private investigator to track his activities, but the one man I spoke to considered the assignment too time-consuming and warned me it would be exorbitantly expensive. Some child advocates suggested I feed the story to a reporter in Pittsburgh. I liked that idea, but a reporter would need sources and none of the other victims were willing to go that route.

The prospect of a public spectacle scared me, too. I imagined the questions—from the media, the camps, my colleagues—about why I'd stayed friends with Farinella, why I'd gone to work for him as an adult. I feared I'd be the one put on trial in the court of public opinion.

WITH NO OTHER help in sight, I turned in desperation to Andrew Vachss, a New York City attorney who was paid by the state to represent abused children. But it was his other gig that had gotten my attention. Vachss was the best-selling author of crime thrillers about a private eye named Burke, an ex-con who operates outside the law to wreak bloody vengeance on pedophiles.

I had just read *Strega*, the second Burke novel—there would be eighteen in all—in which the ex-con destroys a child porn ring that operates via telephone modem. This was 1987, a decade before Internet porn was a thing. Vachss's novels not only conveyed the depravity of pedophilia, they did it through the eyes of a man who'd been abused and was living out my fantasy of an avenging angel.

I'd read interviews with Vachss. He'd done community organizing in steel towns and had run a maximum-security facility for violent juvenile offenders. With his black eye-patch and hard-boiled demeanor, Vachss moved easily through the Times Square underworld where his child clients were easy prey for the "maggots," as he called them. His wife worked for the Queens DA, prosecuting sex crimes. The two of them were on a mission to make the world a safer place for children. If anyone knew what to do, it would be Andrew Vachss.

"Fuhgeddaboutit," he growled, when I reached him on the phone. His voice, like Farinella's, suggested a New York truck driver. "The DA's not going to bring a case unless it's open and shut. Those are rare. And the FBI? They couldn't catch a cold without informants."

Finally, someone who got how things actually worked. The authorities wouldn't move on Farinella unless a gift-wrapped case fell onto their desks.

"So what do I do?" I asked. "Just give up and walk away?"

"Let me handle it. We know people down in Pittsburgh," Vachss said, suddenly sounding like the vigilante protagonist of his novels. "Send me your file on this guy. And give me his address and a photo. I'll put them on the wire. We'll make sure he knows we're watching him."

I had no idea who Vachss meant by "we." I didn't ask what the "wire" was or what "watching" would entail. All I knew was that Farinella operated in the shadows and so did Vachss.

IT WAS CLEAR that the FBI in Pittsburgh was done with me when the Farinella file made its way back to New York. One day in late 1987, out of the blue, I got a call from Agent Faye Greenlee at the FBI field office in lower Manhattan. The file had landed on her desk, and she was trying to make sense of it.

"How come this case was never prosecuted?" she asked.

"You tell me," I said. "I haven't heard from your Pittsburgh office in eight months."

Greenlee was part of a two-person team working to develop sexual abuse cases. I liked her right away. She was heartfelt and direct. When I met with her and her partner, an NYPD detective, I shared the backstory and she brightened or groaned at each twist and turn.

"Unbelievable!" she exclaimed, when I got to Farinella's move into the restaurant business. "I'm so sorry. If this was in New York, we'd be all over it. But it's outside our jurisdiction. They don't have enough personnel in Pittsburgh to investigate unless victims come forward first." She smiled ruefully. "You're looking at the only two people in all of New York who investigate guys like Farinella." They spent most of their time trying to get kids to talk.

"It's amazing you got adult victims to sign statements," she said. "You don't know how unusual that is. But boys are even tougher. Boys who have been abused are tougher to crack than murderers. You try all the tricks and they just don't break."

I knew. Nothing would have gotten me to break at fifteen. I raised the idea of getting a private investigator to develop a case. Greenlee laughed.

"Stephen, you'd get a kid talking faster than any investigator," she said. "But even if you could get him to talk, you still have to get him and his family to cooperate. That's a tough business. And even then, you'd have to get a judge who understands the threat of abusers. A lot of them don't."

"So, what do I do, just pray that he isn't abusing boys anymore?"

"Oh, he's abusing them," she said. "The average molester abuses 117 kids in his life. There is no literature proving they can be cured. It's likely Farinella is still at it."

"Jesus Christ," I muttered.

"The best thing to do is keep the pressure on. You can help change his behavior by making him paranoid. Write him a letter. Tell him you're talking to us. It may make him too scared to do anything, or it may force him into making a mistake and giving himself away."

She sounded more like Andrew Vachss than an FBI agent. I respected her in the same way: she was on the front lines and telling it like it was.

"Anything else?" I asked.

"Someone needs to write about this. It's bigger than your case, Stephen. There are thousands of Farinellas out there. We're never going to change things until people wake up to how prevalent this is. Then the agencies and law enforcement and the courts will start changing. You've seen it all firsthand. You told me you're a writer. Why don't you tell your story?"

WHAT I WROTE was a fourteen-page single-spaced letter to Farinella. I had thought it would be short and to the point, telling him that I was still talking to witnesses and passing evidence to the FBI.

But I kept coming back to our phone conversation and how

oblivious he'd been, or pretended to be, to the suffering he'd caused. I wanted him to face what he had done. For that, I had to assemble my jumble of memories into a linear narrative—something I'd never attempted before. I began locating each vivid event in time by cross-checking it against the calendar, other memories, and accounts from the other men and witnesses.

I wrote of his predatory behavior during that first summer and fall of 1968, tracking how methodical and manipulative he had been. I recounted his words and actions, showing his claims of "good intention" to be self-serving lies. I wrote of the decades of aftershocks. Finally, I told him I was continuing to meet with the FBI and signed off with this:

> You ask me to stop hating you. I will not. I don't find it consuming or immobilizing as you suggest. On the contrary, I find my hatred liberating. I savor my hatred of you because it means I am free of your diseased power over me. It means I no longer need to blame myself. I was held hostage by a sick and violent person. As long as you are alive, I will hate you. That is a promise.

The letter sat on my desk for two weeks while I regressed by years, paralyzed by what I'd written. Each night I dreamed of betrayal, combat, imprisonment in an airtight cell, and my own grisly death. Each morning, I woke up wrecked. I was able to work, barely, but my waking life seemed less substantial and less consequential than the soldiers and executioners in my dreams.

I decided to show the letter to my mother and Ken. I wanted them to know what Farinella had done to me, even if we never discussed it. Two days later, my mother called.

"I read it," she said. "It was wrenching, Stephen. I can't talk about it. But I hope you mail it. I hope it destroys him."

The letter seemed more likely to destroy me. The emotional violence I'd unleashed in those fourteen pages had boomeranged. But at the point when I couldn't bear another minute of self-loathing at my own inaction, I walked to the mailbox and dropped the letter through the slot.

When I got back to my apartment, I packed all of my law enforcement files into a box: two years of digging, of phone calls and meetings, notes, journals, news clippings, and letters. I'd tried everything in my power to stop Farinella. But after talking to Agent Greenlee, I had to concede that the FBI was not going to prevent him from preying on children. I was crushed.

I never spoke with Andrew Vachss again. I took him at his word that someone in Pittsburgh had his eye on Farinella. I had no further contact with the FBI or the Allegheny County DA or the Pittsburgh police department. I stopped calling victims, witnesses, sexual abuse experts, and employees at various camps.

The legal quest that had consumed my life was over. I taped the box of files shut and stuffed it in a closet.

# 31

It was Bruce, the first camper who'd agreed to help me, who delivered the news that Farinella had died of throat cancer. The finality of it was hard to grasp. My immediate thought was *No more boys hurt*. My second was that I wouldn't have to kill him.

The call came six years after I'd given up my quest to stop Farinella. Like me, Bruce had been struggling all that time to move on from the past.

"I keep going back over what happened," he said on the phone. "It won't leave me alone."

"I know. I used to think it would stop. But I'm starting to think it never will."

Months after my meeting with FBI Agent Greenlee, Susan and I had moved west to make a new start. In San Francisco, I joined one of the first therapy groups for male survivors of sexual abuse. Seeing my experience mirrored in the lives of other men was profoundly helpful.

But Farinella was always there, lying in wait. I imagined those boys in the restaurant kitchen in Pittsburgh. I played out fantasies of courtrooms and retribution. I heeded Greenlee's advice to keep the pressure on by mailing Farinella anonymous envelopes containing news clippings about child predators, some of whom were killed by their victims. I'd begun to notice more stories like that.

At night, dreams of my tormentor could still trigger barely submerged terrors. Every few months I would wake up, my identity gone, mistaking the woman I loved for a rapist. During one daytime episode, the room began spinning and I couldn't breathe. Susan called an ambulance. At the emergency room they could find nothing wrong and sent me home with tranquilizers.

BUT THAT WAS all done now. Farinella was dead. As the days passed after Bruce called, the news felt more and more like deliverance. So much of my fear and rage had orbited around the physical person: the half man, half beast of my dreams who had taken me hostage at thirteen. He couldn't hurt me or anyone else now. Death had solved the problem. I could have my life back.

I was thirty-seven years old. I'd put in a decade of intensive therapy and, despite the intermittent panic attacks, I was hitting my stride in the world. I made a good living in the public interest sector, advocating for causes I felt passionate about. Susan and I had gotten married in a small ceremony conducted by Huyen Viet, my monk friend from Songkhla, who was now abbot of the Vietnamese Buddhist temple in Port Arthur, Texas.

We had a son, born on my father's birthday. It felt cosmic, this closing of the circle, and deeply healing. To mark my sense of rebirth, I reclaimed my family name—Mills—the one I'd scrawled on the pegboard behind my desk in East Meadow.

Moving from California, we built a pastoral homestead of cats, dogs, chickens, and gardens in the New Mexico high desert. I was blessed with good health, loving family, and close friends. There were years still ahead of me and life was good.

THAT SURE SOUNDS like a happy ending, but it wasn't. No matter how successful I became in my work, no matter how much my wife and son loved me, my invisible wound ached terribly. The secret kept a firm hold on me. The urge to hide from human contact was powerful. Inexplicably, I felt depressed, broken inside, and prone to self-loathing. I couldn't seem to shake my near-constant companions of shame and hypervigilance.

I pretended to be fine. I told myself I *should* be fine. My denial reflex was uncannily strong. But every so often, when the force of feeling grew overwhelming, my body would bring me face-to-face with the truth.

One night I had terrible chest pain and my extremities went numb. Certain I was having a coronary, I rushed to the emergency room, where doctors told me my heart was fine.

Lying there hooked up to an EKG, I reconsidered the very first assault in the Camp Ella Fohs infirmary. I'd always thought of it as a life-altering event, a break in reality—and it was. But it was also something simpler: my nervous system had gone haywire that afternoon and, decades later, it was still on high alert, as easily triggered as an overly sensitive smoke alarm.

I had desperately hoped that I would arrive at some point, like after Farinella's death, when all that pain would be behind me, gone, and I could declare myself healed. But the past refused to cooperate. The assault on the child still lived in my body—always present. My nervous system would never magically reset to that long-ago day before I walked into the infirmary.

I had no choice but to tend to the mind and body I had: know them, care for them, and alleviate their distress before the alarms went off. This didn't happen overnight. It took years. It's still ongoing.

There are many ways to begin healing from trauma, for feeling whatever needs to be felt in a safe environment. I explored bio-energetics, Rosen Method bodywork, sacred dance, somatic therapy, and other modalities. All of them helped me turn toward the terror, grief, and anger roiling my body. Some of it I'd already experienced on Ecstasy and many times since, but there was so much more. I'd catch myself thinking: *For God's sake, this again? How come I'm still feeling this? What's wrong with me?*

One somatic therapist I saw kept a quotation on her wall from the Gospel of Thomas: "If you bring forth what is within you, what you bring forth will save you. If you don't bring forth what is within you, what you do not bring forth will destroy you."

For years I misunderstood this wisdom, imagining there was some great revelation to be unearthed or some authentic self that would finally emerge, leaving me transformed and mended. What came forth instead was a child's pain, releasing me from the past and creating space for spontaneous joy, gratitude, and love in the present.

Squalls of fear, grief, and shame still blow in. But the practice of mindfulness—deepened in silent meditation retreats—helps me to observe these intense thoughts and feelings without their tormenting me or cascading into panic. Invariably, they pass through. I suffer less. I am rarely depressed. I haven't had a night terror in a decade. I've faced the enormity of what happened to me at thirteen and it has a weaker hold on me than it ever did.

Today I know that my journey out of childhood sexual abuse will not end until I draw my final breath. That is not a problem; it is a truth I accept.


As MY DENIAL receded, our collective denial was eroding, too. In the mid-1990s, a steady trickle of news reports began to appear about sexual abuse in the Roman Catholic Church. New research revealed the astonishing fact that some one in six men had been sexually abused before the age of eighteen. It turned out I was less alone than I'd imagined.

Most of these men were still in hiding. Our culture said guys were supposed to be tough, able to protect themselves. If boys *were* abused, supposedly they weren't hurt by it in the same way as girls, and they were expected to bear their shame in silence. One research paper, memorably titled "See No Evil, Hear No Evil, Speak No Evil," confirmed what I knew intimately: men were much less likely than women to disclose abuse and much more likely to deny the impact on their lives.

At the same time, public health studies were documenting the lifelong damage to men, drawing a straight line from childhood sexual abuse to increased rates of alcoholism, drug abuse, depression, divorce, and suicide attempts.

Then in 2002, the *Boston Globe* launched the investigation into abuse in the Catholic Church that finally broke the dam. Three searing documentaries—*Twist of Faith*, *Deliver Us from Evil*, and *Mea Maxima Culpa*—exposed how the Church had sacrificed children to protect pedophile priests. A succession of headline-grabbing scandals, including those of the Boy Scouts and Penn State, forced a reckoning with the epidemic of abuse of boys by men in positions of authority. The taboo on seeing, hearing, and speaking about the scourge was lifting.

This new public awareness helped open lines of communication with my mother, too. When she'd call and say, "Did you see the piece in the *Times*?" I knew she was talking about the sexual abuse story du jour. She had become fluent in the recurring themes: the wielding of power to exploit children, the institutional cover-ups, the victims held hostage into adulthood. We talked about a new development: men stepping forward to file lawsuits and demand justice. But she hadn't uttered Farinella's name in years. It was still off-limits, as was pretty much everything from my childhood.

So I was caught off guard by what happened next. When my stepfather, Ken, died suddenly of a stroke, my mother began reminiscing, with equal suddenness, about my father. The same woman who had once bristled at the mere mention of her first husband would now, unprompted, tell me about a romantic weekend they had spent in the Catskills after the war.

I'd often wondered why my parents had chosen to have a child, given my father's dire condition and prognosis. Now, at age eighty-one, my mother told me.

"I wanted a baby so badly. I wanted life to go on after he was gone."

My father tried to dissuade her, but she carried the day. Then, when she returned home from the hospital with me in tow, she realized what she'd taken on: a colicky, screaming newborn and a debilitated husband. "I had some kind of nervous breakdown," she said. Aunt Delle and Uncle Harold moved in with us until she was on her feet again.

It sounded like my mother had meant to keep my father's memory alive. Yet by the time I turned six she was bent on erasing it. Once, I would have held this revelation against her, but becoming a parent had humbled me. I'd gained a new appreciation of my mother's limitations, of the ways in which her own ungrieved losses had shaped her. I cared only that she doted on my son and that they shared a passion for books. Her love for him was beautiful and uncomplicated.

One day, as we talked in her living room, my mother unburdened herself of decades of torment about Dan Farinella. She begged my forgiveness, and I was relieved to finally grant it. I reassured her that I was okay and grateful for all I had. I could tell she wanted to believe me.

Soon after that, I asked my mother to come with me to my father's grave. I'd been there many times, but she hadn't been back since the day he was buried, when a lone bugler played "Taps." At the cemetery I wept, as I always did, and my mother was present for me in the way I'd always hoped she would be.

When she was diagnosed with colon cancer two years later, it spread quickly. On her deathbed, I could see the remorse in her eyes, her regret at having failed to protect me. But there was love between us, too, untouched by my abuser and all he'd taken.

After my mother died, I was struck by how much easier it had been to forgive her than to forgive myself. Even now, there would come moments when I would hate myself and hold the world at bay, as if concealing a hideous crime—my crime.

Then, while going through some old family photos, I came across a snapshot of myself at age twelve, the year before I met Dan Farinella. In the picture, I'm hanging upside down from a branch of the tall maple tree that stood in the front yard of our home in East Meadow. I'm wearing a blue New York Mets jersey and beaming at the camera, exultant.

I remembered that moment, me floating in midair. I remembered that boy. "You were so innocent, you were just a child," I said to the boy, and, suddenly, I was filled with love for him.

# Epilogue

## 2021

I TURNED ON THE TELEVISION one night in 2017 to view the sentencing hearing for Larry Nassar, the disgraced doctor for the USA Gymnastics team. A year earlier, Rachel Denhollander, a former gymnast, had stepped forward and accused Nassar of sexually assaulting her when she was fifteen years old. Hundreds of other women followed in her wake.

Now I watched as 156 of them confronted their assailant in court with the terrifying truth of their experience. It was one of the most remarkable displays of raw courage I'd ever seen. Soon, the gymnasts would hold to account the powerful institutions that had shielded Nassar: Michigan State University, USA Gymnastics, the US Olympic Committee, and the FBI.

As this cathartic legal drama unfolded, I was haunted by the fact that I and the other boys abused by Dan Farinella had been denied the chance to face him in a courtroom, call him out as the soul destroyer he was, and find some kind of peace.

The last thing I expected was a second chance. But when New York State passed the Child Victims Act in 2019, it reopened the courtroom door that had been slammed in my face three decades earlier.

Like legislation in several other states, the new law addressed the daunting problem I'd run up against: it could take decades for victims of childhood sexual abuse to overcome the fear, shame, and trauma to seek criminal or civil justice, but by then we were blocked by statutes of limitations. The Child Victims Act changed all that by allowing people longer periods of time to file criminal charges and to bring civil action until they turned fifty-five. I was over the age limit, but the law also opened a one-year window—later extended to two years—during which people like me could bring a civil action against their abusers and the institutions that had enabled them, no matter how much time had passed.

Dan Farinella was dead now and beyond the reach of the law, and so was the criminal case I'd hoped would put him behind bars. But I could file a civil lawsuit against UJA-Federation, which had owned and controlled Camp Ella Fohs, as well as the Young Men's and Young Women's Hebrew Association (YM-YWHA) of the Bronx, which had run the camp. At last, I could compel those two organizations—and indirectly, the Jewish Council for Youth Services in Chicago and the Jewish Community Center in Pittsburgh—to confront the buried truth about Farinella, a serial predator to whom they had entrusted the welfare of thousands of children.

I was encouraged by the fact that the Jewish community, like so many others, was waking up to the pervasive threat of sexual abuse and the need for accountability. More than a hundred rabbis and other Jewish leaders had signed a public letter in support of the Child Victims Act. They called on their congregations to stand with victims in our quest for justice, which they argued would help prevent abuse in the future. "We also painfully acknowledge," they wrote, "that rather than being a source of healing . . . religious institutions have too often been a part of the problem."

In New York, I met with James R. Marsh, a trial attorney who had brought groundbreaking cases on behalf of victims of sexual abuse, campus rape, and child pornography. As I related my story, I found that I had submerged most of the details of my pursuit of Farinella in the 1980s. Susan also had trouble recollecting them. We'd sealed off the ordeal so thoroughly that we'd rarely spoken of it since.

I had to dig deep in the recesses of my office closet to find the box labeled FARINELLA/1986–87. When I sliced it open for the first time in three decades, a gray envelope containing something hard and rectangular was sitting on top: the audiocassette of Farinella's phone call. I'd have to buy a cassette player just to listen to it.

Beneath that envelope were dozens of file folders. I had forgotten the volume of material I'd amassed. Here it all was—every lead, every phone call, every witness—waiting for me to finish what I'd started.

I knew that bringing an action against UJA-Federation and the YM-YWHA would be a lonely venture. When I contacted other victims, only one responded. The web of silence that Farinella had spun fifty years earlier—ensnaring boys, families, colleagues, and institutions—was still holding strong, as if he maintained it from beyond the grave.

Part of me, an insistent part, was reluctant to go to court and risk another heartbreaking failure. But then I recalled some wisdom that Andrew Vachss had imparted decades before. *Surviving is not a big deal*, he'd said. *Survival is luck. It's what you do after you survive that counts. If you can make it to adulthood and still care enough to help protect other children, then you've transcended your abuse.* I thought of Rachel Denhollander and how her resolve had allowed a generation of athletes to cast aside their shame and make their sport safer. I had to act, even if no one else followed me through the courthouse door.

As it turned out, someone else stepped forward first. In early 2021, an anonymous John Doe filed a complaint in New York against the YM-YWHA of the Bronx. The man alleged that Dan Farinella, director of the East Tremont Y, had sexually abused him for two to three years, beginning around 1960, well before Farinella arrived at Camp

Ella Fohs. John Doe, twelve years old when he was first abused, came from a broken home and had little contact with his father. He used to visit the East Tremont Y several days a week after school. Later, he went to work in the kitchen at Camp Willoway, where Farinella was the director and where the abuse continued.

Reading John Doe's complaint was like watching the prequel to a horror film I'd seen a hundred times. His account foreshadowed my own fate with sickening accuracy. There was a legal connection between our cases as well: the East Tremont Y and Camp Ella Fohs were both run by the YM-YWHA of the Bronx and both were affiliates of UJA-Federation.

I understood why John Doe, now in his seventies, opted for anonymity so many decades after Farinella stole his boyhood from him. The secret was all-powerful. But I couldn't hide anymore.

WHEN I BEGAN Hebrew school in fifth grade, in preparation for my bar mitzvah, we studied Hebrew, the Bible, and Jewish history. But the book I remember most vividly was a gray paperback called *To Do Justly*. It took its title from the prophet Micah: "You have all been shown what is good, and what God requires of you: Do justice, love kindness, and walk humbly with your God."

Our teacher used this book to help translate Micah's lofty admonition into social justice in America, circa 1965. We could advocate for civil rights, help feed the hungry, and aid the less fortunate. My copy of *To Do Justly* was dog-eared from repeated readings. By the time I turned thirteen, the year Dan Farinella began sexually abusing me, I was volunteering to mentor children in a low-income housing project, marching twenty miles in solidarity with Cesar Chavez and the Delano grape workers, and running a makeshift carnival in the backyard to raise money for children with cerebral palsy.

In all this, I was a perfectly ordinary child of my time and place. Our generation of Reform Jews was weaned on the doctrine of helping others who had been less fortunate. That credo was the reason my mother worked for a social service agency and why she lionized a social worker like Farinella. She and Ken donated each year to UJA-Federation because no group did more to help the needy. They sent me to Camp Ella Fohs because of its original mission to serve poor, inner-city kids, unable to leave the city in the sweltering summer.

The dark genius of Daniel Farinella, a half-Jewish, half-Italian son of the Bronx, was in deftly exploiting this peculiar affinity for social justice. How better to gain the confidence of Jewish agencies and unquestioned access to their underage charges?

My civil claim wouldn't turn on the question of whether he had sexually abused children. That was well established by multiple victims and by his own admission. The pivotal legal issue is whether UJA-Federation and the YM-YWHA knew or should have known that I and other boys were in danger. According to John Doe, Farinella's inappropriate behavior at the Y in the Bronx was "open and obvious," and that, on one occasion, an employee walked in while he was being abused. Certainly, the campers and staff at Ella Fohs knew that Farinella targeted boys for improper attention and brazenly groped them. Many Ella Fohs employees—waiters and kitchen boys—knew much more than that. They were victims themselves.

The records of UJA-Federation and the YM-YWHA could show what those groups knew, and the only way to open their files and depose former administrators was by going to court. My action might also prompt more victims in New York and untold numbers in other states to seek accountability. We were all chosen by a serial predator hiding in plain sight, protected by a culture that preferred to look away. UJA-Federation and the YM-YWHA were the first links in a chain of silence and complicity that spanned five camps, six states, and multiple social service organizations.

The Child Victims Act affirms the principle that it is never too late for justice. Until men and women like me resolve to seek that justice, these organizations are unlikely to remove their blinders.

Until they are compelled to face this chapter of recent history, conduct thorough investigations, and apply the lessons learned, they will be ill-equipped to safeguard the children in their care.

At age sixty-six, I'd have preferred not to go to court to prompt that reckoning. I have no desire to dwell in my past. I certainly do not want my life reduced to episodes of sexual assault that occurred a half century ago. But I will not stand by while the institutions that employed Dan Farinella pretend these events never happened. I will not allow a predator to prevail, absolved for all time by a tacit and repugnant code of silence.

# ACKNOWLEDGMENTS

WRITING THIS BOOK TURNED OUT to be a multidecade undertaking. I am indebted to the many people who sustained me, body and soul, as I wended my way toward completion.

In New York, Doctors Kenneth Greenspan and Stuart Kantor probably saved my life, or at least made a life possible. Long before I had a clue, Kantor insisted I would write this story. In the San Francisco Bay Area, I was fortunate to find therapists Richard Carlson and Eugene Porter. Porter's pioneering group of male survivors was both revelation and refuge. In New Mexico, Cameron Hough showed me the way to emotional truth in the body and through the act of writing. Finally, Dr. Julie Brown Yau has been a Skype goddess in helping me fend off my demons during the final, pandemic phase of this project.

I bow to my spiritual brother, Thich Huyen Viet, who gave me shelter from the storm and who continues to lead and serve by selfless example as abbot of the Lien Hoa Temple in Houston. My everlasting thanks to meditation teacher Shinzen Young for showing me the nature of mind and how to untangle suffering.

It has been my great privilege to work alongside so many remarkable and dedicated colleagues at the Natural Resources Defense Council. A special shout-out to John Adams, Mitch Bernard, Joel Reynolds, and Gina Trujillo, who have had my back for half a lifetime. Linda Lopez was not just my inspired partner at work but a steadfast friend and trusted confidante through the writing process.

It would have been impossible to complete this journey without the help of those brave men—victims and witnesses—who stepped forward in 1986 and called on law enforcement to do its job. We may have been thwarted, but I am forever grateful for their solidarity. In addition, I want to acknowledge the many former campers and employees from Camps Ella Fohs, Henry Horner, and Emma Kaufmann who have been incredibly generous with their time, memories, and moral support.

On the legal front, special thanks to attorneys James R. Marsh, Vincent Nappo, Tatiana Akhund, and Mollie Cearley—a dream team that has spearheaded my effort to win justice under the Child Victims Act.

When it was time to go public with the book, I knew I could entrust Gail Ross, my agent and old friend, with this most personal of projects. She is simply the best. Her belief in my unfinished manuscript sustained me through completion, and she displayed her trademark finesse and discernment in finding *Chosen* the perfect home at Metropolitan Books.

Riva Hocherman, my brilliant editor, was heaven-sent. She dared to take on a story that many in publishing shied away from, and then fully inhabited the world of the book and envisioned what it could be. Her extraordinary insight and craft helped shape every facet of *Chosen*. She's the editor every author prays for. I'm grateful as well to the entire, talented team at Metropolitan Books and Holt for shepherding this book out into the world.

My cousin, David Mills, has been urging me on since the 1990s, convinced that other families might be spared this scourge if only they knew how pedophiles operate. I have relied on Dave's keen memory, close readings, and unfailing support. This book is proof that our childhood bond, forged in the brotherly love of our fathers, was far stronger than the man who sought to destroy it.

My sister, Donna, has been there for me with open arms since the day we met. In the course of writing, I asked her to revisit some difficult times with me and she always did so with honesty, warmth, and compassion. I love you, Sis.

I'm indebted to those friends who agreed to read and comment on the manuscript: Geraldine Brooks, Leslie Corzine, Dana Davis, Tanya Horwitz, and Pesha Rubinstein. The inimitable Annmarie Dalton was my design angel. Jeff Norman deserves special mention. Beyond his thoughtful read of the first draft, he has always been there for me, standing ready to ease my pain with a trip to the World Series of Poker. It never failed to work.

On countless afternoons and evenings these last two years, the beach bike posse—Jessy Greene, Rami Jaffee, Susan, and Valentine—rolled with love and light, rescuing me from the past and setting me free.

Two lifelong friends and writers died before I could finish. Tony Horwitz was as bighearted as his books. Our last back-and-forth was about Miss Peanuts Butter. How I wish he were here so that he, Josh, and I could dispute the summer of '78 all over again. When we were kids, David Wong Louie showed me how words could work magic, then grew up to conjure dazzling prose. Our friendship took root in innocence, before darkness descended, and bloomed for half a century. I miss him every day.

Finally, there are two people who lived the story with me, then made possible the retelling. Josh Horwitz has been my closest friend for fifty years. In our heedless youth, no one got me into and out of more life-threatening spots—the stuff of memoir. In adulthood, he's been my rock. As if that weren't enough, he's a savant of narrative structure. From draft one, page one, he was story adviser, writing coach, and shrink. Without him, there would have been no page two. No author has ever been luckier in friendship.

My wife, Susan Emmet Reid, has been my loving mainstay throughout. As Van Morrison once sang, "It's a real heavy connection." She had to relive the roughest episodes of my story along with me during the writing of this book. She did so with grace and unwavering devotion to emotional truth. She read each page of the many drafts, calling bullshit on every false note, and thank God for that. I'm so grateful she's still lighting my way on this journey.

To my son, Sky, whose commitment to justice is an inspiration: your grandfather is smiling down, as proud of you as I am.

Finally, to those, known and unknown, who suffered at the hands of Dan Farinella: this book is my way of healing, and mine only. I respect your own experiences and choices, whatever they may be. And to all my brothers and sisters who are still in thrall to a terrible secret: you are not alone. May we all be safe, peaceful, and free.

# ABOUT THE AUTHOR

STEPHEN MILLS is the coauthor with Roger Fouts of *Next of Kin: My Conversations with Chimpanzees*, a *Los Angeles Times* Best Book of the Year. He has worked with the Natural Resources Defense Council since 1983, building campaigns that have mobilized millions of Americans in support of environmental protection. He lives in California with his wife, Susan.